ST★R
STRUCK

Also by Leonard Maltin

ST★R STRUCK

My Unlikely Road to Hollywood

Leonard Maltin

GoodKnight Books
Pittsburgh, Pennsylvania

GoodKnight Books

© 2021 by JessieFilm Inc.

Published by GoodKnight Books, an imprint of Paladin Communications, Pittsburgh, Pennsylvania.

Printed in the United States of America.

ISBN 978-1-7352738-1-5

Library of Congress Control Number: 2021936194

First Printing

Dedicated with love and gratitude to Alice, Jessie, and Scott, who listened patiently as I rewound the events of my life over dinner, night after night. I am truly blessed.

And to dear Mercy Ingles, who takes such good care of us all.

Contents

Introduction: Take One

I met my first movie star when I was 13 years old. Actually, he was more than a star: he was one of my heroes, Buster Keaton. My best friend and I read that he was making a film in downtown Manhattan and managed to track him down. It was an experience we will never forget.

Good timing and luck have defined my life from that day to this. How else can I explain getting my first book published when I was 18 years old or being hired to work on a hit television show when I never dreamt of a career in broadcasting? Even my academic career, teaching at the USC School of Cinematic Arts, came about by chance: the man who was hired to take over a popular, long-running course was having personal problems and they needed a replacement fast.

I chalk it up to serendipity, which the songwriting Sherman Brothers once defined as "the art of happy accidents."

Over the years I've met many people I grew up admiring as well as today's leading lights, but one thing has never changed: I remain an unabashed fan.

This seems to hold me in good stead with the people I encounter. I didn't understand why at first. Then I learned that the interviewers stars face on press junkets aren't always fans or buffs. Sometimes they haven't even bothered to watch the movies they're supposed to be asking about!

Actors and other luminaries respond to genuine enthusiasm. They'll tell stories they don't often share if they believe I'm truly interested in hearing them. Morgan Freeman explained how he got his first job in movies, as a background extra in Sidney Lumet's *The Pawnbroker* (1964). Lumet needed people to walk down a street on the upper West Side of Manhattan while the film's star, Rod Steiger, stared through a chain link fence at a playground. With each take, Lumet used fewer people; he didn't want a crowd, just a sampling of passers-by. In the end he used only one person. It was Freeman, who did what no one else in the crowd had thought to do: he paused in his walk and lit a cigarette before continuing on. This completely natural moment caught the director's eye.

Years later, as a star, Freeman accosted an extra on one of his sets and asked him where he was going. Nervously, the fellow said he was headed from point A to point B. "But where are you going and why are you going there?" Freeman persisted. The flustered man said the assistant director had told him to cross from one spot to another. He didn't understand Freeman's point: a believable extra should know who he's supposed to be and where he's heading. I hope someday he figured it out.

I've had many odd, funny, and unusual experiences from the time, at age 14, that I was allowed entry into the underground world of old-movie buffs in Manhattan to attending my first Cinecon convention the following year (in Baraboo, Wisconsin); from my stumbling attempts to make 8mm silent movies with my friends (long before the invention of video) to several years of traipsing around the country giving college lectures. Once I appeared in a Midwestern campus ballroom that seated several thousand, but there were only 11 people in attendance. The promoters told me I drew the best turnout they'd had all week. When I asked students at another school how they had happened to book me, they explained that they had a certain amount left in their annual speaker budget so I was whom they could afford. I now think of these as character-building experiences.

I never kept a journal, but every now and then after a special day I've been smart enough to jot down my thoughts. I'm awfully glad I did; it's one reason I can recreate so many incidents in detail. For the rest, I've trusted my memory, with a little help from my family. So, step into the Wayback Machine with me as we travel through one lucky guy's life experience.

Circulation: 3

As a boy I never considered myself unusual. Yet, instead of delivering newspapers, I had a *TV Guide* route. My father read two newspapers a day, but I never got into that habit, preferring to devour his weekly edition of *Variety*. I couldn't hit or throw a baseball, but I devised my own comic strip. At 12 I received rejection slips for my gag cartoons from *The Saturday Evening Post* and *The New Yorker*. I guess I wasn't usual after all.

The first movie image I clearly remember is the last scene of Walt Disney's *Snow White and the Seven Dwarfs*, which was reissued to theaters in 1955 when I was four. Movies were shown on a continuous basis in those days, so the minute a throng of parents dragged their kids out of the theater, my mother took me by the hand and led me inside before the current showing was over. That's why the first image burned in my brain is the final shot of Walt Disney's film, with Prince Charming leading Snow White toward a gleaming golden sun.

I'm pretty sure that took place at the Guild Theatre, the art deco movie house that stood—as a seeming afterthought—behind Radio City Music Hall on 50th Street in Manhattan. Several years later my parents took me back to the Guild to see Robert Youngson's 1958 compilation feature *The Golden Age of Comedy*. There was a life-sized standee of Stan Laurel and Oliver Hardy with Jean

Harlow outside the theater, and it made a vivid impression on me, almost as vivid as the hilarious silent-comedy excerpts I got to see on the big screen. I was hooked, to put it mildly. (Years later, I got to know Bob Youngson and had the opportunity to thank him for making such a difference in my life.)

I became obsessed with silent comedy, which even turned up as kiddie-show fodder on television in those days. In 1959 Charlie Chaplin reissued his feature-length films, and I got to see *Modern Times* on a theater screen. It was a time of great discovery for me.

I also acquired my first home-movie projector as a birthday present. It cost $9.99 and was advertised in a mail order catalog as being "battery operated." In fact, only its tiny bulb used a battery: to make the pictures move you had to turn a metal crank, which made a terrible racket. This proved to be an early lesson in false advertising. Eventually, I got permission to use my parents' Bell & Howell projector, which they had acquired to screen our family home movies. From that point on I saved my money to purchase 8mm editions of vintage films with Charlie Chaplin, Buster Keaton, Laurel and Hardy, and other giants of the silent era. I needed no persuasion to show them on any and all occasions. (They also spurred me to try making my own silent shorts with a group of friends when we were in junior high school. This taught me an important lesson about how hard it is to create comedy, even if you have a supply of cream pies on hand.)

I was born in Manhattan; that gives me a lifelong right to call myself a native New Yorker. The hospital where I was born is now a condo apartment building on West 49th Street. We left the city when I was four, but I clearly remember living in our apartment house on West 77th Street just off Amsterdam Avenue. There was a friendly neighborhood fruit vendor named Dominic, whose apples came in fancy tissue paper. I also recall that one of the grocery stores we frequented on Broadway was a former movie theater, which I found confusing because it retained its marquee out front. I always hoped we were going to the movies when, as often as not, we were just going shopping for dinner.

Our first, boxy console television set had slots on both sides of the wooden cabinet to allow sound to emerge from its cloth-covered speakers. It reminded me of a piggy bank, and I would drop coins into the slots from time to time, occasionally causing minor havoc with the set. One of my earliest memories is of an Indian-head test pattern, which I later learned was the only thing available to watch on TV until *Howdy Doody* signed on every weekday afternoon. I never sat in that show's famed Peanut Gallery, but I did get to visit backstage with a local New York TV personality, The Merry Mailman, who was portrayed by genial Ray Heatherton. It turns out that Ray was my father's first client when he started practicing law, so that gave us an "in." (Ray's daughter Joey later made a splash as a sex-kittenish musical performer.)

When my brother was born, we moved to a two-story house in Teaneck, New Jersey, a nice place to grow up in the 1950s and '60s. It was a bedroom community, just five miles from the George Washington Bridge, though many of my friends never crossed the Hudson River to spend time in the greatest city on earth. We visited often, especially when my grandmother lived on the Upper West Side. I remember staying overnight at her apartment so we could walk to Central Park West and see the Macy's Thanksgiving Day Parade. (I even have a dim recollection of seeing Hopalong Cassidy in the parade, shaking hands along the way.) When I started driving, I could be in midtown in 20 minutes flat.

My father was a special hearings officer for the U.S. Immigration and Naturalization Service, as it was known in those days. He came home at the exact same time every day and never brought his work with him, although he was a soft touch and often took phone calls (even at dinnertime) from people who needed help with immigration problems. Toward the end of his 30-year hitch with Uncle Sam, one of his cohorts successfully petitioned to have him and his colleagues officially called judges.

My mother had been a nightclub performer when she was in her teens, singing and playing an accordion. She joined the chorus of the original Broadway production of *Carousel* in 1946 and stayed with the show nearly a year. She always spoke about how thrilling it was to stand in the wings and watch John Raitt sing "Soliloquy" every night. She also appeared on the popular radio show *Arthur Godfrey's Talent Scouts*, and we had a transcription disc of the broadcast. Apparently, fellow contestant Vic Damone was slated to win, but the producers were forced to call it a tie because she got as much applause as he did. After marrying my dad, she gave up her career but still took occasional club dates and sang at local charity and community events.

People often ask me if my parents inspired my interest in movies. The answer is no, but I did grow up in a house where there was a keen awareness of show business. My Uncle Bernie was a professional pianist and songwriter. He died when I was a year and a half old, and my father inherited the copyrights for many songs he wrote. About once a year, Captain Kangaroo would play an old 78 rpm record of a novelty song called "Professor Spoons," and Lawrence Welk would perform another of his numbers on his popular network TV show. Those were big days in our household because, my father explained, it meant his ASCAP rating would go up that quarter and so would his royalties.

Most important for me was the fact that my dad subscribed to *Variety*, known in those days as "the show business Bible." It arrived in the mail every Thursday. For years my hands were smeared with ink from its pages as I pored over movie news, nightclub reviews, and the comings and goings of stars in columns labeled "NY to LA," "NY to London," etc. (Having read the nightclub reviews by "Jose," which evoked so much glamor in my eyes, it was a shock some years later to meet their author, the very unglamorous Joe

Cohen, although when embracing an attractive publicist he did use a line I've never forgotten: "Quelle broad!")

We lived on a pleasant, tree-lined street called Grayson Place. I had to walk four blocks to my elementary school. The public library was just another block away, and that's where I spent a great deal of time. The librarians in the children's room were friendly and encouraging, and I devoured entire series of books like Hugh Lofting's *Dr. Dolittle*, Robert McCloskey's *Homer Price*, and Jay Williams' Danny Dunn adventures. I also learned how to use the Dewey Decimal system to find what few film-related books and biographies were available in the adult division.

The first book I remember taking home was Mack Sennett's 1956 autobiography, *King of Comedy*. It transported me to the rough-and-ready days of silent moviemaking, and I loved it. (I later came to learn that many of his stories were inaccurate, or at best apocryphal, but they captured the spirit of that freewheeling period and that's what appealed to me most.) I would check it out again and again, as I did other books that came along like John McCabe's *Mr. Laurel and Mr. Hardy*, published when I was 10 years old. Another book I read and reread was Bob Thomas' *The Art of Animation*, which taught me about the workings of the Walt Disney Studio at the time *Sleeping Beauty* was in production.

I was devoted to my daily installment of *The Mickey Mouse Club* and to the weekly hour-long show, *Disneyland* (later called *Walt Disney Presents* and then *Walt Disney's Wonderful World of Color*). I felt such a strong connection to Disney that in an illustrated book of *Grimm's Fairy Tales* I owned, I added words in crayon at the end of a story: "A Walt Disney Production." I was Disney's ideal target audience. When he promoted an upcoming movie, it whet my appetite to see it, and I don't think I missed a single one.

I felt the same keen sense of anticipation for each new Jerry Lewis movie. While spending our summer at Bradley Beach, New Jersey, I saw "that kid" on the screen for the first time in his first film without Dean Martin, *The Delicate Delinquent*. I was sold.

In those days, before multiplexes and 3,000-screen opening weekends, movies followed a predictable trail. They usually opened in Manhattan and then gradually expanded to the suburbs. I came to know the "personalities" of every theater in my area, which included Hackensack, Englewood, Ridgefield Park, and Fort Lee as well as Teaneck. The Oritani in Hackensack tended to show Warner Bros. cartoons, so that was good reason to favor it. The Fox and the Teaneck would show Terrytoons or those awful, repetitious Casper the Friendly Ghost shorts. Ugh. The Fox in Hackensack also ran newsreels, which at that time held absolutely no interest for me.

Saturday matinee kiddie shows were a big part of my adolescence. Around midweek I would call local theaters to see what they planned to show. It took me time to realize that theater managers gave little thought to the content of these programs; they were comprised of whatever prints happened to be sitting in the local film exchange. That's how I saw all the Francis the Talking Mule and Ma and Pa Kettle comedies, along with cheesy science fiction movies and even Cecil B. DeMille's *The Greatest Show on Earth*.

One time, a local Thom McAn shoe store on Cedar Lane sponsored a free kiddie show at the Teaneck Theater that promised 25 cartoons. Needless to say, I arrived early. The flyer advertising the show featured head shots of various characters, including Bugs Bunny and Mickey Mouse, but all we got were Tom and Jerry cartoons—including some that reused footage from shorts we'd just seen minutes earlier. Even worse, there weren't 25 shorts, only 18. I knew because I'd been counting. (Didn't everyone?) Filled with righteous indignation, I lingered in the lobby afterwards to register my annoyance with the manager, but he never showed his face. He would have had to contend with a furious 12-year-old.

So many aspects of moviegoing have changed since I was a kid. When I went to the movies with my family, no one ever bothered to call ahead or check a timetable in the newspaper. We simply marched into the theater and sat down right in the middle of a film. We'd see it through to the end, followed by a cartoon, a travelogue, and some coming attractions, take in the second feature and then the first feature. At a given moment my mom or dad would say, "This is where we came in," and we'd leave. It's utterly unthinkable today but it was commonplace back then. Peter Bogdanovich has written about this phenomenon, and I even traded memories with Martin Scorsese, who laughed in recognition of the same experience he had growing up.

The first price I paid for a Saturday matinee was 35 cents. It soon went up to 50 cents, then 75 cents, and then a dollar. If you went to Radio City Music Hall in Manhattan before noon, it cost only 99 cents! My memories of the Music Hall are mixed, because we often stood in line for the Christmas show in freezing weather, shivering for well over an hour on 50th or 51st Street as the crowd occasionally inched forward. My mother would take me by the hand as we entered the palatial auditorium to see movies like *The Music Man* or a new Disney release. I remember the Rockettes, of course, and the theater organist, who emerged from a curtained alcove on one side of the screen.

When I wasn't busy at the movies, I spent my time reading comic books—mostly the funny kind, although I also liked Superman—and watching TV. I was so addicted to television that I could barely bring myself to turn it off from the moment I got home from school. There were great local kiddie shows, a constant parade of cartoons, and of course *The Mickey Mouse Club*. That was all before dinner and prime-time programming. On Monday night, CBS had a strong comedy lineup, and while I didn't care for *The Danny Thomas Show*, it didn't pay to turn the set off for a measly half hour while waiting for *The Andy Griffith Show*. What could you possibly accomplish in 30 minutes' time when you had to check your watch every couple of minutes?

Television was also my portal to the past. In those days, TV was a living museum of movies, with vintage cartoons and comedy shorts comprising the bulk of children's programming. I watched Laurel and Hardy and the Little Rascals every day of my life for years and years. No wonder I committed so many of their shorts to memory. I got to sample cartoons from every studio: Warner Bros., Max Fleischer, Terrytoons, Van Buren, Ub Iwerks, you name it. Like kids of the video generation, I didn't mind watching them over and over. Familiarity did not breed contempt.

In my adolescence, when my interests broadened, local television enabled me to see countless movies from the 1930s and '40s that didn't ever turn up at the Museum of Modern Art, The New Yorker Theater, or other revival houses I haunted in New York. More than once I went to bed early and set my alarm for 2:30 a.m. in order to see a rarity like *Twentieth Century* or *A Message to Garcia*, then try to fall back to sleep so I could function in school the next day.

It's amazing to me how much I remember from my years of constant TV viewing: moments on game shows, talk shows, kiddie shows, and variety programs. A little while back I met the wonderful singer Marilyn Maye and told her that I remembered when *The Mike Douglas Show* surprised her by flying in her 12-year-old daughter to perform a song from the show *Sweet Charity*. Marilyn was amazed that I retained that memory and informed me that her daughter was then 60!

The events of November 22, 1963, are still crystal-clear in my mind. I was in eighth grade typing class when our principal spoke to us on the public address system about President Kennedy having been shot. While many have written and spoken about the events of that day and its aftermath, no one talks about a media phenomenon I've never experienced since: every television show was canceled for the next four days. The networks played somber classical music and resumed broadcasting only when there was news to be updated. I was watching "live" that Sunday morning when Jack Ruby shot Lee Harvey Oswald and frantically called my parents into the room. I couldn't believe what I'd just seen—and there was no such thing as "instant replay."

What motivated me to publish my own magazine? I really don't know; I hadn't seen *Citizen Kane* at the age of 9. I guess I needed to express myself. When I was in the fifth grade my best friend Barry Ahrendt and I created a journal called *The Bergen Bulletin*, a newspaper-ish moniker indicating our location in Bergen County, New Jersey, and my lifelong fondness for alliteration. Our first issue had a circulation of three: one original and two carbon copies. (If you don't remember carbon paper, I'm sorry.)

To be honest, Barry and I weren't all that interested in reporting news. My passion at that time was drawing cartoons, and *The Bulletin* (as it was soon renamed) gave me a place to display my work. Barry liked to write. We passed around our three copies to classmates, and the feedback we got fueled our determination to publish on a regular basis.

It was at this crucial point that we invested $3.95—no small sum for a couple of fifth graders—in a quaint device called a hectograph. It was a 9x12 vat of hardened gelatin in a tin casing about a quarter of an inch deep. When we wrote or drew on a ditto stencil—the kind our teachers used at school with ditto machines, the precursor to photocopiers—and rubbed the slick ditto paper facedown on the hectograph, it left an impression in the gelatin. By gently sponging down the surface and placing one sheet of coated ditto paper on top, then peeling it off, we could make exact copies. (If someone had told us about a future world in which personal computers could enable any child to create graphics, photos, and type fonts, we would have called it science fiction.)

The gelatin vat was called a hectograph because the prefix "hecto" means "hundred" in Latin. We renamed it the "35-o-graph" because our copies started getting blurry once we reached that number of reproductions. Still, we were happy to have 35 copies to circulate around our school.

Barry, who was a straight-A student, wrote some news-related articles, and his older brother contributed a few erudite essays about world affairs. As my interest in show business grew, I started writing profiles of some of my favorite entertainers. We produced a new issue every other week throughout our fifth- and sixth-grade years. Then we retired the publication, figuring that when we entered junior high school that fall, we would join its newspaper staff.

We received a rude awakening when we learned that as seventh-grade freshmen, we didn't rate a place on the paper. Barry lost interest, but another friend, Barry Gottlieb, joined me in launching a new magazine-format publication called *Profile*. My father's cousin, who was in the printing business, gave me a used mimeograph machine. All that was missing was a feeding mechanism to load blank paper into the printing drum, so we had to find a way to do that by hand. (Using the edge of a typewriter eraser—another relic of days gone by—made it easier.) The mimeo machine, a staple of schools and civic organizations, was an evil contraption that had to be hand-inked, which guaranteed black stains under our fingernails, but it could make an infinite number of copies from one stencil. We ran off a whopping 100. Typing on the stencil was fairly simple, but drawing on it required a stylus and a delicate touch.

Barry's father was associated with a local advertising agency and its friendly co-owner, Ernie Vigdor, allowed us to mess around in his office. One of his staff artists even custom-designed a logo for *Profile*. I will never forget watching in fascination as he took stock lettering and painted out some of the thickness of the letter P in order to create a unique typeface.

In league with that, we decided to produce a professionally printed wraparound cover for our humble magazine. With photographs on the front, back, and inside covers, we felt we'd made a giant leap toward legitimacy. Barry's hobby was magic, so he contributed articles about famous magicians while I embarked on writing about film history. My surveys of the careers of Buster Keaton, Mary Pickford, Douglas Fairbanks, and other silent stars were workmanlike rehashes of facts one could find in books. I did my best to personalize them where I could. When I found a London mailing address for Douglas Fairbanks, Jr., in my go-to resource, the library publication *Current Biography*, I wrote to him to ask if Pickford ever gave him any advice about his own career. Being the gentleman he was, he answered my query. I'll never forget the special air-mail envelope in which it arrived. As it turns out, he had little to do with his stepmother while growing up but said nice things about her. I didn't gain much material for my article, but it certainly was exciting to get that letter.

When I wrote articles about the *Superman* TV series and Warner Bros. cartoons, I drew on my own youthful observations, with "facts" gleaned from obsessive TV watching rather than library research. There were virtually no sources where I could learn about such pop culture topics, and it was exciting to try to piece the puzzles together for myself.

I also got a crash course in magic, working as Barry's assistant at some kids birthday parties. It was fun to go to Louis Tannen's famous emporium in Manhattan on Saturday mornings, where salesmen demonstrated tricks for customers, even kids like us. I especially enjoyed a memorable interview Barry conducted with the renowned magician Milbourne Christopher, who was exceedingly kind to us. He welcomed us into his apartment on Central Park West, which was filled with wonderful memorabilia, and ended our conversation by producing a burst of fire using flash paper. He even presented both of us with signed copies of his book on the history of magic.

I started writing fan letters to people I admired around this time and got some promising replies. Cartoonist and caricaturist Al Kilgore invited us to visit him at his home in Queens Village. I had first seen his work in *Mr. Laurel and Mr. Hardy*, which featured Al's beautiful renderings of Stan and Ollie. It turned out that Al was an avid movie buff and collector, so we had much to talk about. His day job was writing and drawing a daily syndicated Bullwinkle comic strip. Following a long and lively conversation, he sat at his drawing table in a tiny basement workroom and drew a souvenir portrait of Bullwinkle reading a copy of *Profile*. When he finished, he signed it for Barry and Leonard. Knowing that there was no way for us to share this treasure, I sheepishly asked if he would do another drawing for me. This time he drew the villainous Boris Badenov tearing up a copy of *Profile* (a whimsical touch typical of Al's imagination) and signed it for Leonard and Barry. I kept the original Boris and settled for a photostat of Bullwinkle, while my friend did the opposite. (That began a deep and lasting friendship with Al, one of the dearest people I've ever met. In the years to come he would contribute cover art for several issues of my magazine *Film Fan Monthly*, and he devoted as much time to these freebies as he did to any paying gigs. Al died, much too young, in the early 1980s and I spoke at his memorial service.)

I still didn't think in terms of a career; that was far off in the future. I never consciously planned anything that happened during these exciting years. Publishing a magazine, going to Manhattan at every opportunity, and seeking out interesting people just seemed like the obvious thing to do.

Looking back, I realize how fortunate I was to meet so many generous, gracious individuals. There were only a few rotten apples, like a couple of movie studio publicists who couldn't be bothered with my amateur efforts. When I wrote a letter requesting still photos from Charlie Chaplin's upcoming film *A Countess from Hong Kong*, an executive at Universal Pictures took the time to compose a formal response saying that the company didn't find my magazine a suitable outlet for their publicity campaign. "However," he concluded condescendingly, "so your letter shouldn't be a total loss, here are several stills." If he was going to send the photos anyway, what did he gain by being so unkind? I'll never understand people like that, especially in the field of publicity.

I learned another valuable lesson early on: if there was any way to dodge publicists and reach the person directly, my chances of success were infinitely better. In 1969 I learned that the esteemed director George Stevens was coming to New York City to appear at the opening of a retrospective at the Museum of Modern Art. They would be showing such classic films as *Gunga Din*, *A Place in the Sun*, and *Shane*. At age 18 I hadn't yet made solid connections at MoMA, so I called several leading midtown Manhattan hotels and asked for Mr. Stevens. I scored on the second try, as I recall, and left a message that I wanted to interview him.

Imagine my astonishment when during dinner a day later the telephone rang. It was George Stevens returning my call. I told him how much I admired his early work at the Hal Roach studio and wondered if he'd be willing to grant me an interview; he invited me to join him for breakfast at his hotel the next day.

To my annoyance, the MoMA tribute began in 1935 and completely ignored Stevens' work as a cameraman and director at the Hal Roach studio, where he worked with Laurel and Hardy and got his first break on a series of short subjects called *The Boy Friends*. Far from being dismissive of these early films and the others he made at RKO, Stevens seemed to revel in talking about them. I told him how fond I was of his two-reel comedy *Air Tight*, which he remembered shot for shot after nearly 40 years. (I later loaned him my 16mm print of the short and had to beg to get it back. I gather he ran it more than once.) I subsequently published my interview in the *Directors Guild* magazine and drew on that conversation for my 1971 book *The Great Movie Shorts*.

And all it took was one phone call.

"Is This About You...or Me?"

When a popular New York radio host looked me in the eye and uttered those words, I was taken aback by his bluntness—and embarrassed that I had, in fact, been prattling on about myself.

I was 13 years old and through the extraordinary kindness of a public relations man for WNEW radio (whose name I still recall after all these years—Bernie Ruttenberg), I had been given the chance to spend the day at my favorite station and meet the hosts I listened to every day. I must have written a pretty persuasive letter, or perhaps it was the novelty of a 13-year-old who liked Peggy Lee and Mel Tormé. WNEW had a stellar lineup of personalities who did more than spin records; they talked about events of the day, joked, and interviewed the occasional celebrity. In fact, they became celebrities in their own right.

Barry Gottlieb and I got up around 8 a.m. and took an early bus to Manhattan that day so we could arrive in time to watch the station's popular morning team, (Gene) Klavan and (Dee) Finch, conduct their impromptu program and ad-lib their way through live commercials. Finch was the nominal straight man who would conduct wacky conversations with Klavan, who assumed various identities on the spur of the moment. We were shown to a quiet spot in their spacious studio and tried to blend into the scenery, but at one point Gene Klavan encouraged everyone to sing along with the jingle for a company called Econo-Car. Our collective voices rang out on one of New York City's most listened-to radio outlets. This was heady stuff for a couple of kids.

During a lunch break I read the handout biography of early afternoon d.j. Bob Landers, which mentioned that one of his hobbies was collecting 16mm films. When I sat down with Landers and turned on my tape recorder, I began our conversation by saying that I collected films too—not on 16mm, which I couldn't yet afford, but 8mm, and I'd accumulated a number of silent films.

That's when he asked, "Is this interview about you or me?"

I was embarrassed but tried not to show it and continued our interview. I was miffed that I'd been put down by someone I enjoyed so much on the air, but I have never forgotten that moment and its object lesson. No matter whom I talk to—on television, onstage, in front of a camera, or over the phone—I constantly remind myself that the conversation is about them. I cringe when I watch someone conduct a Q&A session and inject too much of themselves into the proceedings. They may not be aware of the quiet groaning and eye-rolling in the audience, but I am.

I was an inveterate letter writer in those days before texting and the Internet. I would obtain mailing addresses from issues of *Current Biography* or try reaching people through their TV networks or movie studios. I got some remarkable responses.

I'm embarrassed when I look back at some of my missives. They often began, "Even though I am only 12 years old, I am a big fan of your work…." but apparently my sincerity came through.

Dick Van Dyke was kind enough to handwrite on the bottom of my letter a reply to a query about Laurel and Hardy. "Laurel and Hardy were the funniest duo to ever set foot in front of a camera," he wrote, with perfect penmanship, "before Liz and Dick became real comedians." This was 1963 and Taylor and Burton's antics on the set of *Cleopatra* were prime fodder for jokes at the time.

Carol Burnett wrote that she was too busy for an in-person interview but would be happy to answer me by mail. I immediately sent a list of four or five questions, and she sent short, self-deprecating answers, signing just her first name to the typed letter.

Steve Allen also invited me to interview him by mail, and when I sent him the finished piece in *The Bulletin*, which I was then publishing with my friend Barry Ahrendt, he wrote the most remarkable letter I'd ever received. "Thank you for sending that copy of *The Bulletin*," he wrote on his letterhead. "I think you did a fine job and I believe I'm qualified to judge, because when I was about your age I published a similar magazine at school, and I don't think mine was half as professional as yours." I was floored.

From this experience I developed a belief I've never had reason to contradict: anyone who would take the time to write a personal letter to a young fan must be a nice person. Having met the people just named and others I wrote to when I was a kid, I know it's true.

At that time my ambition was to be a cartoonist. At the Teaneck Public Library I spent lots of time reading and rereading Jack Markow's *Drawing and Selling Cartoons*. It was a practical, no-nonsense guide to developing both the skills and discipline to submit panel cartoons to magazines. I even bought the exact type of India ink and pen nib he recommended to create my amateurish samples.

Undeterred by my lack of skill, I submitted some of my gag cartoons to such publications as *The Saturday Evening Post* and *The New Yorker*, with the recommended self-addressed stamped envelope, and duly received printed rejection slips. The fact that I got the same response as a working professional made me feel good even though they'd turned down my work.

I also wrote fan letters to cartoonists I admired. Chic Young, creator of *Blondie*, wrote some sage words of advice on the back of a printed card featuring Blondie, Dagwood, and the cast of his durable comic strip. Jules Feiffer handwrote an eloquent letter of advice ("Read," he said, "read incessantly....") out of respect for my fellow Teaneck resident, cartoonist Bob Oksner, who had given me Feiffer's address and had been an early booster of his work.

The most memorable reply came from Charles M. Schulz, on *Peanuts* stationery from his studio in Northern California. His lengthy typed letter offered me encouragement, urged me to take art lessons in order to refine my ability, and to persevere. He enclosed a hand-signed original of a *Peanuts* daily strip! This would be hard to top.

I finally met Schulz some 30 years later when United Features Syndicate (now United Media) hired me to interview him on camera for a video presentation that would accompany a touring show commemorating *Peanuts'* 35th anniversary. As we settled into our seats in his comfortable Santa Rosa studio, I told him the story of my youthful fan letter and his generous response. "Well," he said, rising from his chair, "we've got to get you something more current." He went to a nearby desk and shuffled through some Sunday originals until he found one he especially liked, and signed it to my wife and me. Instead of writing his full name he used the nickname by which he was known to his friends and family, Sparky. What a wonderful moment that was. (As for the interview, I didn't need to do any research or preparation: I'd been waiting my whole life to ask him about his work on *Peanuts*. A transcript of the interview was later included in an anthology called *Charles M. Schulz: Conversations*, published by the University Press of Mississippi.)

Not everyone I wrote to answered my letters and I tried to be philosophical about that, though every day I raced home to see if there was a "special" envelope in the mail. (I even tracked the path of our friendly letter carrier Freddy as he made his way up the steep hill to our house, hoping he would have something for me in his satchel.)

I acquired some amazing pen pals along the way. Imagine being 12 years old and receiving a letter on embossed Bullwinkle stationery from Jay Ward, who presided over the Los Angeles studio where cartoon stars Rocky and Bullwinkle were created. He not only wrote a friendly letter but enclosed a handful of goodies, such as "Statehood for Moosylvania" decals and a membership card in the Bullwinkle Fan Club, Chowder-Marching and Moosewatching Society. This was just the first of many clever mailings and notes I would receive from the puckish producer, just because I was an enthusiast and he took a shine to me. When I printed my first article about him in *Profile*, he sent me an elaborate commemorative ribbon emblazoned with these words: "Exceptional Adequacy Award for helping to promote public apathy toward The Bullwinkle Show."

About six years later when I made my first trip to L.A., I got to meet Jay Ward in person—no small achievement it turned out, because he was notoriously shy. When I walked into his Sunset Boulevard headquarters, with a giant Bullwinkle and Rocky statue outside, a receptionist called his office to say I was there. The buoyant, walrus-mustached animation mogul came out to greet me and plugged in a gigantic circus calliope that sat in his waiting area "to announce my arrival." The ancient mechanical instrument literally shook the building, to Jay's delight and my astonishment.

I also happened to be there at a historic moment: a staff artist showed Jay his design for an official Bullwinkle watch, which required his approval. The men agreed that the design made it difficult to tell the time "unless it was 12:30 or 6:00," but Jay concluded that if you wore a Bullwinkle watch, you didn't really care what time it was. I later purchased one and he was right.

Jay introduced me to his supervising director, a lovely man named Bill Hurtz, who walked me through the animators rooms, where they were working on a Cap'n Crunch commercial, and took me to lunch. When we returned and I said goodbye to Jay, I asked if I could take a snapshot and he said, "Actually, no." I thought he was kidding, but he wasn't; he was famously camera-shy, and I apologized for putting him on the spot. He didn't seem to mind and bid me goodbye with a warm smile. All this because I wrote him a fan letter when I was 12.

During my adolescence I pursued two other avenues for getting interviews: scanning the Manhattan telephone book and waiting at stage doors. The first time I tried the latter technique was after attending a matinee of Neil Simon's *The Odd Couple* on Broadway at the Eugene O'Neill Theatre. I was 16, and it was a spur-of-the-moment idea after reading costar Eddie Bracken's biography in my *Playbill*. It claimed that he had been in the cast of *Our Gang* during the silent film era, long before achieving stardom in such famous films of the 1940s as Preston Sturges' *Hail the Conquering Hero* and *The Miracle of Morgan's Creek*. This piqued my curiosity and gave me the idea to try for an interview. I approached the stage door, and a not-unkind guard asked me what I wanted. When I told him, he said to wait. It was a chilly day, but I was not going to leave without getting an answer. After a while, someone came out and said that Mr. Bracken would be happy to see me after the following Saturday matinee. I was elated.

But I was not prepared—at least, not enough. I researched Bracken's career as best I could, but there was no time to track down and view any movies and I'd only seen a few. I also wasn't qualified to deal with a man who pleasantly, even charmingly, made things up. To my relief, he owned up to the fact that he wasn't really in *Our Gang*, but rather an imitation series called *The Kiddie Troupers*. However, he claimed to have created Francis the Talking Mule, which I was never able to verify anywhere, and made other grand generalizations during our chat.

Mr. Bracken couldn't have been nicer, but I wasn't an experienced enough interviewer to get everything I could from him, nor was I prepared to ask specific questions about more than a couple of his movies. (He did admit that it was frustrating that everyone thought of him as being the good-natured schnook he played for Sturges, as opposed to an actor inhabiting a role.) I had enough material to run the interview in *Film Fan Monthly*, but I couldn't help wondering how much better off I would have been if I'd spent time doing my homework before even approaching the actor.

At this time, the summer stock or "straw hat circuit" was still in full bloom. I'm sure actors miss the opportunities this network of theaters presented to young people wanting to learn their craft and veterans who still wanted to work. Both Christopher Plummer and Frank Langella have written warmly about their early experiences in stock in their memoirs.

Paramus, New Jersey, was adjacent to Teaneck and was home not only to some of the nation's first shopping malls but also to a summer stock theater called Playhouse on the Mall. Its artistic director was a man who later forsook the theater world for greener pastures: his name was Robert Ludlum and he went on to write many best-selling novels, including *The Bourne Identity*. (I'm sorry I never got to meet him.)

A married couple who knew my parents handled publicity for Playhouse on the Mall and expressed great enthusiasm for my early publishing efforts. "If there's anything we can ever do, please have Leonard call us," they insisted.

I noticed that Chester Morris and Maureen O'Sullivan were coming to the Mall in *The Subject Was Roses*, and I dropped the publicists a note saying I would love to interview either or both of these veteran stars. When I called to follow up a week later they told me that, unfortunately, neither one would be available.

I tried again a month or two later, and then once more. It was only then that I came to the conclusion that these "nice" people had no intention of bothering their actors with my requests.

I grumbled about this to a friend who said, "You don't need to make an appointment. Anyone can walk backstage there." So, after watching a Friday night performance of *Spofford* a week or two later, I marched backstage to knock on the dressing room door of its star, Hans Conried. No one stopped me or even asked where I was going.

Mr. Conried answered the door himself, whereupon I launched into a hurried speech about my magazine *Film Fan Monthly* and my desire to talk to him about his film career. He thumbed through an issue I handed him and said, unforgettably, "We cannot presume to delude a person as young as yourself that I ever had anything resembling a film career." I assured him that I was interested all the same, and he invited me to come back an hour before curtain time Monday night.

Luckily for me, the role of Spofford didn't require much make-up or preparation, and for an hour this magnificent actor and ra-conteur regaled me with stories. At five minutes before curtain he said, "Why don't you come back tomorrow night?" Which I did. Also the night after that. It was one of my all-time happiest experiences.

By this time in 1969, I had become an old-movie fanatic and was much better prepared to ask specific questions about the actor's work. I had laboriously gone through the old trade annual *Film Daily Year Book* to compile a list of his screen appearances, which I consulted along with notes I'd made on the ones I'd seen. His friendly manner made me feel more confident as an interviewer. At one point I said, "Will you forgive me if I don't recall what you did in *Bus Stop*?" and he immediately responded, "I won't forgive you; I'll be very grateful if you don't recall it." Conried needed little prodding to produce a never-ending string of colorful anecdotes about everyone from John Barrymore to John Wayne, related in his engagingly theatrical manner.

For many film buffs the pinnacle of Conried's film career was the elaborate musical fantasy devised by Dr. Seuss (Theodore Gei-sel), *The 5,000 Fingers of Dr. T*, in which he plays a tyrannical piano teacher. "It was a great, beautiful picture," he recalled sadly. "They cut over eleven musical numbers and reshot for one whole week. I had never had any such part before, never have since, and probably never will again. We rehearsed for eight weeks before I was engaged to shoot for eight weeks, which was an extravagance that I as a bit player had never known. To make this very long and tedious and somewhat tearful story short for me, the picture never made its print money back. It was comparable only to *Wilson* as one of the great money losers of all time. It would stop conversation for some years thereafter at any Hollywood social gathering. If it had been a success, with my prominent part in the title role, it would have changed my life. The general public thinks of a break as being an opportunity. No. A break is an opportunity that pays off."

I tried to stay in touch with Conried, and he was nice enough to phone me from the road when he was touring in *Can-Can*, but we never got to meet again. I will never forget his kindness and hospitality. (To my all-time regret, I never asked him about his work in radio, which wasn't of interest to me at that time.)

I forget who told me that the Manhattan phone book was a great resource, but he was right, at least in those more innocent times before (well-justified) celebrity paranoia. The problem was determining whether or not the Claudette Colbert listed therein was the actual movie star or someone who simply bore the same name. Seeing that the woman in question lived in Harlem, I came to the conclusion that it was the latter.

There were two Reuben Goldbergs listed, and I figured one of them had to be the world-famous cartoonist whose name had become synonymous with fanciful contraptions. I loved his book, *How to Remove the Cotton from a Bottle of Aspirin, and Other Problems Solved*, and figured I had little to lose by trying the two phone numbers listed. The first one, in midtown, rang once or twice and a man answered. I don't remember exactly how I asked if he was *the* Rube Goldberg, but somehow I did and he told me he was. We made an appointment and a week or two later I was escorted into his studio, which was filled with large bronze pieces of his own creation, his distinctively silly-looking characters brought to three-dimensional life. That day he was working on a new piece in clay. If only I had brought a camera! He was gruff but pleasant, we had a nice conversation, and he was happy to sign my copy of his book. I wish I could tell you what we discussed, but at this distance all I remember are the sculptures, the white-haired gentleman wearing an artist's smock, and the thrill of meeting the one and only Rube Goldberg.

A letter went out to another Manhattanite I admired for different reasons, actress Celeste Holm. The address seemed legitimate, but I didn't receive a reply. Then, several months later, I got a call from a Broadway show publicist named Lisa Lipsky asking if I would like to interview Miss Holm after a matinee performance of *Mame* at the Winter Garden Theatre. Of course I would.

On the appointed day, I showed up at the stage door and was met by Miss Lipsky, whose interest in me was nil. We stood backstage together and my attempts to make conversation were greeted by stony silence. When a member of the cast came by, she magically came to life, her face animated and engaged. Then, silence. The performance was now over, but Miss Holm wasn't ready for the interview just yet. "You want some ice cream or something?" the publicist asked dully. I said no thanks.

Then a signal came, and we climbed several flights of stairs to the star's dressing room. Miss Holm was reclining on a divan and sipping hot tea, as her voice was raw from that day's show. With no reference to my original letter, she asked if I'd seen the performance and I (candidly? foolishly?) admitted I hadn't. She expressed regret, saying, "I always think it's a waste doing an interview when you haven't seen the show." I told her that I was primarily interested in discussing her film career and this brought an even sharper retort. She made a disparaging remark about her work in movies and said, "I'm only interested in the present, not the past."

"Well," I said, in a bold attempt at cleverness, "I'm presently interested in discussing your movie career." This didn't go over well, so I changed tactics and asked when she had made her Broadway debut. A better entrée, this opened the door for Miss Holm to talk about her early work onstage and her great success in Rodgers and Hammerstein's *Oklahoma!* By faithfully following this timeline, I knew it would lead me to Hollywood, and it did. Sure enough, when it came time to talk about going to work for 20th Century Fox, she had interesting and witty things to say. (When a producer told her they were having trouble cutting her second film, *Carnival in Costa Rica*, she suggested, "How about right down the middle?")

At this point Lisa Lipsky, who had remained in the corner of the dressing room silent, said, "We have to wrap things up."

I was distraught. I hadn't gotten to the films that really mattered like *All About Eve*! Begging for a few more minutes, I managed to extract a few anecdotes from the actress, including a charming memory of working with Ronald Colman (on *Champagne for Caesar*), who told her, "Never lose your amateur's enthusiasm."

Finally, I asked if I might have an autographed photo. Miss Holm had a supply of 8x10s at her side and told me that she would only sign if I made a contribution to UNICEF. I don't remember how much I handed her, but she dutifully signed, "To Leonard, thank you on behalf of UNICEF, Celeste Holm."

Lisa Lipsky walked me downstairs and bid me a curt goodbye. (I've never forgotten her name; what does that say about me?) When the stage door closed behind me, I wanted to scream in frustration. I was never able to use the interview because it ends so abruptly and covers so little ground.

But at least my letter to another party listed in the phone book hadn't gone unanswered. And at least it gave me a good story to relate, even if it did take years to do so.

My Fanzine and My Future Wife

At the foot of Grayson Place at Teaneck Road, there was an establishment we called a candy store. It's where I bought all my comic books and Bazooka bubble gum. One day a colorful magazine called *Famous Monsters of Filmland* beckoned to me. *Famous Monsters* and its editor, Forrest J. Ackerman, introduced me and a generation of baby boomers (including Stephen King and Steven Spielberg) to the history of horror and fantasy films. Rare photos of Lon Chaney, Boris Karloff, Bela Lugosi, and others fired my imagination and my desire to see these tantalizing movies.

Famous Monsters also changed my life. In one issue Forry invited a man named Oscar Estes, Jr., to review a handful of fanzines, amateur publications whose existence would otherwise have remained unknown to me. Two of them sounded especially interesting: *The 8mm Collector*, published by Samuel K. Rubin in Indiana, Pennsylvania, and *Film Fan Monthly*, which Daryl Davy published in Vancouver, British Columbia. I submitted articles to both of them "cold." In short order I received friendly replies expressing interest in publishing my pieces. There was no money involved, as these publications were labors of love, a hobby for all concerned. Having placed the articles I then "confessed" that I was 13. Sam Rubin, a furniture dealer by trade, told me it didn't matter to him, and Daryl Davy, a budding sportswriter, replied that he was 19!

The piece I wrote for Sam was the first in a proposed series of columns called "Research Unlimited," in which I boldly offered to answer readers' questions about silent films, which they (like I) collected in the 8mm format.

How dare I take on such a task? I marvel at my chutzpah. The first query that arrived in my mailbox was from a man acknowledged to be the country's foremost Laurel and Hardy fan, Mike Polacek from Huntington, West Virginia. He was trying to identify a bit player who appeared in a handful of films with Stan and Ollie. Even Stan Laurel couldn't remember his name. How was I going to maintain a research column with stumpers like this?

Fortune smiled and on one of my Saturday jaunts to Manhattan I stopped at Entertainment Films, a small 8mm distributor with an office in midtown. It was there that I met the eminent film historian William K. Everson. Not only did I secure an invitation to attend a screening at his secret-handshake film group, the Theodore Huff Film Society, but when I asked if he knew the mystery man from the Laurel and Hardy films he answered, without hesitation, "Oh, you mean Leo Willis." Bingo!

Not only did this allow me to establish my bona fides with readers of *The 8mm Collector*, it introduced me to a man who became my hero and unwitting mentor. Bill Everson was unassuming, very British, and generous to a fault. I was just one of many beneficiaries of his kindness.

I'm sorry I never got to meet Daryl Davy face-to-face. We lived on opposite ends of the same continent, and I mailed him my monthly submission for his magazine. After two years he wrote to me, explaining that he was now living on his own with a full-time job and couldn't devote the time to a monthly publishing schedule. Would I want to take over *Film Fan Monthly*?

There were so many reasons to say yes: he had a paid circulation of 400 (whereas my *Profile* reached only 100 people), mostly in the United States and Canada but also in Australia, New Zealand, and even western Europe. What's more, his magazine was professionally printed—no more mimeograph machine to contend with. He told me there was $400 in the treasury and suggested a sale price of $175. That's how I "bought" a magazine and its mailing list, by accepting a check for $225. (Daryl's life ended prematurely in 1973; he was only 32.)

My first issue came out in May 1966 and was numbered #59. I was 15 and about to finish tenth grade. I continued to edit and publish *FFM* for the next nine years, winding up with issue #168.

Once *Film Fan Monthly* came into my life, I had little interest in schoolwork, especially math and science, where I fared poorly. An aptitude test placed me in advanced math, to my frustration. I even failed a take-home, open-book exam! I did slightly better in physics class because my teacher gave multiple-choice tests. I chose "c" for each answer, figuring my odds were better than they would have been if I tried to determine the correct response.

On the whole I was a B student. Almost everything mattered more to me than classes and homework. I started a Motion Picture Club at Teaneck High School, worked on the AV squad, volunteered for stage crew, and in my senior year became editor of the yearbook. Even my doodling was movie related: I would draw classic movie studio logos or try to list all 75 of Bogart's films.

When I was 12 I made two friends who are close to me still. Dennis Reer was a cut-up who shared my love of Laurel and Hardy, Stan Freberg, and *The Honeymooners* and first exposed me to the wonders of *Firesign Theater*. He was a Mr. Fix-It and spoiled me for life by rescuing tape recorders and other electrical equipment without breaking a sweat. He and his wife, Carol, still live in New Jersey, where he does wonderful work with students who care about science and the world around them. When we were 13 we read about the newly formed Laurel and Hardy appreciation society called Sons of the Desert, which had "tents" instead of chapters. We were the first sanctioned "junior" branch of the organization, The Tit for Tat Tent of Teaneck.

Louis Black (no relation to the comedian Lewis Black) was a guy who marched to his own drummer. We shared the same interests and went to Manhattan almost every weekend to comb the used bookshops on Book Row (then located on 4th Avenue, now sadly gone) and attend screenings at the New Yorker Theater on Broadway and 88th Street and at the Museum of Modern Art.

A brief digression: young people don't believe this, but it's true. MoMA followed a New York state law that forbade them from selling movie tickets to anyone under the age of 16. We could pay our $1.75 to get into the Museum, but they wouldn't let us have the free movie ticket that went along with the price of admission. The result: I would stand on 53rd Street and wait until a friendly looking adult came along. I'd quickly explain our dilemma with money in hand and never failed to find a nice person to get us our tickets. One rainy day when this transaction took place inside the lobby, the perpetually nasty ticket seller growled at our benefactor, "You know you're responsible for him now!"

Louis was a talented writer and comic-book aficionado who attended the first comic book conventions in Manhattan. I chose not to go because I wasn't nearly as interested. I also felt I spent enough time with "characters" in the world of movie buffs and didn't need to expand my circle of oddball acquaintances.

I have a snapshot of Louis and me at the first "grown-up" Sons of the Desert banquet in 1966, which was held at the venerable Lambs Club on West 44th Street in Manhattan (now gone, sad to say). Stan Laurel's widow, Ida, was there along with Stan's longtime attorney and manager Ben Shipman and such celebrated performers as Orson Bean (a founder of the Sons), Soupy Sales, and Chuck McCann. The pictures I took with my flash camera that night are so washed out you can't make out details of any faces, but they still rekindle a happy memory for me. Several guests performed from the dais, and I don't think I've ever laughed so much or so hard.

Louis and I have been through a lot over the years. He followed a girlfriend from Boston to Austin, Texas, decades ago and threatened to become the world's oldest hippie grad student. Then a friend asked if he'd like to be editor and co-publisher of an alternative weekly newspaper, and *The Austin Chronicle* was born. Several years later he and his partner invested in a start-up venture called South by Southwest. It has grown exponentially and along the way Louis became a major force in the cultural scene of Austin, which he remains to this day.

My classmate Warren Dressler volunteered to handle the business end of running *FFM*, maintaining subscription rolls and our bank account. When he left for college my father offered to manage the shoestring operation. Somehow the magazine always managed to pay for itself. The longer we kept publishing the more back issues we had to sell, and that floated the operation. We even reprinted older issues to maintain a steady supply.

At first I wrote every page of the magazine, but after a year I began to receive submissions from capable writers who didn't care about being paid because I provided an outlet where they could write about the Golden Age of Hollywood. Our specialty was spotlighting character actors and underappreciated stars. Among our cover subjects were Nigel Bruce, Jane Greer, Robert Donat, George Zucco, Miriam Hopkins, and Dwight Frye—the kind of people who still fascinate me today. On several occasions the great Al Kilgore contributed cover art that money could not buy.

Al was so incensed by Richard Schickel's venomous book about Walt Disney called *The Disney Version* that he painted a moody rendering of Mickey Mouse with a stake through his heart impaling him on a book titled *The Schickel Version*. He also wrote an essay excoriating the book.

I appreciated all these contributions and was especially proud to publish articles by William K. Everson and my new friend

Jeanine Basinger, who found the magazine, got my phone number from Information (remember dialing 411 to get a number?), and called me. We've had a mutual admiration society ever since. She has become legendary, teaching and mentoring several generations of students at Wesleyan University in Connecticut. Her alumni include such successful grads as Joss Whedon, Bradley Whitford, Miguel Arteta, Alex Kurtzman, and Paul Weitz. She also has written a number of influential books, including *A Woman's View: How Hollywood Spoke to Women 1930–1960* and *The Star Machine*. She is the smartest woman I know and has been there for me at key junctures in my life. Alice and Jessie share my warm feelings for her and her loving husband, John. And to think that I had her byline in my humble fanzine.

My pal Louis Black asked why he received no credit in the first issue. I said, "You didn't do anything," but he still protested. In the masthead of the next issue I wrote "Friend in Need: Louis Black." The following month I wrote "Friend Indeed: Louis Black." He received a different credit line every month for the next nine years.

In the early days of *FFM* I would type every article on an IBM Selectric typewriter in Ernie Vigdor's office. Then I would draw a line along the right-hand margin and put marks between words to indicate that I should skip a space when I retyped everything. That's how I wound up with justified copy—a mark of professionalism, it seemed to me. I also became adept at using transfer lettering for headlines. When I think of how easy it is to accomplish all that and more on today's computers, my head spins.

Meeting Bill Everson and being invited to the Theodore Huff Society was a turning point in my life. The first film I saw there was *The Singing Fool* (1928), Al Jolson's follow-up to *The Jazz Singer*. Bill printed program notes on a ditto machine, and I diligently saved them in alphabetical file folders. Now they're all available online in seconds, thanks to NYU, where Bill taught for many years. (I can even look up the date of that momentous night: August 31, 1965. I was 14 at the time.)

My mother drove me to that screening and continued to do so until I was old enough to drive there on my own. (Back then, New Jersey issued licenses at age 17, but I couldn't cross the George Washington Bridge until I was 18.) She enjoyed most of the films we saw (except for Preston Sturges' *The Great Moment*, his only out-and-out failure, which she hectored me about for years) and never tired of the floor show: a motley assemblage of men, many of whom could charitably be described as social misfits. Yet there was more knowledge of film history in that room than one could find in any library. As I got to know these fellows and their specialties, I drew on their expertise for articles and books I was writing.

Bill Everson was the soul of patience and a constant source of information. He didn't hesitate to lend his 16mm prints to anyone who asked. He also provided homemade scores for silent films using a repertoire of instrumental record albums and a portable phonograph. Many stories were associated with the Huff Society, which used to meet in a rented room in a building at Union Square. Later it moved to an amphitheater room at the School of Visual Arts on East 23rd Street.

One night my mother noticed a man in front of us whose windbreaker jacket had a life of its own. That's because his rhesus monkey was scrambling about inside. We figured that Bill let the man come because the monkey seemed to be watching the films.

Not every selection at the Huff was a gem. I didn't care for a 1937 Republic picture called *The Wrong Road*. Richard Cromwell and Helen Mack play young lovers on the lam, accused of a crime he didn't commit. At the end of the film Mack says she doesn't want to run anymore; she wants to be able to laugh again. Just then Lionel Atwill, who's been pursuing them with Javert-like determination, peeks out from behind a tree and says, "You kids can start laughing right now." Curtain.

As the lights came up I muttered, *sotto voce*, a mocking "You kids can start laughing right now." A man behind me said, "I started laughing the day I sold Bill that print." That's how I met Herb Graff, who became a close friend—and my matchmaker.

Herb worked in the garment district for Lucky Girl Shirts, but his great love was movies, which he collected in 16mm. One evening I ran into him on my way to the Huff and admired the topcoat he was wearing. "You like this?" he replied. "This cost me *Top Hat*." It was a rare instance when practicality won out over a chance to acquire a great movie for his library.

Herb was a wonderful character. A student once called him on the recommendation of a film professor and boldly requested to set up screenings of all the Fred Astaire–Ginger Rogers musicals for a term paper he was preparing. Rather than expend needless energy devising an excuse not to do this, Herb said, "I don't have any of them. I only collect Westerns." This brought the conversation to a definitive end. That line of Herb's has become a mantra for Alice and me.

In time Herb found ways to pursue his love of movie history and make some money on the side delivering lectures. For several years he taught an adult education course at NYU. I was one of his guest lecturers and that's where I first met Alice Tlusty. She approached me at the end of the evening and paid me a compliment on my talk. I was polite but (apparently) standoffish, and she concluded that I was either gay or simply not interested.

Some weeks later I ran into Herb as he was leaving the School of Visual Arts. He said he didn't feel well and asked me to look out for Alice, the girl I met at his class. I confessed that I didn't remember her, but he said I'd have no trouble spotting her; women were rare at the Huff Society. When she appeared at the entryway of the amphitheater, I waved hello and we sat together through two silent features: Maurice Tourneur's *The Whip* (1920) and Paul Bern's *Out All Night* (1924) with Adolphe Menjou and Raymond Griffith. It didn't count as a date, but we did chat during intermission and enjoyed watching the program together.

About a month later the New York Tent of the Sons of the Desert had its annual banquet. Alice was there with the other man Herb had introduced her to, the very knowledgeable John Cocchi. She had gone out with him several times, but as we sat opposite each other at a large table she only had eyes for me, so she says.

I invited her on a bona fide date, to a jazz organ concert at Carnegie Hall, which she will never let me forget. I made no effort beyond the concert—no dinner, no pickup in my car—because I was feeling burned by several women I had pursued, only to have our budding relationships end platonically.

Alice was different. She was warm and funny. After the concert we went to eat at Wine and Apples, a longtime establishment (now gone) on 57th Street. Something sparked between us. Our first official date was July 1, 1974, and by Labor Day we were engaged. We just knew we were meant for each other. What more can I say?

Alice likes to say that she saved me from life in a dark room. I counter that I rescued her from spinsterhood. She was 30, seven years older than me, about to be written off by her family as a goner. Somehow we found each other and thank goodness we did. I married my best friend and so did she. She changed my life for the better, and we appreciate that we still love each other after all this time. We can be sitting in the same room reading and enjoy each other's company. We often joke that we can never break up as we are the only people who get each other's pop culture references.

When I met Alice she was working in the credit department at Bantam Books, ironically the publisher of my rival Stephen Scheuer's *Movies on TV*. She was a worker bee and not career oriented. Her youthful dream of performing in musical theater was thwarted when during her second year of college she had to drop out to have a thyroidectomy. It knocked her for a loop.

One day she accompanied me on my rounds as I prepared an

issue of *Film Fan Monthly*. She met my typesetter and layout man and my printer. When we finished, she told me she'd never met anyone who enjoyed what they did for a living. Her father came up during the Great Depression and had to put his dreams aside to earn a living wage as a window cleaner. He worked hard his entire life, and while he and I got on great I saw the bitterness just below the surface that never left him.

My future bride proved her mettle when I took her to some peculiar places to see old movies. The secretive Huff Society eventually faded away as Bill Everson launched a Friday night series at the New School for Social Research on 12th Street (where I would later teach a class on animation). That auditorium was a palace compared to the primitive charm of The Cooperative Film Society, better known as Joe's Place, on 40th Street west of 9th Avenue behind the Port Authority Bus Terminal. As W.C. Fields said in *Mississippi*, "I cut my way through a wall of human flesh" to make it halfway down the block toward 10th Avenue, where we would duck into an unmarked entryway. Inside were rows of padded bench-like seats installed by our host, a likable electrician named Joe Judice. (I'm told he appropriated his power for the screening room from the building upstairs.) It was called the Co-op because members could bring prints they owned or had borrowed to screen and make a few bucks by passing the hat during intermission.

A nice man named Don Koll, an actor by trade, also ran double features every weekend in his apartment on East 3rd Street, not a neighborhood you'd want to linger in. I could usually find a parking space (one of its few advantages), but when I arrived at Don's building I would take a deep breath and vault upstairs to his second-floor apartment, sighing a breath of relief upon my arrival. The smell of urine was always evident in the hallway, although Don's place was neat as a pin, like Don himself. But where else would I have seen Charlotte Greenwood in *So Long Letty* or the 1930 version of *The Desert Song*?

I can't overemphasize how difficult it was to see certain old movies back then. If they didn't turn up on local television or on the revival circuit, you were out of luck unless you were plugged in to the underground network of collectors. Some were sharers and some were hoarders, though most of the people I encountered were eager to share, and some went out of their way to do so.

When I embarked on my second book, *Movie Comedy Teams*, I faced the challenge of locating the films of Wheeler and Woolsey, all but forgotten today but fairly popular in the 1930s. No problem, said my pal Chris Steinbrunner, a member of the Co-op and a veteran programmer at WOR-TV. Since WOR was owned by RKO General, Chris had access to prints of every RKO title. True to his word, he scheduled double features of Wheeler and Woolsey movies at Joe's Place until we had exhausted their filmography.

For my next book, *The Great Movie Shorts*, I borrowed prints from Milt Menell's Select Film Library and ran them at Joe's, but I had to extend my search. On a number of occasions, I left my house at 6 a.m. to catch the early Metroliner train to Washington, D.C. Upon arrival at 9:30 I'd climb the hill to the Library of Congress and screen 35mm prints (originally deposited at the Library for copyright purposes) all day long on a Steenbeck flatbed viewer, furiously scribbling notes until they were about to close at 4:45. Back down the hill to Union Station I'd trudge and board a 6:00 train home to New Jersey. It was a long day but a highly productive one. Sometimes my movie-crazy friend Jon Davison would volunteer to drive for one of these marathon sessions, and we'd stay overnight in D.C. (Lest you think he wasted his time on these jaunts, he went on to produce *Airplane!* and *RoboCop*.) This wouldn't be everyone's idea of a good time, but we had fun.

Alice and I got married on the Ides of March in 1975 and settled in a brand-new apartment building at the corner of 79th Street and Amsterdam Avenue. It was 17 stories tall and we were among the original tenants. Many of us became friendly, and in time we got to know all our fellow dog walkers in the neighborhood. The apartment was euphemistically described as a "junior four," which means it was three-and-a-half rooms—but it was on the corner of 78th Street and set back from the sidewalk, so we had the advantage of natural light streaming in on both sides, which made it cheerful. I worked at home, using the "half room" as my office. Alice had left her job, so we spent all our time together. We were endlessly affectionate newlyweds and we loved our life on the Upper West Side.

In December 1977 I had a very productive month of freelance writing, including an overnight assignment from the *Soho Weekly News* to pay tribute to Charlie Chaplin, who died on Christmas Day. A messenger came to pick up my typed copy on December 26. January came and we were struggling to keep up with our bills because no one who had hired me in December had paid me yet. After Alice heard me fumbling on the phone with one of my editors about getting paid, she set me straight on how to handle the situation. She not only had superior haggling (or to use the Yiddish expression, hondling) skills she'd inherited from her father, she'd also worked in the credit department at Bantam Books. I felt threatened and became defensive. Finally, I sputtered, "If you're so good at this, why don't you do it?" My response hung in the air for a moment, and then we realized the answer: of course she should do it. She had a gift for handling people in this kind of situation and I did not.

It changed our relationship (for the better) and proved to be highly effective. She talked to the accounts payable person at the *Soho Weekly News*, who admitted they were having cash-flow problems and added, "I'm sure you wouldn't want a partial payment."

Alice immediately responded, "I'd be happy to take partial payment right now. When could I follow up with you for the rest?" Alice is a canny negotiator who knows when to be firm and when to use humor. She gets the job done and everyone walks away happy.

I wrote a feature story about animation art for a slick magazine called *Museum*. They offered $500, which was a good sum in those days, but I'd foolishly signed a contract that specified I be paid upon publication instead of on acceptance of the article. By the time the issue came out, *Museum* had left Manhattan and set up shop in Westchester County, just north of the city. It wasn't a good sign. Alice's calls to the editor-in-chief were futile, so she hopped in our car, which we parked on the side street in those days, and drove to Small Claims Court in Westchester. I had just started commuting to Los Angeles, so when the form she was filing called for a court date, she told the clerk that she couldn't guarantee when I would be in town.

"Listen, honey," the clerk said matter-of-factly, "it doesn't matter. They always settle the day before."

Sure enough, one day before our court date the editor called her and said he was putting a check in the mail. When Alice asked why he'd put her through the wringer, he said dispassionately, "We didn't have the money."

Come to think of it, I may have been the only contributor to that issue who got paid. Since then I've called Alice "The Closer."

It's a wonderful feeling to have a life partner who is also my business partner, because there is complete trust between us. We make a good team. I married well. Any success I have achieved as an adult is because of Alice's smarts and encouragement. I would be lost without her.

When friends got to know us as a couple, they remarked upon the fact that we were so openly affectionate with each other. Herb Graff's wife, Anita, said, "It won't last." Forty-five years later, we remain affectionate.

My Two Unlikely Careers

You can't predict when something important is about to happen. Life-changing experiences don't usually announce themselves.

I was a senior at Teaneck High School in New Jersey when a nice woman named Jacquie Egan, who taught English, stopped me in the hall one day and said she wanted me to meet an old friend of hers who was an editor at Signet Books. Ms. Egan had seen the monthly magazine I was publishing, and it inspired her to play matchmaker. "I think the two of you would hit it off," she said, urging me to call her friend and make an appointment to see him after school one day.

I did just that and brought several copies of *Film Fan Monthly* with me when I went to see Patrick O'Connor at New American Library in Manhattan. I had no idea what this meeting might lead to, but naturally I had dreams about writing movie books. I dared not ponder this too seriously.

Patrick (Mr. O'Connor to me) welcomed me into his modest-sized office, which was cluttered with books and manuscripts. When he noticed the magazines on my lap, he asked what I had brought. I told him and he said brightly, "I love your magazine." I wondered how he knew of it. Apparently, he had once subscribed when he was an editor at Popular Library.

Then he asked if I was familiar with a paperback book called

Movies on TV by Steven H. Scheuer. I said I was. I used it every day, as it was the only compendium of movies around, filled with facts, reviews, and ratings.

"What do you think of it?" Mr. O'Connor asked.

"It's good, as far as it goes," I replied.

"What would you do differently?"

"Well," I responded, "I'd put in more cast names; he only gives two or three at most. And I'd add the director's name. I'd say whether the film was in black and white or color and give the original running time so you'd know if a station was cutting the film." I was able to rattle off all this because I knew the book inside and out.

"How'd you like to do it?" he asked.

"Do what?"

"I've been looking for someone to produce a rival version of that book. How'd you like to do it?" he elaborated.

I was thunderstruck. Days later, I signed a contract in the name of *Film Fan Monthly* so my father wouldn't have to co-sign it and Patrick didn't have to reveal to his superiors that he was hiring a 17-year-old to produce a movie reference guide. (Come to think of it, the contract probably wasn't valid, since I was a minor; no one ever brought that up.) Little did I dream that this idea would take root, establish my reputation, and shape my life for the next 45 years.

Patrick had only a few instructions for the book, which had to be completed in a matter of months: the reviews should be written in terse, telegraphic style and accompanied by a star rating. I told him how much I disliked that idea but he was adamant. "People love it," he insisted. "It's a shorthand they respond to."

He was right, as I would learn, although readers interpreted the stars in different ways. A few years later, within the same week, I was stopped on a New York street by a guy who told me he liked the book but doubled my ratings to align with his opinions and another guy who told me he cut my ratings in half for the same reason!

I hired a person to churn out reviews by the bushel—James Robert Parish, who worked with a nice woman named Florence Solomon. It was Jim who noticed that many reviews in *Movies on TV* were identical to those in an industry publication called the *BIB Sourcebook* (BIB being Broadcast Information Bureau). He advised me to check all my write-ups so I didn't inadvertently copy anything from Scheuer, which was easy to do when describing a formulaic programmer from the 1940s. How many ways could one describe a plot like "Crooked lawyer murders his wife and takes it on the lam aboard a ship bound for Havana"?

I heeded Jim's warning and made certain that never happened. Sure enough, however, when Scheuer got wind of our upcoming book he called Patrick and threatened to sue for plagiarism. I wish I could have seen Patrick's face as I told him that we'd anticipated this problem and worked around it. That was one happy man. He met with Scheuer, showed him some of our book, and sent him on his way.

But Scheuer had something we didn't: a good title. His book had originally been called *The TV Key Movie Guide*, plugging the television listing service he offered to newspapers. This was too close to *TV Movie Guide*, which is what we wanted to call our enterprise. He then rechristened his paperback *Movies on TV*, another perfect name. We wound up with *TV Movies*, which neither my editor nor I was crazy about. It was the best we could do, and we made do with it.

None of this was remotely foreseeable when I had that first meeting with Patrick in 1968. He was the one who suggested that I hire people to help me compile the first edition of the *Guide*, which boasted 8,000 reviews. He also warned me not to spend all my $10,000 advance—a wise tip I wish I had taken more seriously. But I used the money well: I bought a reconditioned IBM Selectric, the Rolls Royce of typewriters, which served me beautifully for many years. I also had a chance to purchase a complete run of my favorite trade magazine of the 1930s, *Motion Picture Herald*. Until then I'd only been able to browse its beautiful color advertising pages at the New York Public Library: now I had my very own copies. I still look at them every day. (My daughter teases me about my nerdish idea of a spending spree.)

Without my knowledge, Signet and Patrick hired a copy editor and fact checker to go over my submission. They were both movie buffs and many times over saved me from being humiliated. It was then that I learned the first rule of working on a reference book: every detail is important and should pass under several sets of eyes before going into print.

Back then, it was said that 70 percent of all book sales took place on Fifth Avenue in Manhattan. One day Patrick said, "You are only allowed to make two complaint calls a month about your book not being in the window of Doubleday's Book Store." That rule was hard to stick to. I couldn't help nosing around every bookstore I encountered, at home or on the road, to see if they carried my "baby." Many stores didn't have a section of books about movies in those days.

It was five years before Signet asked me to update the book, which I was eager to do. Here was my chance to correct mistakes, expand the write-ups a bit, and make it a better book. My new editor didn't seem to mind. I also started building a team of contributors, most of whom stayed with me for decades. I owe an awful lot to Mike Clark, Rob Edelman, and Bill Warren (all of whom have passed on in recent years), as well as Pete Hammond, Luke Sader, Spencer Green, Joe Leydon, Michael Scheinfeld, Jerry Beck, Casey St. Charnez, and my daughter Jessie, who cut her teeth writing reviews of youth-oriented movies and Rob Schneider comedies. My assistants over the years have also worn the hat of managing editor, and I'm grateful to Margaret Black, Ben Herndon, and Darwyn Carson for keeping the book afloat.

By the time I married Alice and moved into an apartment on West 79th Street in Manhattan, we had devised a system for making additions and corrections to the *Guide*. Our dining room table became a workspace. We cut up a copy of the existing book and glued each review to a separate piece of paper. If we wanted to add a name to the cast or change a running time, we wrote it in the margin using a ballpoint pen and put a caret where it was to be inserted. This process was cumbersome (and required Alice to run to Woolworth's on the corner of Broadway and 79th Street for more glue sticks on a regular basis) but it worked.

Come to think of it, the history of my *Guide* parallels the advances in technology and communication over five decades. I never dreamt of a day when computers would replace typewriters, and a hand-held device could hold an encyclopedia's worth of information. I lived through the era of fax machines, the malling of America and arrival of bookstore chains, the debut of videocassettes, laserdiscs and DVDs, and streaming. I witnessed the decline of bookstores and the coming of Amazon.

For years the bane of my existence was running times. When a new movie opened you could consult five major newspapers and the Hollywood trade magazines and find five entirely different accounts of its length. I cultivated a network of contacts at the studios, people who understood the importance of getting it right. It might be a publicist or someone in the print traffic department. Once I called United Artists and asked how they determined a definitive running time for their movies. "Uh, we use your book," the man answered. It was flattering but not useful. Then home video came along and made it possible for us to glean the answers ourselves.

With *TV Movies* under my belt, I had an open door to pitch other book ideas, first at Signet (which became New American Library) and then Crown, which was a hardcover house. I wrote books on subjects near and dear to me: *Movie Comedy Teams*, *The Great Movie Shorts*, and *The Disney Films*. What a golden opportunity. I collaborated with my friend Richard W. Bann on a book called *Our Gang: The Life and Times of the Little Rascals* that Crown had no faith in, especially after it was turned down by the Nostalgia Book Club. But to their surprise it kept selling and selling, requiring Crown to go back to press repeatedly. We made extensive revisions for a paperback reprint a decade later under the title *The Little Rascals: The Life and Times of Our Gang* and again it defied their expectations, eventually selling more than 100,000 copies, an almost unheard-of number for any book about old movies.

Patrick O'Connor gave me another extraordinary opportunity when he left New American Library to run a paperback company called Curtis Books, and then moved upstairs (literally) to their sister imprint, Popular Library. He wanted a series of original film books but hadn't the budget to hire me as an editor, so I became a book packager instead, hiring authors to deliver manuscripts which I then sold to Popular Library. I midwifed more than a dozen good books on such varied subjects as Abbott and Costello, B Movies, Stanley Kubrick, directors Don Siegel and Mitchell Leisen, and animation genius Tex Avery. It was a wonderful gig while it lasted.

Patrick lived a long and fruitful life, and I was lucky enough to reconnect with him when he and his partner, Andrew Ciesielski, moved to Pasadena. I even wrote the foreword to his colorful memoir, which was published posthumously. (In it he tells a completely different version of how he came to hire me, but Patrick never let facts stand in the way of a good story.)

But how am I to respond when someone asks me how to break into publishing?

I first appeared on television when I was in my teens, promoting my magazine, *Film Fan Monthly*, on New York City's legendary *Joe Franklin Show*. Later, as a published author, I made annual book tours, appearing on local radio and TV shows from coast to coast.

I had many colorful experiences on local shows. Once, a friend from Columbus, Ohio, warned me that the program I was about to do had a studio audience that "skewed toward death."

But television would prove to be my friend. It was my appearance on the *Today* show one morning in 1982 that led to my being hired by *Entertainment Tonight*—a roller-coaster gig that somehow lasted 30 years.

Timing in life is everything. A man named Garry Hart, who worked in the research department at Paramount Television (and later became its president), saw me on *Today* and contacted the newly hired executive producer of *ET*, which was then struggling to find its footing. Jim Bellows was a legendary newspaper editor who chanced to meet Paramount chairman Barry Diller at a party. Diller offered Jim an opportunity to try his hand at producing television and giving the new show some journalistic credibility.

If I had tried to get on the show in its earlier incarnations, they would have slammed the door in my face. Instead, the telephone rang in our Manhattan apartment. Alice answered and asked who was calling.

"Bruce Cook, from *Entertainment Tonight*."

"May I ask what it's in reference to?" she asked.

"Employment," he replied.

"Yours or his?" she asked.

"His," he responded.

"In that case I'll put him right on."

That's my Alice.

Bruce and I chatted for a few minutes. His original intention was to have me audition at their studio in New York, a smallish satellite operation. He called back the following Monday and said they had decided it would be better if I came to Los Angeles so we could meet each other and I could see how the program was put together. I asked when and he answered, "Tomorrow."

I had a terrible cold, but I felt I shouldn't say no. The next day I was flying from JFK to LAX, sniffling all the way. I picked up a rental car and followed directions to the Beverly Hilton Hotel. As I approached the front desk a well-dressed couple cut in front of me to ask, "Where is the Milton Berle event?" I felt reassured that I was now in Hollywood.

The next day I drove to *ET*'s offices on Vine Street, in a building and studio owned by Merv Griffin. I was taken to Jim Bellows' office, where he said, "You know, we brought you out here to do movie reviews. Do you think you can prepare two reviews for tomorrow morning?" At that moment, I swear my mind flashed to an archetypal scene I'd read about from the silent-movie days. In the morning an assistant director would go to the front gate of the studio where a crowd would be waiting. "You!" he'd say, pointing to a particular fellow. "Can you ride a horse?" If the man wanted to work that day, he'd answer, "Yes." I wanted to ride a horse so I told Jim, "No problem."

As it happens, I had seen a couple of films that were about to be released, *Annie* and *Dead Men Don't Wear Plaid*. I was assigned a producer named Steve Paskay, who walked me through the procedure for a television review, allowing for a film clip and then a voice-over to cover more footage before returning to me on-camera. Early the next morning I showed up at the studio and recorded them both, surprising the staff by being able to swivel my body toward an imaginary movie screen that they would later insert electronically.

The show's line producer, Vin Di Bona, said, "If it were up to me I'd hire you right now, but we have to hear from the Paramount execs." He assured me that they'd have an answer soon. With that, I flew home. The next day, Alice and I boarded another plane to Columbus, Ohio, for Cinevent, a gathering of film buffs and collectors we'd always wanted to try.

On Saturday I was browsing through posters and stills in the dealers' room when someone I didn't know said, "You were good on TV last night."

This didn't register right away. "What was I doing?" I asked. "A movie review?"

"Yes," he said.

Here we were in the middle of Memorial Day weekend with no one to call to find out more. I had signed a piece of paper that gave them the right to air my two pieces, for which I'd be paid union scale, $500 apiece. But it would have been nice to tell me they were going to show one of them.

When we arrived home late Monday, our answering machine (then using reel-to-reel tape) was nearly full with messages of congratulations. My friend Jerry Beck told me that the show's host, Ron Hendren, even welcomed me as their "new movie critic."

I couldn't wait till Tuesday morning to call Bruce Cook, the man who had first called me from *ET*.

"Does this mean I have the job?" I asked.

"No," he replied. "But we had the review and the movie just opened so we thought we should use it. We're still waiting to hear from Paramount."

So that was that, until they aired the second review on Wednesday night, again without informing me.

Alice looked into her crystal ball and said, "You know what's going to happen? Next Monday when they realize they don't have another review ready to go, they'll call you." That's just what they did.

"Can you come out tomorrow and tape some more reviews?" asked Bruce.

"No," I replied.

"Why?"

"Because I haven't seen any other movies."

"Could you fly here later this week?"

"Sure."

Thus began a year and a half of transcontinental flights. At first I'd be home for two full weeks, then I'd fly to L.A. on Sunday night, show up for work first thing Monday morning and come home either Thursday or Friday late afternoon. If the schedule had remained like that I might still be commuting, but before long I was traveling every other week. Then I was spending a ridiculous amount of time finagling my calendar.

"If I see this movie in New York, I can wait another day before going back to L.A. No, wait. I'll miss the L.A. showing of this other film...."

Finally, Alice said, "Enough."

We were used to spending all our time together and what's more, she was trying to get pregnant. So we moved to Los Angeles, temporarily, on November 2, 1983. We sublet our apartment (legally—the only people to do so in the history of the city) and rented a nice little house in Studio City, a short distance from my work in Hollywood. Following the advice of a friend, we brought our own bed and a few other pieces that would make us feel at home. We settled in and even had a New Year's Eve party. One guest was dumbfounded at how we had decorated so quickly and settled in.

"I've been out here for five years and I haven't gotten this far," he marveled.

We eventually bought a house not far from the one we'd been renting. That's when we packed up the rest of our New York belongings. A few years after that, with a baby now in the picture and Alice's mother living with us, we realized we needed more space and rebuilt a house in Toluca Lake, a lovely neighborhood we described to friends as "Bob Hope adjacent." Our daughter, Jessie, grew up there, and we all have many fond memories of that home. (Every Halloween we made sure Jessie trick-or-treated at the Hope residence, where she would be given a tchotchke sporting Bob Hope's caricature. One year it was a paddle ball, another year a kazoo.) Eventually we downsized a bit and moved to Sherman

Oaks in the San Fernando Valley. Jessie and her husband, Scott Hadfield, live in a basement apartment and we meet in what we call Middle Earth, also known as the kitchen.

There were 120 people on staff at *Entertainment Tonight*, and we shared a collegial bonding experience as the show grew to become a bona fide hit. It was the first show of its kind. When I joined it, we aired on independent station KTLA in Los Angeles every day at 4:30 and again at midnight. Many of the staffers gathered around the news desk to watch the late afternoon broadcast, and I joined in. We cheered each other on and sometimes made fun of pieces that seemed cheesy. It was genuinely exciting. The immediacy of planning and taping a piece, then seeing it on the air the same day was a novelty for someone like me who had spent years working on books. Sometimes I'd stay awake in my hotel room and watch the rebroadcast at 12 a.m.

It didn't take long for me to meet the only other die-hard movie buffs on the staff: Luke Sader, who had just moved out from New York, and Pete Hammond, a native Californian who has saved the ticket stubs from every movie he's ever seen in a theater. My kind of guy. (He married a terrific woman, Madelyn Hammond, a savvy entrepreneur and Jessie's godmother.) The three of us became unofficial musketeers at *ET* and have remained close ever since.

But how am I supposed to respond when someone asks me how to break into television?

By the time I made my debut on *Entertainment Tonight*, I had published a handful of books and enjoyed modest success in the realm of film history. But it was nothing compared to the impact of appearing on television. After moving to L.A. in 1983, Alice and I received an invitation to the AFI Life Achievement Award dinner, where Lillian Gish was being honored. A friend who had attended these events before urged us not to leave the moment the program was over. Having been to the Beverly Hilton Hotel ballroom, he knew that it took time for the most important guests to make their way to the exit, so we took his advice and lingered. Michael Caine eyed my wife—which she has never forgotten—and then we spotted Fred Astaire standing to one side with his wife, Robyn, waiting for the crowd to thin out. We approached them and I made small talk about what a lovely tribute it had been.

Mr. Astaire looked at me and said, "Have we met before? Your face is so familiar."

Robyn gave him a little jab and said, "Oh, Fred, that's Leonard Maltin. We watch him all the time on *Entertainment Tonight*."

There is only one word to describe that moment: thrilling. It was not the last time someone famous recognized me, and let me assure you, it never gets old.

What's more, for Alice and me, every day seemed like a trip to Fantasyland. One day she returned from a shopping trip all agog. "I just saw Dana Andrews in the frozen food section of Ralph's," she exclaimed. Another day she recognized a nearby car lot as the site where Janet Leigh rented her vehicle at the beginning of *Psycho*! (It has since been rebuilt.) We'll never forget the evening we made a wrong turn at a confusing crossroads in Culver City and found ourselves staring at the plantation facade we knew as the trademark on David O. Selznick's films—like *Gone With the Wind*.

It was all magical to me, seeing Penny Singleton (who played Blondie in the long-running movie series of the same name) leaving a local supermarket or braking my car so I wouldn't run over Billy Curtis, the star of *The Terror of Tiny Town*, who frequented a coffee shop just down the street from Merv Griffin's studio.

One day I picked up the phone and dialed a number a friend had obtained for me. In a moment's time, I found myself talking to Pinky Lee. When I was very young, he had a popular children's show on national television, and I thought he was the greatest thing I'd ever seen. Now I was actually talking to him—and he knew who

I was! We arranged to tape an interview in a few days' time, and I asked if we could make dubs of some video copies he had of his 1950s show. He was reluctant to let them out of his hands, but I assured him that if he came over to our offices we could transfer them right in front of his eyes.

The morning he came by we said a friendly hello. Then, as he reached into a paper bag to pull out the tapes he'd brought along, he started getting nervous. "Where was that first show?" It was right where he put it, on the desk in front of him. "Did I already give you the second tape?" "No, you haven't taken that out yet." He made us all nervous for no reason at all.

In the afternoon the crew and I went to his apartment, where he gave me a good interview. The manic nervousness of the morning dissipated. I had to admit, I didn't remember that much about him or his show; I just knew that I was crazy about him when I was four years old. At the end of our chat, I asked if he would put on his famous checkered hat, look directly at the camera and recreate his sign-off. As he did, the years melted away and I remembered why I loved him so much. What's more, he still had it in him to summon that feeling. It was a glorious experience.

I made my big-screen debut in *Gremlins 2: The New Batch* in 1990, in which I was attacked and presumably killed by the angry creatures. This novel experience was payback for having given the original *Gremlins* a bad review on *ET*. (It also earned me a spot on two Topps gum cards telling the story of *Gremlins 2*.) Director Joe Dante and I had met when we were teenagers back East, and while never close, we were friendly and spoke the same language as movie buffs. This marked the first time I was put in the position of reviewing a film made by someone I knew—and telling the world I didn't like it. What an awkward situation. It caused a rift between Joe and me, which I completely understand. No one enjoys being criticized—even me. At a newspaper or magazine, I would have recused myself and had another critic review *Gremlins*. At *ET* there was only me. I debated whether I should soft-pedal my response to the film but ultimately decided that I had to be honest. Telling the truth about how I felt was essentially my job description. I couldn't waffle.

The story had an eventual happy ending: Joe's producer Mike Finnell called me a few years later and asked if I'd be willing to appear in *Gremlins 2: The New Batch*. "I think I owe you that," I replied. That's how I wound up on a soundstage at Warner Bros. being directed by Joe, who said "Just use your own words." Holding a copy of the VHS cassette of *Gremlins*, I gave it a bad review all over again, until the creatures slung strips of 35mm film around my neck and yanked me back in my seat. Steven Spielberg, who served as executive producer on the film, wanted to use my scene in the trailer, but I thought that would spoil the surprise.

This is the reason I try not to get friendly with actors and filmmakers, even when it's tempting to do so.

My next (and possibly final) screen appearance was in an ingenious mock documentary called *Forgotten Silver*, directed by a then-little-known New Zealander named Peter Jackson. The contact was made by our mutual friend Rick Baker, the multi-Oscar-winning makeup artist who lived down the street from me in Toluca Lake. Peter coached me by explaining the points he wanted to make about a fictional film pioneer named Colin McKenzie. Like Joe Dante, he encouraged me to use my own words. The response to this hoax has been gratifying over the years. I've turned down other similar projects because I don't want to wear out the joke.

The most satisfying phone call I ever had relating to my publishing career came after I had been on *Entertainment Tonight* for two years. I'll never forget taking that call in my tiny corner of the *ET* offices on Vine Street in Hollywood and listening to my new editor, Arnold Dolin, back in Manhattan. He told me that Penguin had just concluded its fall sales meeting and wanted to make two changes, if I agreed: putting my name above the title and my photo on the cover. My life, and the fate of that book, was about to change, all because I wound up on a hit TV show.

It was also Penguin's idea to publish the book annually, to keep up with the mushrooming popularity of home video. That was a smart move, although it had a major impact on my life. Every spring was now deadline time, which involved a lot of work under pressure. Travel plans took a back seat to reading galley proofs and updating entries week by week, but the book is still paying me rewards today. By the time the Internet and social media put us out of business in 2014, *Leonard Maltin's Movie Guide* had sold millions of copies. I still can't quite believe it.

Hollywood: The First Time Around

My family tended to take auto trips along the eastern seaboard, so I was jealous of my friend Barry Ahrendt, whose family drove out to California two summers in a row. The idea of visiting Hollywood seemed exciting, even exotic, to me; we never went much farther than Niagara Falls. Most of all, it was the home of Disneyland. (Barry was kind enough to bring me souvenirs from the park, which I still have: original cels of Chip 'n' Dale and Ludwig von Drake from the Art Corner at Disneyland. They cost $2.98 back then, before animation art became collectible—and expensive.)

When I was 14 my parents allowed me to travel by myself to St. Louis, Missouri, to rendezvous with a nice man named Bud LeMaster, whom I'd met as a pen pal, and who stayed at our home when he visited New Jersey. He offered to drive me to Baraboo, Wisconsin, for the second annual Cinephile convention. The Society for Cinephiles was a group founded by Sam Rubin, publisher of *The 8mm Collector*, and it was Sam's idea to launch a yearly gathering where like-minded film buffs could get together. The grownups who populated this group were remarkably welcoming to my teenage self and never made me feel self-conscious about my age. And it was the Cinecon that enabled me to make my first trip west in 1968.

All of the visiting Cinephiles stayed at the fabled Hollywood

Roosevelt Hotel, which had grown a bit seedy. That's where I had my first official "star sighting." When our 16mm projector broke down in the wee hours of the morning, a group of us ventured into the hotel's Cinegrill, and there was Broderick Crawford hunched over the bar, his arm around a young blonde whom I am tempted to describe as a floozy. It was an odd but memorable milestone.

I called on my only real contact in "the business," Bob Thomas, the longtime Hollywood correspondent for the Associated Press. He kindly provided me with two precious local connections: cigar-chomping comedian and home-movie entrepreneur Ken Murray, who screened a 16mm print of his Oscar-winning novelty feature *Bill and Coo* for me in his living room, and the great comedy performer Billy Gilbert. Gilbert was one of my comedy heroes. Not only was he a naturally funny man, famous for his comic sneeze (which landed him the job of voicing Sneezy in *Snow White and the Seven Dwarfs*), but he'd worked with seemingly everyone in show business, including Charlie Chaplin, Laurel and Hardy, and Our Gang. By the time I went to visit him at his home in North Hollywood he'd suffered a stroke, but his loving wife, Ella (known as Lolly), knew all his stories and happily prompted him along.

I soaked up a lot of show business lore during that wonderful afternoon. Billy had a gigantic scrapbook with signed 11x14 photos of stars with whom he'd worked, and the images sparked his failing memory. With one glance at Shirley Temple he broke into a broad smile, remembering how much he liked her. He felt the same about dancer Eleanor Powell: "and then she had to marry that no-good son-of-a-bitch," meaning Glenn Ford.

I also got a lesson in show-business perspective. When I told Billy that I'd first seen him on the Andy Devine kiddie show *Andy's Gang*, the name didn't ring a bell. Then Lolly remembered it and explained that he'd shot all his scenes for an entire season of the program in just one day. It was a mere speck of sand in his vast career, but it meant the world to me. I'm sorry I didn't get to visit with the Gilberts again, but Billy did me the honor of writing (with Lolly's help) an introduction for my book *Movie Comedy Teams*.

When I decided to return to Los Angeles during the next few summers, I worked hard to arrange interviews before my arrival, using what few contacts I had made, like a friendly *Film Fan Monthly* subscriber who happened to work in publicity at the ABC Television Network. In those days I had to find pay telephones several times a day to make follow-up calls and update my schedule. (I felt it was bad form to admit I didn't have a number where they could return my calls.) It didn't help that I was dependent on friends to drive me wherever I needed to go; if you're under 25 you can't rent a car, even if you can afford one. I made some excruciatingly long walks by Los Angeles standards, but I survived.

I pursued mostly character actors and unsung heroes during these early trips, and had wonderful conversations with Joan Blondell, Grady Sutton, Edgar Buchanan, Una Merkel, and unappreciated directors Mitchell Leisen and Gordon Douglas.

My most awkward moment arose during a lovely conversation with Una Merkel, whose honeyed Southern accent was fully intact. I had on my lap a typed list of all her movies in chronological order. One by one I asked about the famous people she worked with, from Jean Harlow to W.C. Fields. She couldn't have been sweeter as we worked our way through her career, but the dialogue came to a standstill when I asked how she came to make a short subject in the 1940s with comedian Harry Langdon. She stared at me and said, "I never worked with Harry Langdon."

I knew full well that she did. Not only did I have an 8x10 still from the two-reel short, I had screened a 16mm print of it. As I searched for something to say, she added, "I was a great fan of Harry Langdon's. I certainly would remember working with him." With that, I skipped ahead to the next notable movie on my list.

Afterwards, I pondered this conundrum. Why had she blanked out? Then I realized that this short and another that she headlined for Columbia Pictures may have been the low point of her Hollywood career. After all, she had been a prominent second lead at MGM in the 1930s and would wind up on Broadway in the 1950s and '60s, even winning a Tony Award. Perhaps something went wrong in between. Since then I've learned that her mother committed suicide in 1945, and she tried to follow that same path seven years later. Fortunately, a nurse caught her overdose of pills in the nick of time. No wonder she might have erased a stressful period of her life and forgotten a three-day gig filming with an aged Harry Langdon.

I can't resist adding a postscript: in the early 1970s, onetime stage-and-screen star Fifi D'Orsay made a heartwarming comeback on Broadway as one of the stars of Stephen Sondheim's *Follies*. A contributor to *Film Fan Monthly* named Don Stanke asked if I'd be interested in publishing an interview with her, and I said yes. I added, "Be sure to ask her about working in a Columbia short with Harry Langdon," which she did in 1942.

She had no memory of him.

Of the people I spoke with on my first trip to Los Angeles, one became a dear friend: comedy actress Dorothy Granger, a leading lady in comedy shorts and mostly a bit player in features—scores of them. I came to the conclusion that supporting players often had the best stories. They weren't blinded by the spotlight and had a more interesting point of view than many stars. Dorothy was a perfect example, an ebullient woman with fond memories of working with Laurel and Hardy, watching Spanky McFarland's original screen test, and so much more. Every now and then while watching Turner Classic Movies, we'll see a movie from the 1930s and '40s and one of us will cry out, "There's Dorothy!"

She retired in the 1950s and married a nice man named Jack Hilder who ran a successful upholstery business. The walls of her workspace were dotted with framed 8x10 photos, including one of her on a date with Clark Gable and another I never forgot. One night while watching television, she happened to see herself in a small part as a nurse with Robert Mitchum in the 1952 movie *One Minute to Zero*. On a whim, she wrote him a note asking for an autographed photo, nearly 20 years later, and he obliged, inscribing the picture with these words: "For Dorothy—I grieve that you denied me your body."

I returned to Los Angeles in September 1975 with my bride. Alice and I had married in March, and Dorothy and Jack insisted on taking us to dinner at their favorite restaurant, Trader Vic's in the Beverly Hilton Hotel. We had a wonderful time together, and Dorothy pointed out Burt Reynolds at a nearby table. But Alice and I were more excited to see Mr. Show Business, George Jessel, exiting the establishment with what used to be called a young chippie. "Did you take a doggie bag?" he inquired as they passed by our table. We were in heaven.

I put Dorothy on camera just once for *Entertainment Tonight* as part of a story I was doing about Laurel and Hardy's foreign-language films. In the earliest days of talkies, Hollywood didn't know how to deal with the huge overseas market. No one thought of dubbing back then, or if they did, they concluded that it was too cumbersome a process. Instead, several studios made alternative versions of their films. The most famous example is the Spanish-language *Dracula*, which was shot at night on the same sets that Bela Lugosi and director Tod Browning used during daylight hours. Laurel and Hardy and the other stars (even the Our Gang kids) voiced their own dialogue, with help from coaches and phonetic scripts written out on blackboards. Audiences in France, Spain, Italy, or Germany accepted their less-than-perfect accents as part of the comedy.

For *The Laurel-Hardy Murder Case*, Dorothy had such a small part that she persuaded the powers that be to let her speak her own line in multiple languages, a feat that she was justifiably proud of. I was equally proud to have testimony from an actress who was still alive to tell the tale.

To shoot our brief interview Dorothy came to the *ET* studio. We were located on the west side of the Paramount studio lot— the part that had been RKO Radio Pictures way back when. As I escorted Dorothy to our stage, she stopped dead in her tracks. She recognized the entrance to a soundstage across the street and dug in her wallet for a precious snapshot she carried with her. Sure enough, she and her longtime costar Leon Errol were standing on that exact spot in the late 1940s—40 years earlier! She kindly allowed me to make a copy of the photo, which I treasure.

Incidentally, I also interviewed the Spanish *Dracula*'s leading lady, Lupita Tovar, in her beautiful home. She was married to the powerful agent Paul Kohner and traveled in the best Hollywood circles. Her daughter, Susan Kohner, enjoyed a brief but notable acting career and married fashion designer John Weitz. Her grand-children are filmmakers Paul and Chris Weitz. For our interview Lupita sat beneath original oil portraits of her children painted by her friend Diego Rivera.

An exciting adventure came about in 1970 when, after having my latest proposal turned down by New American Library, my ed-itor mentioned that they were interested in a book about camera-men. I didn't respond at first. What did I know about cameramen? But after a month or so, with my spring semester winding down at NYU, I figured I could at least try to write a proposal, and I did, inspired by reading Arthur C. Miller and Fred Balshofer's informa-tive memoir *One Reel a Week*. NAL bought the book, which I called *Behind the Camera*. Now all I had to do was write it!

As he so often did, Bill Everson came to my rescue: he as-sured me that if I went to Hollywood I'd find a number of vet-erans hanging out at the "clubhouse" headquarters of the ASC, the American Society of Cinematographers. Not willing to leave this to chance, I called the ASC and got through to its president, three-time Oscar winner Arthur Miller, who not only promised me an interview but offered to put me in touch with some of his colleagues. Miller, whose career dated back to the earliest days of silent films (including *The Perils of Pauline*) and continued through Academy Award-winning work on *How Green Was My Valley*, *The Song of Bernadette*, and *Anna and the King of Siam*, was a walking history of motion pictures all by himself, and his contemporaries were in the same league. My friend David Chierichetti acted as a liaison with another old-timer, Hal Mohr, who was married to actress-turned-UCLA-professor Evelyn Venable. On the strength of those two commitments, I headed to Hollywood.

The next few weeks were extraordinary, as I absorbed the history of filmmaking from a cameraman's point of view, day by day, soaking up my newfound knowledge like a sponge. There were some disappointments: I wasn't able to connect with James Wong Howe or Leon Shamroy, although I spoke to Shamroy briefly on the phone, but Arthur Miller lined up interviews for me with modern masters Lucien Ballard and Conrad Hall. (I listened in on his phone calls, and he didn't give them a chance to refuse.) Another living legend, Hal Rosson, was sitting in the ASC clubhouse and agreed to an interview right on the premises.

I had all sorts of misadventures during this trip. I put my audiocassette into the recorder backwards and missed a huge chunk of Hal Rosson's interview, which I then had to piece together from memory. If that didn't test my powers of concentration enough, Lucien Ballard froze up when he saw the recorder and asked that I turn it off. He didn't mind my taking notes, but whenever my pen started flying across the page, he seemed to get nervous. Ballard lived along Pacific Coast Highway in Malibu, where I'd never been before, but I was so intent on capturing our conversation that I didn't pay much attention to the view or my beautiful surroundings. I also thought it would be rude to refuse the beer and tacos his wife graciously offered me, even though I'd never consumed either one before (and haven't since).

Conrad Hall, the youngest of the cinematographers I met, also lived in Malibu, and I got a brief hello from his housemate, actress Katharine Ross, whom he'd photographed in *Butch Cassidy and the Sundance Kid* and *Tell Them Willie Boy Is Here*. It was a rare moment of glamor during an expedition populated by colorful and crusty senior citizens.

One day, David and I came upon a box of old production photos at a Hollywood memorabilia shop, and I purchased the most interesting ones. Several of the stills didn't have captions, so I showed them to Arthur Miller. He recognized the Technicolor specialist Duke Green in one shot and within moments had the very same Duke Green on the phone.

"Hello, Duke?" he barked into the phone. "How are you? I'm sitting here with a young fella who's got a still we can't identify." He then described details of the camera and an actress we recognized in order to pinpoint what movie he was making in the photo, shot some 35 years earlier. What an experience.

Miller also handed me a strip of 35mm negative about six inches long: it was a test shot he had made on location for *Brigham Young, Frontiersman* with Tyrone Power and Linda Darnell. He had devised a makeshift portable darkroom, with cloth sleeves, that would enable him to expose and print a short length of film and see exactly what his camera was capturing before proceeding with a scene. This was one example that he'd saved, and he graciously allowed me to take it with me.

One day while we were chatting, George Folsey (who photographed *Animal Crackers*, *Meet Me in St. Louis*, *Seven Brides for Seven Brothers*, and countless other pictures) popped his head into the office, apologizing for the interruption by saying he just had to say a quick hello to "the master." Imagine my shock when, just weeks after returning home, I read in *Variety* that Miller had taken his own life at the age of 75. I'd never asked any personal questions and had no idea what might have driven him to such a desperate act. I only know how kind and generous he was to me.

That book, which was later revised and reprinted under the title *The Cinematographer's Art*, has stood me in good stead with aspiring filmmakers ever since. A number of young, successful cameramen, from Ernest Dickerson (*Do The Right Thing*) to Matthew Libatique (*Black Swan*) have told me that the book was an inspiration to them: I can't think of a higher compliment except one. In 2005 I was presented with a Distinguished Achievement Award from the American Society of Cinematographers at their annual awards dinner. It was presented to me by the late Allen Daviau, whose credits include *E.T. the Extra-Terrestrial* and *The Color Purple*. To say I was honored would be an understatement.

Alan King and the American Academy of Humor

What? You've never heard of the American Academy of Humor? Join a very large club. Almost no one remembers it from its year and a half of existence in the 1970s, but for me it was a big deal. It brought me into contact with show business at a level I never dreamt of.

It all began with a phone call from an eager assistant at the venerable William Morris Agency who thought I should meet his boss, Karen Hitzig. She was, at that time, the only agent at the firm who worked in both the literary and television departments. This set my head spinning with ideas. Our meeting was cordial but wasn't the stepping-stone I had hoped for. Still, I owe Karen a debt of thanks for suggesting that I contact her husband, Rupert, who was then partnered with Alan King, the comedian, actor, and producer.

Alan and Rupert had produced a prime-time special for ABC called *The Comedy Awards*, and it was successful enough for the network to commission a second annual program. But Alan had a condition: he asked them to cough up an additional $25,000 so he could launch the American Academy of Humor, which he envisioned as a comedy hall of fame. Its proposed location would be alongside the Shubert Theatre in Los Angeles, where ABC was headquartered on the West Coast.

I walked into the offices of King Hitzig Productions on Fifth Avenue at just the right moment. My books and credentials convinced Alan and Rupert that I could turn the American Academy of Humor into an actual organization, instead of just an excuse for a TV special. And that's just what I did. You might call it a dream gig. Alan asked what title I would like, and I suggested "Curator." He approved. (Alan quit school in his teens, started working in nightclubs, and put his brothers through law and medical school, but he was strictly self-educated. I sensed that, as a result, he had ambivalent feelings toward educated people, including me. He needn't have felt that way: he was incredibly smart.)

My first order of business was to expand the membership. For the first Comedy Awards Alan had sent ballots to about 200 voters—friends and colleagues in the world of comedy. I redoubled his efforts (and ghosted a cover letter that he signed) soliciting responses from cartoonists, columnists, playwrights, humorists, screenwriters, and show business veterans. There was no fee involved, just a willingness to vote on the upcoming ballot for "Funniest Movie of the Year" and such. Almost everyone said yes, ranging from veteran writer-producer Nunnally Johnson to Charles M. Schulz. Reading the incidental notes that some of them wrote on the response cards was fascinating. One that's stayed with me all this time was from Frank Sinatra, because he had such beautiful handwriting. Who knew?

I began publishing an AAH newsletter and included a roster of members, separated into three columns. They typed out evenly but there was an extra line at the end of the third column. Here, Alan's comedic savvy came into play. He had me insert the word "and" before the final name, Henny Youngman. Perfect.

A friend of mine worked at Scholastic Magazines and I suggested that the AAH cosponsor a contest for the best humorous essay—with Alan King as the final judge. This was another activity that lent credibility to the Academy and didn't cost a dime.

Then I programmed three nights of panels at the New School for Social Research, where I was teaching my animation course at the time. The first evening dealt with women in humor and featured Anita Loos, Nora Ephron, columnist Chris Chase, and TV writer Susan Silver. A male gathering the next week had *National Lampoon*'s and *SNL*'s Michael O'Donoghue, playwright/screenwriter Peter Stone, and a last-minute fill-in who happened to be Peter's house guest, columnist Art Buchwald. I moderated both panels and it was a heady experience.

For the final presentation I promised—and after a last-minute calendar glitch, delivered—Alan King. Not knowing better, I made no protest when the school had each of us standing at a lectern on opposite sides of the stage. We opened the evening with a film clip of one of Alan's favorite comedians of days gone by, Willie Howard. Then I introduced Alan to the sold-out crowd; that was about all I got to say for the next hour and a half. At first Alan was visibly nervous talking to a so-called college crowd, but the minute he realized they were just an audience he felt at home and held court in high style.

When I got a signal to wrap things up, I said on the spur of the moment, "Printed copies of my remarks can be had for ten cents in coin and a self-addressed envelope." It got a huge laugh, and Alice swore that Alan looked annoyed. If that's true he didn't hold it against me, I'm happy to say.

As the months went by and I continued publishing our newsletter, which featured interviews and guest columns, I was having a wonderful time on the periphery of show biz. That fall Alan and Rupert produced a live, hour-long variety show for ABC called *Saturday Night Live* with Howard Cosell, featuring the bombastic sportscaster who was being positioned as the new Ed Sullivan. I had no involvement with the show, but just by being in the office suite I got to eavesdrop on all sorts of meetings and encounters. A major pop singer didn't want to actually perform—he just wanted to chat with Cosell for his healthy guest-star fee—while George Burns (who was plugging his new movie *The Sunshine Boys*) refused to come on unless he got to perform. I remember the day a painfully shy young comic came in to audition and got the job. It was another decade before Christopher Guest established himself on *Saturday Night Live* and in the movie *This Is Spinal Tap*.

Alan's old friend Herb Sargent was part of the staff, and after half a season of dismal shows and equally dismal ratings, Herb said, "ABC called Howard in and pulled him out from under his rug," as good a piece of wordplay as I've ever heard firsthand. My chief memory of Cosell is that he liked to swat whoever was near him when he got to the punch line of a funny story; my thigh is still sore after all these years.

Toward the end of the calendar year, plans began in earnest for the *Second Annual Comedy Awards*, to be held in January at the Shubert Theater in Los Angeles. There were ballots to prepare, voting to be supervised, guests and presenters to be lined up. I wondered if there would be any place for me. I finally worked up the courage to ask Alan if I would be flying to L.A. with the rest of the staff. "Of course you're coming," he replied. "You're the curator!"

Alice and I had been married less than a year when this fantasy trip came our way. We were in Hollywood for two weeks with no actual work requirements. I sat in on bull sessions with the writing staff, which included legendary comedy writer Harry Crane, Herb Sargent, Bill Dana, and two hot young fellows named Jim Mulholland and Mike Barrie, who spent years writing monologue jokes for Johnny Carson and David Letterman. They pinned file cards to a giant corkboard on the wall indicating celebrities who had been booked for the show—a crazy-quilt of names that looked different every day as people dropped out and others were recruited. This was old news to the writing team. "They always start out with Greta Garbo and wind up with Ruth Buzzi," one of them cracked. (I had no point of comparison, but apparently this process struck Jim and Mike as fodder for a play. A few years later, Alice and I went to a backer's audition in Manhattan where the Alan King figure was played by the gifted Ron Leibman and one of the other writers came to life in the expert hands of character actor Joe Silver. It was called *Good Evening, Ladies and Gentlemen* and we thought it was very funny, but then we could hardly be objective.)

The first session went on for several hours and consisted mostly of schmoozing, with Alan telling hilarious stories of his experiences in the Borscht Belt. Who would dream of interrupting him? The next day he called the meeting to order in a more businesslike manner and all sorts of ideas were floated. The third day began with Alan rejecting everything they'd agreed on the second day. Next afternoon, he announced that he was tired of the same old faces and worn-out ideas. He had called Budd Friedman, who was going to stage a command performance the next night at the Improv in Hollywood. Alice and I will never forget watching Jerry Seinfeld, Johnny Dark, and other talented comics that night, but the guy who walked away with the show was Andy Kaufman— whom Alice had seen at a political fundraiser in the Bronx a year or more earlier. His pièce de résistance was silently mouthing the lyrics to the "Mighty Mouse" theme song.

Carl Reiner was in the audience, and he was so bowled over by Kaufman that the next morning he encouraged Dick Van Dyke to hire the young man for his new variety series. Which he did. Alan also hired Kaufman to entertain the audience at our taping that Sunday night.

The daily writing sessions became a bit more purposeful during the week leading up to the show. Scripting banter for the presenters was stressful when the individuals for whom the lines were hand-tailored changed from day to day. To get major stars to appear as presenters, Alan had to agree to reciprocate. For months afterwards every time I saw him on TV (as on *The Carol Burnett Show*) he was repaying an obligation. He had to call in favors, cajole, and wheedle to get big names to appear. I was present when he phoned Michael Gruskoff, the producer of Mel Brooks' *Young Frankenstein*, to goad him into showing up with Brooks to accept the "Funniest Movie of the Year" award.

Meanwhile, Alice and I were having a great time having lunches and dinners with friends. We stayed at what was then the Hyatt on Sunset and on our first night walked to dinner at Carney's, a railroad car turned hot dog emporium. We quickly learned that no one walks anywhere in L.A.

Gathering material for my newsletter, I arranged to meet Jay Sandrich for lunch. He suggested we come to CBS Studio Center, where he was directing *The Mary Tyler Moore Show*. We arrived just in time to catch some of the rehearsal for an episode featuring guest star Eileen Heckart squaring off with Edward Asner. The minute lunch hour was announced, Jay gave us a friendly hello and drove us to Art's Deli, just blocks away in Studio City. There we saw MTM boss Grant Tinker and TV host Allen Ludden waiting for a table and Alice Ghostley joining a friend. We were starstruck tourists.

Jay Sandrich was a most congenial guy who provided me with good material for our newsletter. Later that afternoon we had a rendezvous with entertainer-turned-director Eddie Buzzell in Culver City but got fouled up on the freeway and realized we were heading in the wrong direction and encountering endless traffic delays. There were no pay phones to be found, and we had no way of sending word of our plight to Mr. Buzzell. Imagine: no cell phones, no GPS. No luck.

The taping of *The Second Annual Comedy Awards* was a black-tie event that dragged on for hours. The audience was subjected to endless delays in what should have been a "live-on-tape" event. Before long, people started filing out of the theater. It seemed like an utter disaster to me, but what did I know?

I spent most of the four hours it took to stage this straight-forward show in the green room, taking the opportunity to say hello to Neil Simon, Steve Allen, Jack Albertson, and numerous other guests. Paul Lynde seemed to be a bit tipsy, which turned out to be the case. He was presenting Carol Burnett with a lifetime achievement award at the end of the show, but it took so long to get there that he was well lubricated and delivered his speech in slow-motion. My office-mate Barbara Meltzer had spent endless hours creating a seating chart; her careful plans evaporated as our well-dressed audience thinned out at an alarming rate.

This was my class in Television 101. When the special aired some weeks later, it was trimmed to a brisk 90 minutes and all the cuts were invisible. You would have sworn it was a lively, well-attended event. Even Paul Lynde's speech played well. It would be some years before I got to edit my own pieces and try out different techniques at *Entertainment Tonight*.

Back home in New York, I waited for word about the future of the American Academy of Humor. Some cynics had said, unkindly I thought, that the organization was just an excuse for Alan and Rupert Hitzig to sell a special to ABC. I found this insulting and said so on more than one occasion. But when ABC failed to pick up its option for a third year, Alan pulled the plug. Naïve as I was, I understood. Producing the show had been a joyless chore. I asked if there was any chance of someone else picking up the idea and saving the Academy, but it was plain that Alan had decided to move on.

I entertained the idea of trying to keep the AAH alive on my own but realized that without Alan's presence—and backing—it would take more effort than I was willing to invest. So, like Alan, I moved on. But boy, it was fun while it lasted.

Sharing Soup with Katharine Hepburn

Whenever anyone asks me if I have a favorite among all the people I've interviewed, I have no hesitation in answering: Katharine Hepburn. In fact, I was lucky enough to meet her on four occasions, but none could compare to my first encounter with the great lady in 1988.

Hepburn had agreed to do two television interviews to promote a movie she'd made for NBC called *Laura Lansing Slept Here*. By some miracle *ET* decided I would be the one to conduct the interview; up to that time, I hadn't done many major figures for the show, so it came as something of a surprise. The deal they struck with NBC was that the interview would be "80 percent about the new movie and 20 percent on other subjects," an equation I couldn't fathom, especially since NBC couldn't show me one scrap of the finished film! They did send along a script, which I read on the plane to New York. It struck me as a flimsy comedy that served merely as a vehicle for Hepburn's formidable presence.

It was February and cold in Manhattan as I joined the *ET* crew gathered on the sidewalk in front of Ms. Hepburn's brownstone on East 49th Street. We were huddling outside because we had been instructed not to ring the bell until the *Today* crew came out. They'd gotten first dibs, and I was annoyed that Hepburn might not be fresh for our interview. I needn't have worried.

69

The moment they left, we headed in. When we opened the door there was a stairway in front of us and to the left a corridor with doorways leading to the kitchen and pantry. Hepburn was standing in one of those doorways, so I went over to introduce myself. "Ah yes, you're the big cheese," she said in a friendly way, shaking my hand and leading me upstairs to show me where we'd be shooting the interview. She indicated her favorite chair, and the crew got busy setting up. Meanwhile, she led me and my assistant, Margaret, into her adjacent living room so we could talk. She asked if I'd had lunch, and I politely answered that I'd already eaten a late breakfast. "Oh, but we have some delicious homemade soup," she added. I was not going to turn down soup from Katharine Hepburn. She called downstairs to have some soup and crumpets brought up for me and then turned to Margaret and asked if she'd like some too. Margaret said yes. "And some more soup and crumpets for his right-hander," she called out in her distinctive Yankee fashion.

Just a few nights earlier, I had met veteran television director George Schaefer at a function at the Academy of Motion Picture Arts and Sciences and told him I was going to be interviewing Hepburn later in the week. He directed her TV movie and was pleased with the results. This, then, was my ice-breaker.

"I ran into George Schaefer the other night and he told me how well the movie turned out," I began, and it got me off on the right foot. From there we talked about other directors, including George Stevens, and she told me a funny story about being discovered by Stevens in a clandestine tryst (or perhaps merely a tête-à-tête) with Charles Boyer on the RKO lot back in the 1930s.

As we continued chatting and I sipped my soup (which was delicious), I realized how straightforward and unintimidating she was. When the crew signaled that they were ready for us, Miss Hepburn was relating a story about the legendary stage actress Laurette Taylor, who'd made a vivid impression on her when she was young. Our director indicated that she was ready to roll, and I told her as casually as possible to go ahead and turned my attention back to our star. I wasn't going to interrupt Miss Hepburn or cause her to freeze up because we were now beginning the "official" interview. I think my ploy was successful, because she finished her story and we simply continued talking.

It was a wonderful conversation. I wasn't very bold in those days and wouldn't have had the nerve to bring up her relationship with Spencer Tracy—a topic she hadn't yet written or spoken about on the record—but I eased into the subject by talking about privacy. Presidential hopeful Gary Hart had recently been photographed with an attractive woman (not his wife) on a yacht, and the notoriety ended his campaign.

Hepburn said he'd been foolish and added, "The press was very nice. But I was very careful and Spencer was very careful. Mrs. Tracy lived in Los Angeles, and I never went out with Spencer, all those 28 years in California, ever. We didn't make a spectacle out of the relationship." They met only at her house or at the home of friends like director George Cukor. (Compare this with today's tabloid celebrities who attract paparazzi outside popular clubs and restaurants and still complain about a lack of privacy.)

She had only good things to say about the powerful moguls she knew—she even called the czar of Columbia, Harry Cohn, a "nice man"—and had especially good things to say about her longtime boss, MGM's Louis B. Mayer. "Louis B. Mayer I think has been maligned by people. Not only was he nice to me, but I knew Mayer fairly well, and he was nice to a lot of other people. I never had an agent when I did business with Mayer, and I used Mayer's lawyer to go over my contract. I said, 'Now, Mr. Mayer, your lawyer wouldn't cheat me.'"

Speaking of her latter-day life on the East Side of Manhattan, she recounted a recent incident about "a man who was going to tow my car away out here on 49th Street, where they're very fussy.

I went up to him and I said, 'You can arrest me anytime you damn please, but if you touch my car I'll shoot you.' He looked up at me and he said, 'You're…, aren't you?' and I said yes, and he threw his arms around me and gave me a big kiss."

The only question she wouldn't answer in a straightforward manner was about which current actors and actresses she liked. Here she hedged, out of politeness or possibly because she didn't really have any names in mind. The one exception was Jack Nicholson, of whom she said, "I never miss. I think he's a brilliant actor, and funny."

By the time we loaded our second 20-minute videocassette, I realized I hadn't asked any questions about the TV movie and began my new tape with that subject. It immediately became apparent that she didn't have much to say about it. I wasn't going to ask her to describe the plot or her character, which would have been a waste of time. After getting the obvious answers to the obvious questions and knowing that I had enough to fill a story or two on the subject for *ET*, I returned to the Good Stuff. Unbeknownst to me, the NBC publicist in attendance was fuming.

As we were launching a third cassette, our director whispered in my ear that this would have to be the last one, as we had promised to be out of the apartment by two o'clock and it was now one-twenty. Somewhere during the course of that cassette I began to notice, out of the corner of my eye, a waving of hands indicating that it was time to stop. Hepburn was in the middle of an anecdote, and I hardly knew what to do. Finally, I managed to say, "I guess we're out of time, Miss Hepburn" and she immediately responded, "But I have nothing to do until four o'clock."

This is the moment I wish I could relive. I told her that we had promised to be out by two, and she repeated that she had nothing to do until four. Had I been more experienced, or more nervy, I would have said, "Good, let's continue," and defied the NBC publicist to kick us out. Instead, I waited for someone else from the *ET* crew to take that responsibility, and no one did. So I made one final volley and said, "You're supposed to be interview-shy, but you're a wonderful interview."

"Well, I'm really not interview-shy," she replied. "I'm terrible when I have to be all alone, so I'm dependent on you. I find it terribly, idiotically difficult to get up and make a speech. Now, I don't understand that because I can come in totally unprepared to you as long as I've had a good night's sleep. I think it's rather fun, actually." So did I. And with that, we packed up.

During that packing-up time Margaret and I continued talking to her informally and asked her to sign our copies of her book on *The African Queen*.

Having seen her shake badly in recent TV appearances, I was impressed by how healthy she seemed. Her tremor was less pronounced than I expected it to be (a result, perhaps, of a new drug she was taking, as I was told) and she seemed as vigorous as ever. I noticed a painting of her on the wall and asked if she had ever seen the famous Walt Disney cartoon *Mother Goose Goes Hollywood*, in which she was caricatured. She immediately launched into an impression of herself as Little Bo Peep from that film and told me that upstairs she had a cel signed to her by Walt Disney.

We finally said goodbye, and Margaret and I left on a high that was hard to dispel. By the time I got back to my hotel and called my boss in California to tell him how well the interview had gone, he had already received several complaints from NBC about my unprofessional behavior, and the fact that I was taxing an old woman by keeping her so long. Ha!

The next day I sent Miss Hepburn flowers, and about a week later NBC had to give her my address so she could send me a thank-you note. It is scrawled on yellow-lined paper and it says how nice it was working with me. Needless to say, I treasure it.

My only regret is that I couldn't air the entire interview intact. Even though I squeezed three or four stories out of it, the show used a total of perhaps 10 to 12 minutes from the 45 to 50 that I shot. Believe me, virtually everything she said was interesting. She talked about her snooty attitude toward Hollywood in the 1930s, including how she had unwittingly insulted Mary Pickford upon her arrival and was banished from Pickfair, Hollywood's social mecca. (Years later she met Pickford on a long flight, sat down next to her, and asked her to tell the story of her life, which she found absolutely mesmerizing.) She talked about the Academy Awards and why she never attended ("I was being my impossible self...."). Wonderful stuff.

I think I impressed her or, at least, put her at ease by recognizing her references and asking her about people I don't think she spoke about too often, such as Lowell Sherman, the actor who directed her in *Morning Glory*, which garnered her first Oscar nomination. She liked him very much, but she hastened to add that her breathless recitation—and explanation—of her name, Eva Lovelace, in that film was copied outright from a performance she'd seen Ruth Gordon give onstage.

I returned to her townhouse for another interview when her autobiography was published. On this occasion I made a grievous faux pas. She'd mentioned being fond of chocolates in her book and I asked her what kind; she told me she had a weakness for turtles from a particular candy shop, and asked if I'd heard of the store. Wanting to sound both knowledgeable and agreeable, I said yes, and she immediately expressed surprise, because it was just a small shop in Connecticut. Lesson: don't bullshit Katharine Hepburn.

I also flew to Vancouver on two occasions to talk to her as she made her final television movies. The first of those visits was pleasant but uneventful, although it gave me a precious souvenir: her autograph on an original cel from *Mother Goose Goes Hollywood*, which I'd found at a Pasadena antique show. I'd removed the glass from its frame so she could sign directly on the mat, and when she spaced her inscription perfectly from one side of the mat opening to the other, she remarked, "I think I did that rather well, don't you?"

My final encounter with Hepburn was bittersweet. She was back in Vancouver filming another trifling television vehicle, *This Can't Be Love*, in 1994. One of the producers explained to me that the actress was somewhat frail and her memory was not what it used to be. He urged me to use discretion and get whatever I could from our conversation. I thanked him for his candor.

I also met a publicist from CBS who seemed pleasant but asked me to focus my attention on the current film. I told her what I had heard about Hepburn and said I'd do my best, but if she wandered off-topic I was not going to stop her. She seemed to understand. Our crew had prepared a two-camera setup, per the producer's instructions, outside the suburban home that was serving as headquarters for the shoot. I ventured the opinion that it seemed awfully chilly but was assured that this was the way Miss Hepburn wanted it.

When the star arrived for our interview, she turned to her producer and said it was simply too cold to sit outside, causing our crew to scramble for an alternative indoors. We had agreed to share our cameras with another outlet and with CBS itself, which was going to tape its electronic press kit interview in tandem with our shoot. I even allowed the other reporter to go first, so I could size up the situation.

Our cameraman did his best to rig up a makeshift "location" in cramped quarters. Hepburn seemed to be in good-enough spirits, but I wasn't so sure about her powers of concentration. I began by noting that she could be sitting comfortably at home by a fireside in Connecticut. Why was she here in chilly Vancouver? She smiled and rubbed her fingers together, indicating money. I couldn't have asked for a better television "moment."

I continued asking her about her health and outlook on life, and when I thought I'd exhausted her limited energy I thanked her. At that point the CBS publicist spoke up. "You haven't asked her about the movie!" With that, the cameraman rolled again and I said, "Miss Hepburn, what is it about this part that made you want to appear in the film?"

She responded, "I haven't the faintest idea."

I made two or three other attempts to ask her about her character and her costars to no avail. She had no short-term memory.

Later that day I spoke to her costars Jason Bateman, Jami Gertz, and Anthony Quinn, and they all expressed enormous pleasure at having the opportunity to work with Hepburn. (I later learned that after several weeks of shooting, Quinn greeted her on the set one morning and she had no idea who he was.)

That is not the way I choose to remember Katharine Hepburn, although I wonder if, even in her somewhat foggy state, she wasn't still expressing her feistiness.

I prefer to think back to that first wintry day in New York City when she offered me soup, sharp memories, and strong opinions, sparing no one, least of all herself.

A Day with James Stewart

To my surprise and delight, *ET* decided to pay tribute to director Frank Capra on the occasion of his 91st birthday in May 1988. What's more, the show arranged to have James Stewart host the tribute and asked me to write and produce it, with my friend and colleague Bob Heath directing. It was an incredible opportunity.

Having interviewed Stewart not long before for Jeanine Basinger's *The It's a Wonderful Life Book*, I had a good sense of how he spoke, and as I sat at my computer I tried to imagine him saying the words I was writing. Apparently it worked, because he felt at ease reading my dialogue and delivered it beautifully. I even put in a trademark Stewart "dialogue fumble," which called for him to get caught up in a flurry of words before resolving his thought and concluding, "Well, why not let Barbara Stanwyck tell you about it herself?" He read it just the way I'd imagined he would.

We tried to anticipate all of Mr. Stewart's needs for the day of the shoot. We asked if he wanted to work with a teleprompter, which he did, but he still wanted to have the scripts in hand ahead of time. But when he arrived on our set, it turned out that he had mistaken teleprompter to mean cue cards; he'd never actually worked with a scrolling prompter before. He felt ill at ease, and we were on the verge of frantically hand writing his speeches on pieces of cardboard when he said he'd give the prompter a try. In just a few minutes he had it down.

More to the point, he did try to memorize or at least be very familiar with the copy. Between each setup he retired to his chair and buried himself in my script. John Strauss, his longtime publicist and friend, told me that he'd learned years earlier not to bother Stewart at moments like that. Jimmy had told him he considered himself a slow study, and therefore felt he had to work especially hard to get to know every script. Being a professional, he wanted this to be done right.

When he rehearsed the first speech and the words were familiar to him, we did a rehearsal and it was perfect. Then Bob called for tape to roll and I noticed that Stewart tensed up ever so slightly; the result wasn't quite as good as the rehearsal. Even this lesser version was excellent, but I had seen the difference.

Bob and I shot each other a look; we both knew the reading wasn't his best but didn't know how to ask Jimmy Stewart to do it again. Then Bob asked if he'd like to see a video playback of his first take. "Can we do that?" he responded with some surprise. We turned one of the set monitors around and showed it to him. Without Bob or me saying another word, he asked to do it again. He knew it wasn't as good as it could have been. We shot it one or two more times, and when he'd gotten it just right, we played it back—to our mutual satisfaction. From that point on, every time he had a good take, he sensed it. Bob asked if he wanted to see one and Stewart shook his head. He didn't need to see it on tape; he already knew he'd nailed it.

We had one piece of business in mind for him, and we weren't sure how he would respond to it. Our set was designed to resemble the living room from *It's a Wonderful Life*. It was my assistant, Margaret, who came up with the inspired idea of adding to the staircase a newel post with a rounded piece on top that would come off in his hand, just as it had in the movie. I pitched this idea to him to see if he would go for it.

My suggestion was that he finish his speech while coming down the stairs and then do the bit of business, look at the camera, smile, and sign off. He scowled slightly, screwing up his face in thought, and said that the newel post had come apart while he was going upstairs in the film and he thought that we should do it that way. Of course, he was right. He seemed unsure of how the bit would play, but I ran it over for him one more time, and he said he'd give it a try.

We didn't roll tape until he felt confident. A final rehearsal sealed the deal. Stewart looked straight into the camera and smiled warmly for the viewers at home, acknowledging the reference to Capra's beloved movie. It was a precious moment for all of us.

John Strauss told us that, as they were being driven to our studio that day, Stewart had been discouraged by the fact that he wasn't feeling that well when just a day earlier he'd been in the pink of health. If this was his performance level on an "off" day, I can't imagine what it would have been like the day before.

During the course of our taping, members of the *ET* staff drifted onto the stage; by the time we wrapped there was a substantial audience on hand, all of whom wanted to meet Mr. Stewart, pose for a picture, or ask for an autograph. He stayed and patiently obliged everyone—including me.

Shake the Hand That Shook the Hand of Buster Keaton

I was 13 years old and about to spend a day in Manhattan with my best friend, Louis Black. Before leaving my house in New Jersey, I skimmed the *New York Times* and noticed a story about Buster Keaton making a movie with the Irish poet and playwright Samuel Beckett "alongside a dilapidated warehouse in the shadow of the Brooklyn Bridge."

I said to Louis, "This is a once-in-a-lifetime opportunity; let's try to meet him." I grabbed some 8x10 stills and we set off on our quest. We took the subway to the Canal Street station, marched up the stairs, and looked around; sure enough, we spotted a reflector and a couple of klieg lights several blocks away. We walked over and noticed a mild flurry of activity but no security guards to keep us off the premises. And there, reading a newspaper in the back seat of a car, was Buster Keaton. His unmistakable porkpie hat was laid on the seat alongside him.

I was just a kid and didn't know how to make easy conversation with a living legend, but I shoved my face in the back window, said hello, and showed him a photo I hadn't been able to identify. "Well," he said without a moment's hesitation, "That's *Parlor, Bedroom and Bath*, but that isn't the gal I did the scene with. This must be from a rehearsal." I asked if he'd be kind enough to sign it for me and he did. After a few minutes, other people started gathering around, and Louis and I backed away, content that we had had our moment.

Since that time, I've gathered Keaton anecdotes from everyone I've ever met who encountered him. I had occasion to talk to Sid Caesar, who worked with Keaton in *It's a Mad, Mad, Mad, Mad World*. Being a great pantomimist himself, Caesar was naturally a great fan of Buster. I asked what he remembered most about meeting him and he replied, "His handshake; it was very strong." Coming from a man of fabled strength like Sid Caesar, this was significant. It also reinforced my impression of Buster as rock solid and nearly indestructible.

I collect lapel pins and select them with care to see if my choice might spark an interesting reaction. Alice suggested that I wear my Buster Keaton pin when I first interviewed Johnny Depp since he'd studied Keaton with Dan Kamins for his role in *Benny & Joon*. It was a felicitous choice, as it was the first thing he noticed and broke the ice for our conversation. The morning I left for the Napa Valley to visit director Francis Ford Coppola and do a story about his film *The Rainmaker*, I decided to wear my Buster pin, because I couldn't think of anything else that related to him. I hoped, at least, Coppola would respond to my homage to another great filmmaker.

Instead, he knocked me off my feet by saying immediately, "I met him, you know."

"You did?" I responded, wide-eyed, and asked when and how. The answer was simple: his father, Carmine (then billed as Carmen) Coppola, was music director for the now-well-chronicled tour of *Once Upon a Mattress* in which Buster starred.

"He played the king in *Once Upon a Mattress*," Coppola recalled, "and he was there with his wife, and they were big buddies with my mother. I think they played—[with] my father—they played Yahtzee together. I was about 15 or 16 and I was interested in theater. And I hadn't yet seen the great Buster Keaton films, and they are indeed very great, so I met him and was very impressed to meet him, but I didn't realize the importance of him as a cinema artist. He was a very sweet man, and he was cute in [the show]. He played the mute king, did a soft shoe dance in it."

That was all—no great revelations, just a nice remembrance.

Two months later, I chanced to meet the director's sister, actress Talia Shire, and mentioned our conversation. She immediately told me that one of her indelible memories was sneaking into a rehearsal one day and spending two hours in the dark unnoticed, watching Buster rehearse a comic fall. "Two hours!" she marveled. "What an artist he was."

You never know where or when a Buster Keaton admirer will turn up. That's how I felt one morning when I saw Betty White on a local Los Angeles morning show promoting her book *Here We Go Again: My Life in Television*. The host asked her to name the most memorable people she'd ever worked with in TV, and to my astonishment the first person she cited was Buster, whom she'd encountered in the earliest days of L.A. television. I couldn't let this rest, so I pursued Miss White and asked her for more details.

"I was doing the Al Jarvis show, *Hollywood on Television*, and we were on five-and-a-half hours a day, six days a week, live. He was also doing a disc jockey job and he had all these friends, so his friends would be our guests. They would come on, and one day Buster Keaton walked in. We went on the air in November of 1949, and Buster had in 1950 a half-hour show of his own. He came over to visit with Al one day, and oh, I was just so fascinated seeing him because even then—I mean, you don't see that kind of comedy talent, it was just different.

"We had a zillion commercials, always, and even at five-and-a-half hours we were always late, so Al interrupted the interview with Buster just long enough to say, 'Excuse me, Betty, would you do the Thrifty Drug commercial?' Thrifty was on twice a day on our show, and they were a big sponsor for us. They had an easel there with nine billion little products all tacked to it, and somehow they expected you to mention them all. Of course, there was no limit on time for commercials, but I knew that they wanted to get back to the Keaton interview, so I just went over and started to buzz through as fast as I could.

"Well, all of a sudden—you feel some presence there, you know—Buster had gotten up and shambled over. He didn't say a word, he was just looking at the easel so closely.... Of course, I was having a struggle to keep it together. Every [product] I would mention, he'd take it out and examine it and he'd try to make it work if he could. The commercial must have gone on—it seemed like it went on for an hour, it probably lasted ten minutes. Then he went back over, never said a word, continued his scheduled interview with Al. Oh God, if they had tape in those days...

"After Al left the show, I inherited it. So I took my courage and invited Buster back over. I told him that we wanted to do something kind of impromptu, if that was all right. He said, 'Sure, whatever you want to do.' So I set up a toy store, a little one in the corner. We didn't have a lot of money, but we set up this whole thing against a flat, like a little store counter. In the interview I said, 'Incidentally, you always knock me out the way you can improvise. Does that come naturally?' He said, 'I don't know.' And I said, 'Well, let's see what happens if—come on over here a minute.'

"I took him over to the toy store and then I just left him there. He was there, 'in one,' and, Leonard, to watch what he [did]... I mean, he just used everything in the set, and I can't explain to you why it was funny. It was the imagination. If his head was made of glass, you'd be able to see the wheels go around, you know?

"Later when I went over to ABC and was doing shows there, I invited him, and we did a silly thing with a trampoline. Those were the only three times that I worked with him. He was so nice; at the end of either the second or third time he brought me in a present. It was a little wishing well about two inches high. God knows where he found it. It had no significance, but he gave it to me as a present. Needless to say, I still have that wishing well."

She then apologized for not having more to say! Even brief encounters with Buster left people with warm and happy memories. "He wasn't playful in the sense that somebody comes out and clowns for a talk show," she said in summing up. "He just participated because it interested him at that point, and he couldn't help but be funny."

My search for Buster sightings went on. I became friendly with veteran actor Elliott Reid, whom I had never thought to ask about Buster. Yes, Reid explained, when he was a young man working a season of summer stock in White Plains, New York, the resident company supported a different star every week. The star would move on to the next town, and the repertory players would remain and memorize a new play. Reid had had some difficulty with a former Hollywood leading man and was still feeling the sting of his wrath when Buster came through in a production of *The Gorilla*, with Harry Gribbon (who'd appeared in *The Cameraman*) in a costarring role. Reid loved Buster on sight and became friendly with him during the week's run. Over lunch one day, he told him of the run-in he'd had with the visiting star a week earlier. Buster pondered this a moment and said of the man, "He was the biggest false alarm that ever hit Hollywood." That was enough to endear Keaton to his younger colleague for life.

One final note: the morning I was to interview Emma Thompson I decided to wear my Chaplin pin, thinking the British connection might be worth a little something. Thompson, as bright and interesting as they come, took one look and said, "Actually, I've always preferred Buster Keaton to Chaplin."

Just goes to show you.

Robert Mitchum's Grass Roots

My first encounter with Robert Mitchum was unforgettable. I was working as entertainment editor on the NYU daily newspaper, then called the *Washington Square Journal*, and was invited to attend a press conference touting David Lean's upcoming movie *Ryan's Daughter* at MGM headquarters in midtown Manhattan. The lure was irresistible: Robert Mitchum would be there in person.

The following day about a hundred student journalists and I filled the screening room at the appointed time, but the actor was nowhere to be seen. Someone decided to screen a promotional short about the movie, but when it ended there was still no sign of Mitchum. Then, quite suddenly, he burst into the room and strode down the aisle carrying a duffel bag. "Hey, I'm sorry," he said, "but I just found out I'm going to take a connecting flight through Chicago and I'm carrying a brick of grass, so I have to sift it before I get on the plane."

With that he took a seat in the front of the theater and began doing just that! Jaws dropped and the MGM publicists looked at each other in total bafflement. One of them approached Mitchum and asked if he'd be willing to go to the podium, which he agreed to do once he recruited an audience member to continue prepping his marijuana. The sound of sifting accompanied everything else that followed.

As Mitchum walked to the lectern one of the MGM staff asked if he'd be willing to speak while they ran some silent behind-the-scenes footage from *Ryan's Daughter*. He seemed agreeable and gave a running commentary, identifying director Lean, then costar Sarah Miles, whom he called "a brilliant actress. Totally unsavory person but a brilliant actress." After a few more remarks, the screen went blank and we in the crowd were invited to ask questions.

This was Mitchum's chance to parry with a pack of cub reporters. The questions were uninspired at best, and when there was a lull I raised my hand and asked what Charles Laughton was like as a director. Without a moment's hesitation he said, "Absolutely brilliant." I then asked about John Huston. The only advice he got from the legendary filmmaker was "a little more, son," which he related in a perfect carbon copy of Huston's voice.

I was pleased with myself and packed away those answers for future use. And with that, the press conference came to a hasty conclusion.

The next day I received a phone call from MGM asking if I would refrain from writing about the events that transpired in their screening room; I assured them I would. And I have, until now.

Decades later, I took a call at *ET* offering me a chance to interview Mitchum in conjunction with a one-hour special about him that was going to run on HBO. I went to one of my producers to get an OK and, to my surprise, hit a brick wall. Talking to Mitchum was a waste of time, he said, as every opportunity they'd taken in the short life of our show had been disastrous. I later screened one of those conversations, which he had done to promote the miniseries *War and Remembrance*. He was drinking from a tall tumbler and was in a feisty mood. Our reporter asked if he would ever agree to appear in a TV commercial, as many other prominent actors were doing at the time. "No way," he said emphatically. "No fucking way!" (He later changed his mind. Remember "beef...it's what's for dinner"?) I could see why that Q&A never aired, and I also understood why my producer didn't jump at the chance to put him on camera again. I persevered and said I thought I had a way to get him to open up a bit, and my boss finally relented.

We shot our interview in a private room at the historic Biltmore Hotel in Santa Barbara near the actor's home. He was dressed in a suit and tie and smoked when he wasn't on camera. As we began to talk I sensed that he was testing me. His first responses were wary and almost curt. Then I said I'd recently watched *The Human Comedy* on TV and was surprised to see him alongside Barry Nelson and Don DeFore in just one scene as soldiers on leave. He didn't even get screen billing. He smiled at this and it seemed to evoke a happy memory.

"You know, they tarped in two whole blocks at MGM [to make it seem like nighttime] and it was really a magical set," he recalled. He was also impressed that director Clarence Brown insisted that the actors all watch the rushes, even bit players like him.

His next break was a costarring role in *The Story of G.I. Joe*. Again, the experience was vivid in his mind. He remembered cutting his hair and doing a test at the back lot in Culver City known as 40 Acres. "I went in and met Buzz [Burgess] Meredith and we did the scene and 'cut!' There's a silence and I looked beyond the camera and Bill Wellman was sitting there crying. He said, 'That's it,' and they used that scene in the film. He was one of the tenderest, most sensitive men I've ever met."

By now he was fully engaged. The ice was broken.

"They found it difficult to classify me," he explained. "At that time a leading man was Tyrone Power; everybody had to be sort of the classy, waitressy type. It wasn't actually until Bogart came along … [that was] the beginning of the ugly leading man, and I did parts to which I was suited."

I asked about some of his larger-than-life directors. He related that Raoul Walsh would never watch a scene being shot after he'd supervised a run-through. Mitchum was greatly amused that he had his back to the actors while they were actually filming. Otto Preminger was "a great producer but as a director he was busy overacting all the time." He regarded Josef von Sternberg as a pompous fraud. And he did dead-on impressions of John Huston and George Cukor.

He called Marilyn Monroe "a dear girl, a friend. I got to know her and she projected no sex appeal at all, really. She had a lot of physical problems which were with her all the time, and she didn't think she was very pretty. One thing I think is rather significant is that all the women who ever worked with her have not one cross word to say about her."

We talked more about Charles Laughton and *Night of the Hunter*. He said, "Charles was a great appreciator; if it was good he was just so ecstatic. He would show a little contrariness when the children were just too much, and he'd give Shelley [Winters] a kick in the rear every now and then, but he was a joy; he had a great vision."

As for Howard Hughes, who took over RKO when Mitchum was under contract, "I had direct communication with him and as a result I was in a very uncomfortable position because I was regarded as teacher's pet on the lot. I got along very well with him."

Hughes didn't abandon Mitchum after he was busted for possession of marijuana and had to serve time in jail. "You gotta remember that Howard wanted to fight the whole thing. Also it was thrown back in the court for lack of evidence. It was all thrown out and the whole case was wiped out, which nobody ever considers to be interesting."

Why didn't it hurt his career? "Well," he said, "A, I was innocent and B, I refused to name names. I said, 'I'll just go quietly' and people thought that was a reasonable attitude."

The worst location he ever endured? "Mount Rainier, I guess, on *Track of the Cat*, under 30 feet of snow. They'd call lunch and it's two steps forward and three steps back. By the time you get to the top, lunch is over. That was tough."

And the best? "Probably *Heaven Knows, Mr. Allison*, the island of Tobago. We'd come down to the beach and John Huston would say, 'Too nice a day. We'll do it tomorrow.'"

At the end of the shoot, I asked if he'd mind signing an 8x10 photo I'd brought along, and he was agreeable. He thought for a moment and then wrote, "For Leonard—The bones are clean—Robert Mitchum." My assistant Ben Herndon explained that his newborn son was named Cassidy after Hopalong Cassidy, which seemed to please Mitchum, who started out doing stunts and small parts in some Hoppy Westerns. "For Cassidy," he wrote, "Bang! Robert Mitchum."

I admired him all the more after seeing those inscriptions.

The HBO special, titled *Robert Mitchum: The Reluctant Star*, featured a number of his leading ladies ("the only ones still alive," he declared) singing his praises. By then the secret was out: his nonchalance bordering on indifference regarding his chosen profession was an act. He was an intelligent man who took pride in his work, especially when the roles were worthy of his talent. He was also a contrarian and provocateur.

I saw him one more time, in 1994 at the Golden Boot Awards, the annual celebration of Western films and television that benefited the Motion Picture and Television Fund. When I first spotted him he looked as if he'd been dragooned into attending. Then he was guided to a chair next to Anne Jeffreys, the still-beautiful woman who had been the leading lady in his first starring Western, *Nevada*, 50 years before. Seeing the charming, ageless actress caught him unawares and served as a tonic. It was just the first of many reunions that night with fellow players and stuntmen he'd known. By the time he mounted the podium to receive his Golden Boot he was genuinely moved and said so.

That's the way I choose to remember him.

A Reluctant Ambulance Chaser

It was the single worst moment of my career. I was driving to an interview at a special effects house in Santa Monica for *Entertainment Tonight* when my boss called and told me to turn my car around and head to Cedars-Sinai hospital.

"Frank Sinatra was admitted early this morning," she said with breathless excitement. "I want you to go there and walk into the emergency room area. He's in bed 3 under the name of Taylor."

My response—a long moment of stunned silence—prompted her to continue in a more soothing tone. "I'm not asking you to do anything a gentleman wouldn't do. Just go and find out how he is."

I murmured, "OK," made a U-turn and was shaking from a combination of disgust and fear. How could I possibly do this? I was a film critic, not a tabloid gumshoe. I called my agent in New York, whom I rarely turned to for hand-holding. "You know you can't say no to Linda," he advised. "But look: by the time you get there the place will probably be crawling with reporters. It's not like you'll be the only one trying to get the story."

He was right, I told myself as I made my way toward Cedars and found a parking meter around the corner from the hospital, where my daughter had been born a decade earlier. When I walked up to the emergency entrance my heart sank: there was no swarm of cameras and reporters. I'd beaten everybody there.

I gingerly walked inside. Strangely, there was no one at the Emergency reception desk, but I damn well wasn't going to sneak inside and look for bed 3. I didn't know what to do. Then I noticed a woman looking around for help; she was clutching an enormous stuffed teddy bear under her arm.

Our eyes met. I said, "Nancy?" and she said, "Leonard?" It was Nancy Sinatra. I'd met her several times and we'd had a nice rapport, so I kissed her on the cheek and asked how her dad was feeling.

"He must be doing better," she responded. "They moved him up to a room on the eighth floor."

I said how glad I was and asked her to tell her father that we were rooting for him. She thanked me and hastened down the corridor to an elevator.

As I walked outside, I saw an *ET* cameraman approaching and told him in a dazed tone, "I just got a scoop." It wasn't terribly valuable because it was 10 in the morning and *ET* wasn't a live show, so my "newsbeat" wouldn't air for seven or eight hours. But my boss didn't let the exclusive get away entirely: she sent another correspondent to interview me about my encounter with Nancy Sinatra. Several other local news outlets talked to me as well, and our cameraman said with a knowing smile, "Now they'll send you out on all these stories."

Thank God that did not come to pass. During my 30-year run at *ET* I had my share of odd and embarrassing moments, but they were relatively few, especially compared to some of my colleagues. I never had to ask, as Bob Goen once did of Anna Nicole Smith, "Is it true your breasts exploded?"

I never felt comfortable asking personal questions, even relatively benign ones by today's standards. One of our staff directors advised me to blurt out the awkward questions instead of pussyfooting around them, but I never acquired that skill. The closest I came was during an awkward interview with Ryan O'Neal when he was promoting a dreadful movie called *An Alan Smithee Film: Burn Hollywood Burn*. My boss had no interest in the picture; she wanted Ryan to talk about a recent headline-making incident involving his ex, Farrah Fawcett, who was having substance abuse problems.

Ryan, whom I'd never met, bounded into our hotel-room studio in a state of agitation, having apparently been assaulted by his previous interviewer. As he sat down he asked me, "Is the movie really that bad? Did you hate it?"

Without missing a beat I replied, "Well, I liked you." It was the truth, and it disarmed and defused him. With that, we had a most enjoyable chat. I even got to ask him about working with Stanley Kubrick on *Barry Lyndon*, which he was happy to discuss.

But I was avoiding the elephant in the room and my director knew it. As our allotted time wound down, he prodded me and I asked, as plaintively as possible, "If you could say anything to Farrah right now, what would it be?"

He didn't seem to take offense and offered a poignant response, saying he hoped she would seek help and pull herself together. The minute he finished I knew I had done my job. With that I shook hands with the actor and sent him on his way. (I was told that one or two interviews later he bolted from the hotel, never to return.)

I cringed over assignments like that and never found a comfort zone. I am not really a reporter, even though I hold a degree in journalism from New York University. I'm a lucky film buff who stumbled into careers in publishing, television, and academia, all of them unplanned.

I landed my first interview by huddling in the cold outside a Broadway stage door when I was 15 years old. I never dreamt that I would spend the next five decades talking to many of my heroes and idols, let alone women I'd had crushes on. I may not be the most aggressive interviewer on the planet, but my knowledge and enthusiasm have proven to be valuable assets.

I also benefit from wisdom that's been passed on to me by people who've been around. Bob Thomas, the noted biographer and Associated Press Hollywood correspondent for more than half a century, told me that he had no friends in show business. He didn't equate business contacts with friends and said this with no bitterness or irony: he recognized where he stood in the Hollywood social order. I was a teenager when I met Bob and never forgot his candid remark. I think of it often when I see wannabes and phonies who try to convince people around them (or perhaps merely themselves) that they're pals with the stars.

One of the highlights of my annual calendar is the Oscar Nominees Luncheon, which is held at the Beverly Hilton Hotel several weeks before the Academy Awards are handed out. What started out as a small gathering now attracts between 100 and 200 nominees who come to celebrate their achievements with their colleagues. I am privileged to attend every year as a friend of the Academy, and it was at one of these events that Tom Hanks paid me a great compliment. I congratulated him on his latest nomination and said how lucky I felt to be admitted to the event on a pass. He said, "No, you're part of this community." It was an extraordinarily kind thing to say, typical of the good guy we all know Hanks to be. After several decades of working the beat in Los Angeles, I suppose he's right—though I still feel keenly aware of keeping a proper arm's-length distance from the people I have to criticize as part of my job.

A few years later, my wife and I were invited to join friends at the trendy Malibu restaurant Nobu. We'd never been there and felt intimidated to go on our own, but they were regulars and assured us that we'd enjoy ourselves once we acclimated to the sky-high prices. The dining room was fairly quiet as we were shown to our table early on a Saturday evening. After we were seated, our friend Joel Beren said, "That's Will Smith and Jada Pinkett sitting over there, and I think they noticed you as we walked in." My wife urged me to say hello, but I refused. If our eyes had connected it would have been different, but I didn't want to bother the famous couple while they were dining.

Within minutes, their waiter approached our table with a tray of four lychee martinis. "These are from my customer, Mr. Smith. He sends his compliments and says his new film, *The Pursuit of Happyness*, opens on December 15."

We all laughed and went to the Smiths' table to thank them. Will explained that many years ago he'd read that this was Elizabeth Taylor's m.o. whenever she spotted a columnist or critic. He'd waited for years to have a chance to emulate her.

As for his inspiration, Elizabeth Taylor, I had one unforgettable meeting with her in 1989 when she agreed to do some interviews to promote a TV production of Tennessee Williams' *Sweet Bird of Youth* she had made with Mark Harmon. I was uncharacteristically nervous about this interview, and a day beforehand I telephoned her lifelong friend Roddy McDowall, who'd been kind to me on several occasions, to ask his help: were there any subjects she enjoyed talking about that people didn't generally know?

"Oh, you won't need to play any games like that with her," he responded, assuring me that we'd get along fine.

Knowing the star's reputation for lateness, my crew and I brought reading matter to the Beverly Hills Hotel suite where the interview was to take place. We were told that we got off easy when Miss Taylor showed up two hours past our appointed time.

From the moment she walked in the room she was graciousness personified. I asked the obligatory questions about *Sweet Bird*, her costars, and Tennessee Williams. She admitted that she didn't watch the 1962 movie because "Geraldine Page is such a brilliant actress. I'm a natural-born mimic; I didn't want to pick up anything. It would have been easy for me. I can't help it; I mimic. It would have intimidated me enormously."

Then I got to the things I was interested in, and she seemed happy to answer my questions about her early career. Was it true that MGM was thinking of testing her brother back in the 1940s? "Yes," she replied. "He didn't want to be a child actor. He was supposed to be tested for a Western, so he stopped by a barber and had his head shaved. I loved it."

She told me she regarded *A Place in the Sun* as the first milestone in her career, calling it "the first conscious time I thought about acting.... George [Stevens] and Monty [Clift] made me aware of the thought process. It was really the first time I observed and probably really listened, because mainly before I had been playing myself with horses and dogs. This time it was with people.

"I never had an acting lesson in my life," she concluded, "so really my school of acting is from watching other people."

To my surprise, she told me she was highly self-critical, which made it difficult for her to watch her own films. "I don't like my voice. I don't like the way I look, I don't like the way I move, I don't like the way I act, I mean period!"

I asked if there were any exceptions, and she said, "I think the only one I thought [well of]—and probably because it was a character part—was *Who's Afraid of Virginia Woolf?* I changed my voice, I wore padding and rubber on my face, so it was almost like watching someone else, I guess."

Then I asked about two of her most memorable films. She called *National Velvet* "a great experience for me because it was an extension of myself. It was no great work or performance for me; it was just kind of being me. I even chose the horse. The studio gave me the horse and I had him with me till he died, so that was great. I was 12 and it was just like being told, 'Live your fantasy.'"

And I asked about *Father of the Bride*, in particular her costar. She replied, "I think Spencer Tracy is probably the greatest screen actor that ever lived. It was incredible working, just watching him.

He was a wonderful man; I loved him dearly. We kept in contact with each other for years, and he was Pops and I was Kitten until the day he died."

All of these answers were interesting, of course, and well expressed, but at the end of each response was a big "period" rather than a sense of give-and-take. I felt flop sweat on my neck because I had to keep the conversation flowing, inch by inch. Miss Taylor couldn't have been more professional, but she was not forthcoming. I guess she'd been burned too many times over the years by the press.

Then something interesting happened. In one of its penny-pinching moves, *ET* had sent only one camera crew that day. My director asked Miss Taylor if she would mind staying a few extra minutes while he reset the camera to get an over-the-shoulder shot of me asking some of my questions. To our great surprise, she said she didn't mind at all.

This procedure is one of the most embarrassing in television journalism, but sometimes it has to be done. The director then explained to Miss Taylor that it no longer mattered what she said since they were only recording me. At that, she flashed a smile and began teasing me, making offhanded wisecracks as we went along, but the sound man had removed her microphone!

This saucy woman with the wicked sense of humor was the real Elizabeth Taylor, the one I'd hoped to capture on camera. I'm sorry that didn't come to pass, but at least I was afforded a glimpse.

The Nutty Filmmaker

Jerry Lewis looms large in my life. One of the first films I distinctly remember seeing in a movie theater was *The Delicate Delinquent* in 1957. The movie opens "cold" in an alleyway as a rumble between two gangs is brewing; the tension grows, enhanced by music that underscores the percolating moment. Then Jerry Lewis bursts out of a doorway, fumbling a metal garbage can and making a terrible racket, blissfully unaware of the commotion he's causing.

It's a great gag, perfectly set up and paid off, and for me at the age of six, a perfect introduction to Jerry. (Only later did I learn that he had been part of a team with Dean Martin, and this was his solo movie debut.)

I immediately became a Jerryholic. I lived for his movies, which tended to appear at my local theater twice a year. This was long before home video or streaming. I contented myself in between biannual doses by reading about him, looking out for occasional TV appearances, listening to his records, and reading his DC comic books.

Reading all the magazine profiles I did and watching him on his disastrous live Saturday night television show in 1963, where his ego eclipsed his talent, I lost some of my zeal for the man, if not the comedian. By this time I was an adolescent.

Some 25 years later, I met Jerry Lewis for the first time. He was about to give an interview in the *Entertainment Tonight* conference room. I tiptoed in while the crew was setting up and introduced myself. I had a question to ask that I suspected he hadn't heard all that often: what was it like to work in 3-D, which he and Dean Martin did in their 1953 movie *3 Ring Circus*. (I'd been gathering 3-D anecdotes for a possible book.) He told me that the lights on the set were so intensely hot that they couldn't shoot more than a minute at a time because his makeup would start to melt. He couldn't have been more forthcoming, but I didn't want to interfere with the *ET* crew, so after thanking him I excused myself and went back to my office.

That night I had a delayed reaction and almost hyperventilated over the excitement of meeting the man who had been my boyhood idol. That was Jerry Lewis!

I had several other opportunities to talk to him privately and publicly over the years—onstage, backstage, over the phone. I was curious how Norman Rockwell happened to paint the artwork for the original *CinderFella* posters, so I picked up the phone and called his longtime assistant, who put me through to The Man, who was sitting at home in Las Vegas. "I'm looking at it right now," he said with obvious pride. He explained that he, Ed Wynn, and Anna Maria Alberghetti had to fly back East to pose for the noted artist, who didn't like working from photographs. Jerry happily explained that it was his idea to hire the quintessential American illustrator to help promote his movie.

He was exceedingly kind to me and, while my nervousness subsided, my feeling of excitement never did. After all, he was a giant in the world of comedy; his accomplishments speak for themselves. More than that, he was the living embodiment of a form of show business that has long since faded away. One night I introduced him to a huge audience of video dealers who were presenting him with a lifetime achievement award in Las Vegas. He didn't join us for dinner because, in best show-biz tradition, he would not sit down once he donned his tuxedo.

In 2003 he agreed to participate in an evening presented by the Directors Guild of America as part of a series called "Under the Influence," presenting young filmmakers in conversation with directors who inspired them. The gifted Miguel Arteta (*Star Maps*, *Chuck & Buck*, *The Good Girl*) served as host, interviewing his hero following a screening of *The Nutty Professor*. Jerry's Q&A session was part interview, part soapbox, part love-fest, and entirely fascinating.

He said he wrote a first draft of *The Nutty Professor* in 1953 and it gestated over the following decade, finally coming to fruition as a collaboration with his longtime writing partner, Bill Richmond. He recalled the 1931 version of *Dr. Jekyll and Mr. Hyde* with Fredric March and borrowed some of its ideas, especially the first-person camera.

His view of the nerdy, buck-toothed Professor Julius Kelp was interesting. "Kelp is everybody," he explained. "I always felt like Kelp as a kid, how silly I looked when I tried desperately to act like a bon vivant."

Nothing stung more than when a newspaper critic wrote that he was obviously getting even with his former partner, Dean Martin, through his characterization of Buddy Love, the slick Mr. Hyde heel to Julius Kelp's Dr. Jekyll.

"That hurt me desperately," he said, to have someone think that he would want to "get even" with "the one human I loved more than anyone on the planet. When I was writing Buddy Love, I was thinking of the most despicable individual I could think of."

There are some who feel that Jerry protested too much on this point. He obviously loved and admired Dean and looked up to him as a kid brother might. While Buddy Love has many loathsome qualities, he also has a kind of savoir faire that Jerry may have envied as a gangly, Kelpy kid. In Dean Martin he may have seen both the good and bad side of that handsome guy who could attract women and intimidate men whenever he chose to do so.

That didn't keep Jerry from harboring a grudge against the critic who had written about the Dean/Buddy connection so many years earlier. It served as a springboard for a tirade against critics in general: "No kid at five years old says, 'I want to grow up to be a critic,'" he said to gleeful response from the filmmaking crowd.

Jerry then told us that he had just finished the 4,000th manuscript page of his long-promised book about Dean Martin. He explained that not every page was complete and that the typescript was probably equivalent to 1,650 pages. He figured he had about 100 pages to go before the book was finished. "I'm gonna make *War and Peace* look like a pamphlet," he said with a broad smile. The book, called *Dean and Me (A Love Story)*, was finally published in 2005 at 340 pages.

He begged off specific questions about *The Day the Clown Cried*, his notorious unfinished film, saying, "I try not to talk about it because it hurts; it's a baby without arms, without legs."

He confirmed a story that he had met Charlie Chaplin (five times, in fact), who had exchanged a print of *Modern Times* for *The Bellboy*. He claimed that he never opened the shipping cases that arrived from Chaplin in Switzerland, maintaining the print just as it arrived at his home so many years before.

He regaled the crowd with stories of his "home movies" of the 1950s, when he and such friends as Dean, John Barrymore, Jr., Mona Freeman, Jeff Chandler, Tony Curtis and Janet Leigh, Betty Grable and Harry James participated in super-productions like *Come Back, Little Shiksa*. He had klieg lights, a red carpet, and deluxe catering for the premiere at his home, which he said cost $50,000.

He called director Frank Tashlin "my director's dream, a Messiah. He was brilliant in everything he did."

Asked about his filming techniques, he explained that he always had two cameras running simultaneously to capture the immediacy of his comedy performances but had them lined up as close togeth-er as possible to expedite cutting between the two shots.

And questioned about published reports that he wears a pair of socks only once before discarding them, he said it was true and made a point of saying that he donates the used clothing to a lo-cal hospital. He asked the audience member, "You know why I do that?"

"BECAUSE I'M RICH!" he crowed in his best Jerry voice. The audience ate it up.

Jerry's work ethic was instilled by his father, Danny, an all-round performer who took his son to see Al Jolson, renowned as the world's greatest entertainer. "I'm watching the man say, 'You ain't heard nothin' yet,' and I sat another two-and-a-half hours after the two-hour show was over. You can't forget that."

But there was more than one facet to this show-business crea-ture. Asked what drove him as a performer, he answered, "Fear," and he wasn't kidding. It's no secret that Jerry had a healthy ego, but he was also extremely sensitive. I talked to him after a terrific evening at the Academy of Motion Picture Arts and Sciences, and he mentioned how hurtful it was whenever someone walked out of the theater while he was onstage. The fact that hundreds remained couldn't salve the sting of even one person leaving.

When he and Dean Martin teamed up, their unique brand of anarchy propelled them to untold heights of popularity on the nightclub circuit, then on TV's *Colgate Comedy Hour*. I was too young to see their appearances on live television and didn't re-alize—until years later—that their movies only captured a frac-tion of their comedic energy. Jerry recalled that a group of comics were gathered at Lindy's in Manhattan, talking about the new duo who were breaking it up at the Copacabana. "And they all said to [Milton] Berle, 'We're gonna see the guys tomorrow night at the Copa.' And one of the comics said to Berle, 'What do they do?' And Berle said, 'They come out and the skinny kid does some jokes and gets the audience ready. Then he introduces the handsome Italian who comes out and sings sweetly to the audience. It's a great beginning.' 'Yeah, but what about the comedy?' 'Oh, you gotta see it.'"

"It was really magical," Jerry recounted, "and nobody could leave the Copa and tell anyone else what they saw. 'You gotta see 'em. You gotta go see 'em.'"

Dean and Jerry never disappointed an audience. As Jerry later told me, "It always worked because the audience knew we were having such a good time."

"You couldn't sit down and design that kind of energy output," Lewis told me in 1992. "You could sit down and design the sketch, the meter, the rhythm, the logistics, but you needed two people who couldn't wait to become Katzenjammer Kids in that frame of reference. That's what we had going for us. We were absolutely having the best times of our lives watching hundreds and thousands of people laughing at that nonsense. Audiences enjoyed our victory—they enjoyed that we pulled it off."

What did come across on-screen was Lewis' unique comedy persona in such early films as *At War with the Army*, *Sailor Beware*, *Living It Up*, and *Artists and Models*. His comedy was, and remains, gut-funny. He is the perpetual child, which appeals to the kid in all of us.

When Martin and Lewis arrived in Hollywood, Jerry became intrigued with the mechanics of moviemaking. He later recalled, "They never could find me the first year. Because I was in editing, I was in the camera department. I was in makeup, wardrobe, miniatures, main titles. I was everywhere but on the set.... I learned about the F-stops and the light. I even learned to load the camera. And I did it on my own production because producers that I worked for weren't crazy about the idea. But I learned to do it. It was a great joy to be able to talk to these 185 [crew] guys on a level you would never have an opportunity to talk about. I learned from what they said, I learned from what they showed me. And they loved that I wanted to learn."

But in the wake of his earth-shattering split with Dean Martin and his evolution into an auteur, or what he called "The Total Filmmaker" in the 1960s, critics began to sound some sour notes. While audiences flocked to *The Bellboy*, *The Ladies Man*, and *The Nutty Professor*, Andrew Sarris said Lewis "has never put one brilliant comedy together from fade-in to fade-out." The French, who became Lewis' biggest supporters, apparently didn't care about sloppy construction, arid stretches between funny scenes, or the banal, sentimental, self-indulgent moments Lewis included in many of his movies. But as Sarris pointed out, "The argument about laughs is irrelevant because laughter in this case is less decisive than love. The French critics love Jerry Lewis. Many Americans do not."

He even managed to impress critics with his performance as mordant talk-show host Jerry Langford in Martin Scorsese's *King of Comedy*.

I am a critic, and I certainly criticized some of Jerry's work, but that pales alongside the deep feelings I always had for him as a performer.

There is no facet of show business he didn't conquer, from nightclubs to movies to the Broadway stage. He taught filmmaking at the University of Southern California and once showed off his modest paycheck for an *Esquire* magazine photo essay about what gave famous people their greatest reward.

He continued performing into his 90th year and remained a headliner—a bona fide star—until the day he died at age 91. Some people only know him for his annual telethon, where he raised millions of dollars for the Muscular Dystrophy Association. His tireless efforts ultimately earned him the Jean Hersholt Humanitarian Award from the Academy of Motion Picture Arts and Sciences.

Fortunately, Jerry's work survives, in part, because he preserved it himself. He kept audio recordings of Martin and Lewis from their earliest days: 35mm footage of the act at the Copacabana, rehearsals and outtake footage, kinescopes, and much, much more—all of which he donated to the Library of Congress. When I asked him what made him such a well-organized pack rat, he replied, "My father. My dad said to me as far back as I can remember, 'If you're gonna do anything, it's important to preserve it.' So I recorded every performance we ever did, on audio. Prior to that, I had every clipping, everything that was ever written about me or Dean. Everything was in leather-bound books. I've got four or five film vaults that must house, I don't know, six or seven million feet of film, because I keep the work print, the dailies, the final cut, the print that's shipped—you're talking about a lot of material. But there isn't anything you might know about that I can't bring you said piece. If you say, 'In 1950, you and Dean played the National Theatre in Detroit,' I'll bring you the clipping, I'll bring you the review, and I'll bring you the ad in the paper that said we opened that day. The only man that had a better library, or at least equal, was Jimmy Durante."

Summing up, he said, "I realized that what we did was so formidable that we have to give it to our grandchildren, let them know what we created, how it worked."

The last time I interviewed him was at the Paley Center in Beverly Hills in 2012, when his 1959 TV special of *The Jazz Singer* was released on DVD.

He disarmed the audience by admitting that at the age of 84 he was starting to lose track of stories, shifting the beginning, middle, and end. Several times during the evening I gently steered him back on course, but just as often he caught himself. More important, he answered questions from me and the audience with rapid-fire zingers and perfect timing. (When I said, "Let's start at the beginning," he interrupted my question. "When my father jumped on my mother?")

Every time I had the privilege of talking to Jerry I tried to learn things I didn't know before. I asked where the caricatures of him and Dean that became their logos originated. He told me that the pen-and-ink renderings were done by "a kid" who worked on the staff of the *Colgate Comedy Hour*—and sure enough, years later I saw similar drawings of Jack Carson, Donald O'Connor, and other series hosts, but I never did find out that young artist's name.

A few days before the public Q&A we spoke on the phone and I asked a question so arcane I didn't think an audience would necessarily care. I always wondered how it happened that these caricature images of him and Dean appeared on dispensers of Tuck Tape. Jerry explained, "Because Paul Cohen, who was the chairman of the board of the company, was a dystrophic and Paul Cohen was the man who gave me the idea to do a telethon. We were very, very close friends, and I struggled with his particular disease. He decided to give Dean and myself shares in the company. Those shares were very meaningful, but of course that became a conflict of interest so I had to tell him, 'No, we will just be there' as we promised to be for him, but with no remuneration."

That night at the Paley Center Jerry knocked me for a loop when he reached into his pocket and presented me with a roll of Tuck Tape! He later told me that he had to reach deep into his trophy case to extract it. What an extraordinarily kind gesture. I may not be six years old anymore, but he's still a hero to me.

Two Decades of Teaching at USC

Around Christmastime in 1997 Rick Jewell took me to lunch. He was then associate dean of the film department at the University of Southern California; I knew of him but we became better acquainted that day. Rick is a straight-shooting guy and he laid his cards on the table. The university had a popular class, best known by its course number 466. Its reputation was unparalleled: former students included George Lucas and Ron Howard. The idea for it was initiated in the early 1960s by the late film critic Arthur Knight, who proposed inviting filmmakers to campus with their latest pictures. At that time Alfred Hitchcock was still working and John Cassavetes was building his reputation; both of them were guests. After many years Arthur passed the baton to longtime *L.A. Times* critic Charles Champlin in 1985. When he in turn retired, the school hired a critic for one of the Hollywood trade papers to succeed him, unaware that he was having personal issues. The fall 1997 semester had been something of a disaster and with the spring term about to begin in January they needed to find a replacement, pronto. He asked me if I'd be willing to step in.

I told him the truth: I was flattered but wary of how much time I'd have to put in. Rick reassured me that someone on staff would book the films and the guests, the teaching assistant would grade the papers, and I wouldn't have to attend any faculty meetings.

"All we need is for you to be there every Thursday to conduct the class," he assured me.

I said I'd be willing to give it a try. More than 22 years later I'm still teaching that class and loving it.

We convene in the oldest screening facility on campus, Norris Theatre, a comfortable venue with superb projection and sound and great sight lines. Many filmmakers have told me they've never seen their movies look as good anywhere else.

In 2002 the auditorium was renamed Frank Sinatra Hall. Sinatra's three children paid to refurbish the theater and donated all his memorabilia to the School of Cinema. I like to point out to guests some of the highlights on the lobby walls and in glass showcases: personal letters from FDR and later presidents, photographs of young Frank on the streets of Hoboken, New Jersey; his two Academy Awards, one for *From Here to Eternity* and the other for participating in *The House I Live In*, a 1945 short subject preaching tolerance. One wall is decorated with an artist's portraits of Sinatra as he looked in a variety of films, and the other features gold and platinum albums. I explain all this to the class so they will appreciate the reason we play Sinatra recordings as they arrive every week.

The class is almost always full, because word is out that we screen some juicy blockbusters that everyone wants to see. I take pains to explain that we also screen documentaries, foreign-language films, and micro-indie productions. I emphasize this because only a fraction of the young people in attendance are film majors; the rest come from all facets of the university. At first I didn't understand the point of this, but it didn't take me long to embrace the idea. This class is "the demo" that Hollywood courts so fervently, and as I tell my students on the opening night of each semester, "I'm here to make you smarter moviegoers." By exposing them to films they might not otherwise see and introducing them to the specialists who work together to make a film, I give them a sense of the bigger picture than they might know about. I also tell them that they can learn as much from someone who's just made a bad movie as they can from someone who's produced a gem. It's absolutely true.

When people ask me why I still enjoy teaching so much I explain that I learn something every week—from our guests and my students. As the gulf inevitably widens between me and those 20-somethings, I challenge myself to remain relevant and aware of the ever-changing world around me—including newly hatched words and jargon. It keeps me on my toes. Every session begins with me talking about whatever is on my mind or movie-related issues in the news. It's nice having a captive audience.

After conducting the class for several years I started feeling my oats. Film history is my first love but I couldn't change the mandate of 466. To please myself as much as anyone I screen a vintage short subject before the feature, often from my own 16mm collection. I'd venture to say that my class is the only place such films as *Marriage Story* or *Ad Astra* were preceded by a Betty Boop cartoon.

The official name of the class is Theatrical Film Symposium, which no one likes, but neither I nor anyone else has a better name, so "466" has stuck. Among the students during my tenure are Ryan Coogler, Jon M. Chu, and Marvel chief Kevin Feige, who has been especially generous in arranging screenings of MCU movies and being willing to field a wide swath of comic book-related questions (all of which he's well prepared to answer).

I'm not shy about inviting people to campus. When I spotted Judd Apatow at the annual AFI Awards Luncheon in 2010, I walked over and introduced myself. He was cordial, and as I started pitching my class he said, "You know, I attended USC and they've never asked me back." I said, "I'm doing it right now." I suggested he bring a favorite film to discuss or one that inspired him, and he chose *Diner*. It played extremely well, and afterward Judd was a great guest. A former standup comic, he enjoys parrying with an audience. But as the clock neared 11 p.m., I knew I had to let students go. Judd looked at them and said, "My wife is out of town. I have nothing to do tonight. I'm not going anywhere!" He stayed onstage with me for another 45 minutes and while the majority of kids remained, he heckled the ones who left by calling after them, "You'll never get anywhere in show business!"

At a subsequent AFI luncheon I pulled the same routine on J.J. Abrams. He said, "I go where I'm invited," and I replied, "I'm inviting you right now." But I had an ace up my sleeve: it turned out that his assistant had taken my class. She became an ally in lining up a date for J.J. to visit. The film he chose as one of his favorites: *An American Werewolf in London*. After the screening he patiently answered all the *Star Trek* and *Star Wars* questions my students could muster.

Alexander Payne and his writing partner Jim Taylor first came to class with their breakthrough comedy *Election*. Since then Alexander has been steadfast and loyal. We've screened *About Schmidt*, *Sideways*, *The Descendants*, *Nebraska*, and *Downsizing*. At his first meeting with the marketing people on a given film, he asks them to set aside a Thursday night when he can come to class.

We've met talented directors at the outset of their now-established careers, like Barry Jenkins, Rian Johnson, Catherine Hardwicke, Jason Reitman, Paul Feig, and James Gray. Guillermo del Toro is one of my most popular guests because he is so passionate and eloquent about his work. He also curses a blue streak, to the delight of my students. And he scores points with me for being so philosophical. After showing *The Devil's Backbone* in 2002 I walked him to his car and said how grateful I was that I liked his movie so much and didn't have to pretend. "Hey," he responded, "a movie is like a blind date. Sometimes you wind up in bed, and sometimes it's just a cup of coffee."

Over the years I've introduced my students to actors, producers, production designers, cinematographers, editors, sound editors, assistant directors, animators, casting directors, composers, costume designers, visual effects supervisors, sound designers, distributors, exhibitors, studio executives, one poster designer, and one property master. Do you see why I say I learn something every week?

January and February are difficult months to book because so few good movies are released at the beginning of the year. The best we can hope for is to snag someone who's in town promoting their year-end releases for awards consideration. One year, at the Los Angeles Film Critics Association awards dinner, I met Marion Cotillard, who was brilliant as Edith Piaf in *La Vie en Rose*. I knew she had been on a treadmill attending screenings for Screen Actors Guild members and the like. Within earshot of her publicist I asked if she might enjoy meeting American students, knowing that even though it was six months old, most of my kids wouldn't have seen a French import with subtitles. Cotillard was openly enthusiastic about the idea and a week later was greeted with a lengthy standing ovation after the students witnessed her magnificent performance. She warmed to them and gave us all a fascinating look behind the scenes of a challenging film. It was a memorable evening, to put it mildly.

That's not the only time a foreign-language film has proved to be an unexpected crowd-pleaser. *City of God* galvanized the class (including the entire football squad, who were in attendance that year) as did its writer-director, Fernando Meirelles. Walter Salles was as riveting as his deeply felt film *The Motorcycle Diaries*. Bertrand Tavernier told the story behind his highly personal feature *Holy Lola*, and Costa-Gavras provided the background for his dark comedy *Le Couperet*. More recently, Florian Henckel von Donnersmarck commanded a similar reaction with his Oscar-nominated *Never Look Away*, photographed by USC alum Caleb Deschanel.

On the flip side of that coin, I learned a valuable lesson when we showed a middling romantic drama called *Message in a Bottle* starring Kevin Costner, Robin Wright, and Paul Newman. Alice and I, as a middle-aged couple, found it diverting and we especially loved watching Newman. He meant nothing to my students, who were downright hostile to the film. I should have seen it coming. Here was a story about a widower and a divorcée playing to an audience that wanted sex, not romance, or at least someone they could relate to. Director Luis Mandoki bore the brunt of that chilly reception. Thank goodness my class has always been respectful to our guests.

We've had many experiences and adventures. Filmmaker James Moll brought his gripping Holocaust documentary *The Last Days* as well as one of his interviewees, Renee Firestone. As a survivor she felt it was her duty to share her story with young people, and they were incredibly responsive. After the screening and discussion, scores of students drifted to the front of the room to meet or, in some cases, touch Renee. I'd never witnessed anything quite like that before.

In 1999 I participated in a press conference for *The Straight Story* on assignment for *Entertainment Tonight*. Having thoroughly enjoyed the film, I asked director David Lynch if he'd be willing to come to class. He pondered this for a minute, and I wondered if I'd overstepped my bounds. Then he asked, "Can I smoke?" "Absolutely," I declared with no authority to back me up. The night of the class he joined me onstage, and after two questions he said, "You said I could smoke, right?" I said, "Yes indeed." I think the statute of limitations has now run out.

That same semester we scheduled *Fight Club* and landed its star Edward Norton as our guest. Having just seen the film a few nights earlier, I went to Doheny Library to read and then walked back to Norris Theatre a few minutes before the film was over, just as Norton was arriving with his companion, Salma Hayek. (She later told me it was their first date!) None of my students had any reason to turn to the back of the room, but if they had I'm sure they would have enjoyed seeing Ms. Hayek sitting quietly in the back row.

Way back in January 1998 I asked my USC contact what film we'd be showing on the first night of the new semester. She told me it would be *Jackie Brown*, which I was happy to hear. "Great," I said. "Can we get Quentin?" "No, he's at the London premiere." As I inquired about other possible guests, it seemed all the principals were going to be in London.

"Well, then who?" I inquired and I was told, "The sound mixer."

I said, "The sound mixer? We have Quentin Tarantino's first film in five years and you're bringing the sound mixer?"

That shows you how dumb I was. This particular sound mixer, whose name is Michael Minkler, has won three Academy Awards (so far). Quentin Tarantino requests him because he's one of the best in the business. What's more, he's a third-generation sound man in Hollywood, with a son who's carrying on the family tradition that began at the dawn of the talkie era. As I watched the film that night, knowing I was going to be interviewing Mike afterward, I thought carefully about the use of sound in *Jackie Brown*. I began to notice things I hadn't paid attention to before. A fair amount of that film was shot at the busy Del Amo Mall. How do you shoot on location in a noisy place, keep the focus of the sound where it's supposed to be, and still capture the ambiance? There's a scene where somebody gets whacked inside a panel truck. How do you record that gunshot and make it convincing?

Mike had interesting answers to all of those questions. It became clear that he put as much thought and energy into his job as Quentin Tarantino did writing and directing the movie. If he were somebody less creative, less aware, less passionate in his work, the results wouldn't be as good. Lesson learned—by me as well as my class. A sound mixer is not a mere technician but a creative collaborator.

That same semester we screened Alfonso Cuarón's remake of *Great Expectations*, which starred Ethan Hawke, Gwyneth Paltrow, and Robert De Niro. Out of curiosity I asked how many in the class had seen the classic 1946 version by David Lean. Only 5 out of 320 raised their hands; one of them asked me how to spell "Lean." (At least she was interested enough to ask!)

It was then I started plotting. I knew I had to get in my licks and give these students a film experience they hadn't had before. In other words, I decided to show them an old movie. In keeping with our weekly format, I would do this only if I could get a pristine 35mm print and present one of the film's principals as a guest.

In order for this to work, I reasoned that my guest had to be someone they would relate to right away as opposed to someone who'd have to win them over. I wanted someone they would recognize. Within moments, the answer came to me. The next step was finding the right film. A call to Universal provided the solution: I asked if they had a 35mm copy of John Ford's little-seen 1932 movie *Airmail*, and I was told they had just struck a brand new print! What's more, the company was willing to let me show it. I kept both the film and the guest a surprise. All I told the class is that we'd be doing something "different."

First, I said we were going to see an old movie. (Some kids groaned. I told them, "Tough!") Then I discussed the various definitions of "old." If you're as young as my USC students—even in 1998—*The Godfather* is an old movie; after all, it was made before some of them were born. I still think of films of the 1920s, '30s and '40s as old. I can't quite apply the term to films from the '50s on—because they came out during my lifetime!

Finally, I told them we were going to see John Ford's *Airmail*, from 1932. I hastened to add that this was not a classic. It was more or less a potboiler that was made without fanfare at a time when local movie theaters changed their bills two to three times a week, and many Americans went to the movies just as often. In those pre-television days, the product that Hollywood turned out was equivalent to today's hour-long TV episodes. The difference was that studios provided new fodder 52 weeks a year.

Thus, *Airmail* was just one more film on the assembly line—better than most, because it had a great director, a good script (by longtime Ford collaborator and former aviator Frank "Spig" Wead), great camera work (by Karl Freund) and special effects (by John P. Fulton, the man who—one year later—would bring to life *The Invisible Man*), and a first-rate cast led by Ralph Bellamy, Pat O'Brien, and … our guest, Gloria Stuart.

Yes, the same Gloria Stuart who earned an Academy Award nomination in 1998 as Old Rose in *Titanic* was the leading lady in this movie—made 66 years earlier.

After the film which, I think, impressed most of the group with its well-crafted storytelling and still-impressive aerial stunts by the legendary pilot Paul Mantz, Gloria took the stage and spoke of her career with candor, humor, and intelligence. She won over the class in an instant.

She didn't look or act like a stereotypical 87-year-old. She disarmed the group by admitting that she didn't think she was terribly good in the film. She found her performances from this period stiff and overemphatic, a leftover from her training on the stage. She hadn't yet learned to relate to the camera.

"Let's face it," she said, "I was hired because I was pretty."

But she was also smart. She learned from experience. She had made waves, by helping to form the Screen Actors Guild, which didn't endear her to any of the studio moguls who were violently anti-union. She also married a screenwriter who happened to be best friends with Groucho Marx, which thrust her into heady company for the rest of her life. (Her husband-to-be, Arthur Sheekman, introduced himself to her on the set of Eddie Cantor's *Roman Scandals* as one of the writers of the film. "Then why didn't you write me a better part?" she replied. His fervor didn't flag, however, and they had a long and happy marriage.)

She reminisced about John Ford and hot-dog pilot Mantz (who

took her for an unforgettable ride when they made *Here Comes the Navy* two years later), explained how she was diverted from a stage career by the lure of a movie contract—and money—during the heart of the Depression. (Her starting salary: $125 a week.) And she told the incredible story of how she went after—and won—the part of a lifetime in *Titanic*. (Other veteran actresses who were contacted considered it an insult to be asked to read for James Cameron. Gloria didn't mind.)

At the end of the discussion period, the class gave Gloria Stuart an enthusiastic round of applause. I hope they got something out of the experience. A remark by one student leaving the theater, overheard by a friend, made me feel I had done my job.

"That," he said, "was really cool."

The evening was a complete success, and a tough act to follow, but I lined up a colorful and interesting roster of guests for our closing-night screenings. I had producer Ronald Neame with *Great Expectations*, Robert Stack with *To Be or Not to Be*, Margaret O'Brien with *Meet Me in St. Louis*, Russ Tamblyn with *Seven Brides for Seven Brothers*, Dick Jones with *Destry Rides Again*, Evelyn Keyes with *Here Comes Mr. Jordan*, Ann Savage with *Detour*, and Patricia Hitchcock with *Strangers on a Train*.

Sidney Poitier agreed to come, but he didn't favor my choice of film, *The Defiant Ones*. He preferred *To Sir, With Love*, so naturally I obliged. I learned that he is not an anecdotal man when it comes to discussing his movies, but before I knew it he launched into the telling of his true-life story. You could hear a pin drop in the auditorium. He held my class (and me) positively spellbound. It is an amazing saga with no equivalent. Afterwards, he remained at the front of the room and looked each student who wanted to meet him straight in the eye and shook his or her hand. It's a night I'm sure they'll never forget.

I pursued Angela Lansbury for seven years. She was always willing but still working steadily or heading to her second home in

Ireland, then mourning the death of her husband Peter Shaw. Finally, fate smiled and she confirmed a date. I decided not to screen *The Manchurian Candidate* but another less familiar title: Frank Capra's *State of the Union*, starring Katharine Hepburn and Spencer Tracy. In it, Lansbury (then 23) plays a Katherine Graham-like power broker who is backing her lover (Tracy) in his presidential campaign. Critics of the film in 1948 felt it watered down the Broadway play by Howard Lindsay and Russell Crouse, but I like it a lot and think it's still punchy (and timely). All of the laughs Capra put into the picture still landed with my young audience, which was especially gratifying to me.

Miss Lansbury invested the time to watch it at home the night before class to refresh her memories of the picture.

Before the film I showed a lovely tribute reel prepared by BAFTA (the British Academy of Film and Television Arts) when they gave her an award several years previously. It covered her entire career, from *National Velvet* to *Sweeney Todd* and beyond. But when she sang the title song from Disney's *Beauty and the Beast*, an audible wave of appreciation swept through the class. They may have seen her in passing on *Murder, She Wrote*, but her performance as Mrs. Potts is what made an indelible impression on my students.

Our question-and-answer session was lively and candid. The actress had warm memories of Capra, Tracy, and Hepburn and explained to the class what it was like to work at the movie factory that was MGM in the 1940s. She also admitted that she left Metro at a bad time, in the 1950s when the bottom fell out of the movie business. Being a worker by nature, she took every television job that came her way. Later, when she felt she had to prove herself on the stage, she realized that she had to learn a whole new set of skills to sing and perform on Broadway.

She spoke openly about the challenge of managing family and a career at a time when most women were homemakers. And she identified the price of being away so much; her son developed a drug habit, completely unbeknownst to her, in the late 1960s. When she realized what was happening she decided to move her family to Ireland. It wasn't easy to reconnect with her children, but in time everything turned out well. She disarmingly explained how she used her clout to get her son a job as dialogue coach on *Murder, She Wrote* and then persuaded the producers to give him a chance as director. He wound up directing a majority of the episodes in a medium not known for tolerating waste or incompetence.

It was a wonderful, wide-ranging conversation. When I took questions from the class, a meek-sounding girl in the back of the auditorium raised her hand and asked, "Could you sing 'Beauty and the Beast?'"

I was about to say that it wasn't fair to ask this of anyone (let alone an 80-year-old woman) at 10:30 at night without preparation, but something inside my head told me to shut up. Miss Lansbury said, "Oh, I couldn't ... well, all right!" And, apologizing for a voice that hadn't been warmed up, she proceeded to sing the first few lines of the familiar song.

Needless to say, the crowd went wild. At that moment, 360 kids fell in love with Angela Lansbury. Later, she stayed to talk to every student who wanted to meet her, giving each one her undivided attention and asking his or her name. The next morning, still on a high, I thought about why she had agreed to sing: she's a performer and has been all her life. She wasn't going to disappoint an audience. And I daresay she never has.

As I write this I am about to begin a new semester, teaching via Zoom during Covid-19 quarantine. It's not nearly as rewarding as looking out at a full auditorium and hearing instantaneous response to a quip or a wisecrack, but it's our only option at the moment. Still, the concept of passing along my thoughts and ideas to a new generation is inherently exciting. I can't wait to get started.

Happy Trails with Roy and Dale

I am a prototypical baby boomer, born in December of 1950, a product of post-WW2 suburbia and part of the first television generation. It was TV that introduced me to Roy Rogers, The King of the Cowboys, and his wife, Dale Evans, The Queen of the West. I was so crazy about Roy that I begged my parents to take me to the Roy Rogers Rodeo when it played at Madison Square Garden in New York. I don't remember much about the show, except that I got to see Roy ride on his golden palomino, Trigger, and laughed at his sidekick Pat Brady, who was there with his jeep Nellybelle.

Fade in, more than 20 years later. My wife and I have recently moved to Los Angeles, and I am covering (and attending) the Golden Boot Awards, an annual event that raises money for the Motion Picture and Television Fund. And there standing in front of me is Roy Rogers, decked out in a beautiful cowboy suit, hat, and custom-made boots. I approach him to ask if he'd be willing to appear on *Entertainment Tonight* with me, and he readily agrees. Then I stick out my neck and ask if he'd walk up to me, tap me on the shoulder and say, "Leonard, can I buy you a sarsaparilla?" He hesitates for a moment and I fear I've been too nervy. No, that's not it: he just wants to know if someone will throw him a cue. You see, he's a professional. As he's about to walk away, he stops and asks me to remind him of my name and I say, "Leonard—same as yours." The former Leonard Slye flashes a smile and does the routine with me to perfection. What a guy! That night he cemented his reputation with me as a hero.

Several years later, I was invited to bring an *ET* crew to the Roy Rogers–Dale Evans Museum in Victorville, California, to help celebrate the cowboy's 82nd birthday. Alice and I decided to take Jessie out of school that day so she could share the experience. I got a personal tour of the memory-laden museum from Roy, who turned out to be a pack rat. He traced his entire life and career through the things he kept—including, yes, his beloved horse Trigger, who was mounted (not stuffed, as I learned) and on proud display.

I wound up on the advisory board of the Golden Boot Awards, which is how I came to know Roy and Dale's eldest daughter Cheryl Barnett, a dear woman who has told her story in a delightful book called *Cowboy Princess*. After we became friendly she asked me a favor: would I be willing to prepare an official obituary for her dad, who was not doing well? I told her I would be honored and set to work. We exchanged faxes of several drafts until we had a piece that she and I were pleased with. I then obtained the contact information for the *New York Times*, *Los Angeles Times*, Associated Press, and several key radio and television outlets.

One day Cheryl called and told me Roy was on his last legs. I told her I was wearing a pager and I'd respond the minute I heard from her. As it happened, the news came via a telephone call at 4:00 in the morning. Her dad died peacefully at home, surrounded by his family.

Alice and I sat in bed with a reading light on, taking in the news, when I shook myself and realized that I had to get busy: I was sitting on a big story! My office was in a separate building in our back yard and I went out there to start faxing and phoning. When I got the man on the AP news desk and told him that I was calling on behalf of the Roy Rogers family to report his death, I could almost hear him sit up straighter and go into high-alert mode.

Jessie was up by now, having heard us talking, and she toddled out to the office to help send faxes. Within the hour I was talking "live" on CNN, which had a short video loop of Roy and Dale they had grabbed from their vault. I explained that this was a special occasion for me, as I seldom dealt with breaking news. My 12-year-old daughter replied, "No, Daddy, you deal with broken news." Out of the mouths of babes…

Roy's funeral was set for Saturday, and we realized we were going to be out of town. I called Cheryl to ask if there was a time we could come by Dale's house to pay our respects. She invited us to visit on Friday and assured us that Jessie would be welcome as there would be countless grandchildren, great-grandchildren, nieces, and nephews running about.

That was the scene we entered a few days later. Jessie, never shy with grownups, fell into a long conversation with Dale, sitting on a recliner lounge alongside her. I told Cheryl, "Tell me if she's outstaying her welcome," and she said, "No, this is good for Mom." In the course of their long conversation Jessie related that she would be having a Bat Mitzvah the following year. Dale replied that she had never been to a Bar or Bat Mitzvah, although she had been to Israel several times and had great respect for the Jewish people. Jessie invited her to the ceremony, and Dale accepted.

Sure enough, the following year, Dale attended my daughter's Bat Mitzvah in Los Angeles, which of course floored many of our friends.

Two friends, married freelance writers and researchers Rob Edelman and Audrey Kupferberg, had come for the Bat Mitzvah from upstate New York. When we saw them later that year they told us they'd never had such a successful summer, and they knew the reason why: Dale had blessed them when they met in June.

I'm sure they're not the only ones who felt that way. Dale Evans was a remarkable woman. She was guided and inspired by her faith, not only in God but in the goodness of people, and folks felt better just for being in her presence.

What impressed us most was her directness; Dale didn't mince words. She was a deeply religious woman, but unlike some people one thinks of as pious, she also had a hearty sense of humor. It was that combination of qualities that made her unique and lovable.

At her funeral, a reporter asked me what set Dale and Roy apart from other stars of their generation. I realized that part of the answer was that they not only allowed but encouraged the line between real life and make-believe to blur: the people we saw on-screen were a lot like the people who got married and raised a family together. Like other Western stars, they didn't isolate themselves in Hollywood; they went on the road and met their fans up close, creating a bond that never existed between moviegoers and such idols as Clark Gable or Bette Davis. Movie, radio, and television audiences felt as if they really knew Roy and Dale. Those of us who were lucky enough to take that relationship one step closer loved them all the more.

Lunch, Dinner, and a Roast with Jackie Cooper

Before I was affiliated with a hit TV show, obtaining interviews with people of note was always a challenge. I'll admit, I wasn't above a bit of subterfuge to achieve my goal. When I read that Columbia Pictures was about to release a horror film called *Chosen Survivors* in 1974, I used my gift of gab to persuade a studio publicist to set up a phone call with one of its stars, Jackie Cooper. It is perhaps some measure of the interest in this film that anyone would think an interview in *Film Fan Monthly* could help its box-office allure.

Jackie Cooper was a big deal to me. I'd grown up watching *The Little Rascals* on TV, as well as his subsequent TV series *The People's Choice* and *Hennesey*. What's more, I was in the midst of trying to complete a book about Our Gang (the original name of The Little Rascals) and having some quotes from him would be very useful.

I dutifully attended a screening of *Chosen Survivors*, not a great film by anyone's standards. A group of disparate people are selected to perpetuate the human race after a nuclear explosion—but their underground shelter is also home to deadly vampire bats. Cooper did a capable job alongside such other pros as Richard Jaeckel, Alex Cord, Diana Muldaur, and Bradford Dillman. When I got through to him in California I asked some perfunctory questions about the movie and then, as casually as possible, steered the conversation back to his childhood.

He was willing to go along and was disarmingly candid. I asked how clear the memories of making his first movies were.

"Well," he said, "I'll tell you something. Sometimes I'll wake up in the middle of the night and I'll hear a voice that sounds familiar. My wife has fallen asleep with the tube on and finally I'll start recognizing the dialogue, look up, and Jesus Christ, it's me, at 14, or 12, or 9, or whatever. Sometimes I'll sit there and watch it and I can tell myself what's coming next. I remember the dialogue, the scene, and the set very well, and then there'll be a part of the picture I never remembered at all.

"Because there were times as a kid, as a teenager especially, when if I'd be terribly occupied in what I was doing—with my boat, or on a circuit of rodeos and horse shows, or with my car—very often on some of this stuff when I'd have to go to work, I'd just give the script a cursory glance. I had no training and I was a quick study, so nobody knew how involved or not involved I was. But I look at that stuff now and I can see I wasn't involved, and I wasn't very good."

Regarding the Our Gang comedies he said, "They made us as unconscious of what we were doing, and the importance of it, as possible. They tried not to tell us where we were going, what we were going to do, and how we were going to do it. I remember as a kid it was always a surprise when we'd get in the car and were going someplace. We never knew if we were going out, indoors or outdoors, or where.

"There were no lines to learn. I didn't learn any lines until I did the first feature, *Skippy*. They would over-shoot and they could always cut to the dog if they didn't have enough coverage. They tried to keep it [as much like] play as much as possible. But there was a respect you had. There were two directors I remember from the year or so I was there: [Robert] McGowan and his son [actually his nephew]. There was big respect for this guy. He was a big father image to all of us, and boy, whatever he said, we did, and we'd be rewarded with ice cream and things. It was terrific."

He also admitted that he still had some ham in him. "I would love to get a good part in a good picture. You know, if a picture makes money it's amazing how many executives like your performance a little better. On *Chosen Survivors* I really got a charge out of it, because as much as I've directed and horsed around with different parts of this business, once you're an actor, you're always an actor. You can stay out of the water for 10 years but if you fall in you can swim. It never leaves you."

A decade went by, and I found myself attending the National Association of Television Program Executives convention, which was held that year in San Francisco. This was the launch pad for syndicated TV sales. I was there representing *ET*, while Jackie was promoting the relaunch of his early 1960s show *Hennesey*. Flying home to Burbank airport I saw him and his wife on the plane and, when we landed, made a beeline for him. We exchanged pleasantries and he said we should break bread together. Hot dog! As it happened, I was entering a period of hectic activity and it was months before I was able to have lunch with him, but he apparently remembered me and we set a date. He said he would pick me up and, as I anticipated from reading about his various hobbies, he was driving a sporty car (stick shift, of course). We went to a nice Italian restaurant and had a relaxed lunch.

I wish I'd had the nerve to bring a recording machine along but I didn't want to formalize what was intended to be a social meeting. He recalled that on *The Return of Frank James*, prickly director Fritz Lang ordered him to pull up his horse to a hitching post and dismount on the animal's right side. Jackie, who'd been riding since childhood, protested that this was the wrong way to get off a horse. Lang exploded at the insolence of his actor—a youthful one at that. Seeing that he couldn't win the argument, Jackie goaded him until the director used foul language, at which point the young star—still a minor—walked over to the studio-appointed teacher/guardian and reported Lang's verboten behavior. She promptly shut the set down. As a result, said Jackie, "All you see of me in that picture is the back of my head."

Another German émigré, William Dieterle, was similarly bull-headed when discussing an upcoming film about the birth of jazz called *Syncopation*. He wanted Jackie to take trombone lessons so he would look natural playing the instrument on camera. When Jackie tried to correct Dieterle, who meant to say "trumpet," the director became furious at his insubordination and wouldn't back down. As a result, Jackie took lessons on the wrong instrument.

I was lapping all this up, and as we finished our main course, Jackie said, "So, tell me what you wanted to talk about." I replied, "Just this—getting to know you and hearing your stories." He hesitated but a moment and flashed a friendly smile. "Great!" he said. (I learned that no one "just has lunch" without an ulterior motive in Hollywood. Thank goodness Jackie didn't mind simply schmoozing.)

A short time later I got a call from someone working with the Friars' Club, the venerable show-business social organization. He invited me to participate in an upcoming "roast" of Jackie Cooper, and I, flattered beyond words, said yes. I inquired who else was going to be on the dais, and he read off a list of comedians, some old and others older. I then realized that he was booking the dais as one would a benefit and asked if he'd considered asking anyone who actually had worked with Cooper. He said Jackie had nixed Mickey Rooney, for fear that he would steal the spotlight. I asked, "What about Hal Roach, who produced the Our Gang comedies?" The fellow said, "Is he still alive?" I said yes and gave him Mr. Roach's phone number.

Came the evening and I had a ball, for all sorts of reasons. Milton Berle did a great job as master of ceremonies, handling his oversized note cards with the mastery of a Las Vegas croupier. Some of the comics were funny, others not so much. I played it sincere, which gave me a niche all my own. But the best story of the night was told by 86-year-old Hal Roach.

He had Jackie under contract in 1930 when Paramount Pictures decided he would be the perfect boy to star in a film adaptation of the popular comic strip *Skippy*. A meeting was arranged to negotiate the loan of Jackie's services. Roach mentioned to his friend, producer Joseph M. Schenck, that a Paramount executive was coming to his office the next day to seal the deal. "No!" said Schenck. "You go to his office."

"Why?" asked Roach.

"Because," Schenck replied, "you can't walk out of your own office!"

Afterwards, the three of us posed for a photo, smiling ear to ear. Jackie later accepted an invitation to the Cinecon when Alice and I hosted it with Randy Haberkamp at the Hollywood Roosevelt Hotel. We showed a rare 1932 feature, *When a Feller Needs a Friend*, which Jackie accurately described as mediocre, and he seemed genuinely pleased when we surprised him by having Hal Roach present him with our award.

By this time he'd been in show business more than sixty years. He had been a child star, a has-been, a Broadway actor, a television star, and a busy TV director. He had even worked as an executive running Screen Gems, the TV division of Columbia Pictures. He'd seen and done it all and had firsthand knowledge of how things operated in Hollywood. But when I asked him to sign my copy of his autobiography, *Please Don't Shoot My Dog*, this is what he wrote, without a hint of cynicism: "Leonard—with respect to a real fan of this terrific business of ours… Best, Jackie Cooper." I admired him all the more for that.

The Unsinkable Gloria Stuart

When you've lived a full life and made it to the century mark, it's hard to complain, but Gloria Stuart still had a special spark even in her 101st year on the planet. Her energy was waning and her mind could wander, but she loved life, including her family, her artwork, her fine-edition books, kites, and bonsai plants. I'm happy that she was able to celebrate her 100th birthday in high style with a series of events including a citation from the Screen Actors Guild, which she helped to found, and a gala evening at the Academy of Motion Picture Arts and Sciences, which positively thrilled her. (I was privileged to serve as host.) She was also feted by Suzy Amis, who played her granddaughter in *Titanic*, and her husband, James Cameron, who treated Gloria like a member of the family.

As much as I enjoyed watching her revel in the attention that *Titanic* brought her—including the opportunity to write a candid and engaging autobiography, *I Just Kept Hoping*—I will never fully understand why Gloria didn't become a bigger star the first time around in the 1930s. She was beautiful and smart. Perhaps she lacked the drive to make it happen, or perhaps she just didn't get the breaks. Her first contract was shared between Paramount, which didn't make good use of her at all, and Universal, which primarily made undistinguished "program pictures," although she did get to work with James Whale and John Ford there. She longed for better material and made her way to 20th Century Fox, where again she worked for Ford but toiled mainly in B movies. (Having married screenwriter Arthur Sheekman, she wasn't interested in the advances of notorious studio chief Darryl F. Zanuck; perhaps that was a factor as well.) It was Hollywood's loss; she brought charm and conviction to even the silliest films she was forced to make.

She held her own in the heady company of her husband's witty friends, including his best pal Groucho Marx. And she succeeded in every one of her non-acting pursuits, from throwing imaginative dinner parties (vividly described in her book) to painting (selling out her first show at the prestigious Hammer Galleries) and finally, to creating her own paper and hand-setting type for her fine-art books.

No life is perfect, but hers was varied and rewarding. And just when she'd stopped thinking about acting, *Titanic* came along. I spoke to her on the phone when she was awaiting a callback from the casting director, and she asked me to cross my fingers for her. When she got the part she was elated; as it turned out, that was just the first step in a parade of unexpected joys, from an Oscar nomination to the enduring friendship of her costar and director.

The one thing Gloria didn't do was live in the past. She didn't mind reminiscing, and for years she was sought after by anyone writing about James Whale, Boris Karloff, or Groucho Marx, but she was more interested in tending to her garden or setting type.

Back in 2004 when Universal Pictures archivist Bob O'Neill (since retired) told me he had just struck a new 35mm print of the 1934 movie *I Like It That Way*, I couldn't resist asking its leading lady if she'd want to watch it. She practically shrieked, "That's the worst musical ever made!" but admitted that she'd enjoy seeing it again. It had never been on television and apparently was never released on 16mm.

Arriving at Universal's main gate Gloria, my wife, and I had to show our photo IDs. The security stop made Gloria think of a time when she and her husband were traveling to Mexico with Groucho Marx. When a border guard asked Groucho his occupation, he immediately replied, "Spy." Needless to say, the entire party was routed from its automobile and searched.

Some films require extensive restoration, but the nitrate negative of *I Like It That Way* survived in great shape. The print we watched was excellent, which is more than one can say for the film itself. As Gloria remarked, Universal dealt in chintz.

Roger Pryor stars in this breezy, grade-B musical about a super-salesman who finally meets his Waterloo. Having worked his charm on female customers galore, he meets absolute resistance from Gloria, whom he chances to meet on the stairway of her apartment building

Gloria is aloof at first and finally agrees to go out on a date with Pryor. She even gets to like him, but when he makes a move on her she puts him off, asking if he wouldn't rather wait until she wanted to be kissed. This concept has never occurred to him before; he falls head over heels and renounces his womanizing ways. Little does he dream that Gloria, whom he now places on a pedestal, is the star of the sexy show at The Plantation Club, a nightclub and gambling joint.

Shirley Grey sings the movie's first (and best) song, "I've Got Two Little Arms" in her apartment. The remaining songs, "I Like It That Way" and "Good Old Days" are ostensibly sung by Gloria in the nightclub. She begins the first song with feathered fans, à la Sally Rand, although she is fully clothed. Her lip-syncing is quite good, but the idea of casting her as a nightclub star when she could neither sing nor dance is one of those wonderful Hollywood absurdities.

The biggest production number revolves around "Good Old Days." It begins with Gloria and the chorus girls wearing and singing about bathing attire of grandmother's era. Then we see them in modern swimsuits. And then, so help me, Gloria and company give us a glimpse of the future—at a nudist colony, where strategically placed shrubbery hides their private parts. (I'd always wondered why Gloria had bare shoulders in ads and sheet music for the film; now I know.)

The film opens with the National Recovery Administration symbol, heralding Hollywood's support of President Roosevelt's short-lived plan to help America out of the Depression. Then we see the Universal biplane and the main credits. The first thing Gloria remarked upon was the name of Lucille Gleason in the cast list, because "she is one of the founders of the Screen Actors Guild." People with just one scene in the film, like young Mickey Rooney and the ever-popular Mae Busch, get billing, in fact.

At the outset of her first musical number Gloria declared, "I may throw up." So how exactly did she find herself in such a film?

"I was under contract. I said, 'I don't sing and I don't dance,' and they said, 'Well, you just stand in front of the chorus and we'll take care of the rest of it.' I remember standing [there] and saying 'I don't want to do this, I'm no good at this.' I'm standing there like a broomstick; they gave me no gestures, they didn't cover me at all. It's embarrassing."

She wasn't any too crazy about her wardrobe, either. "Polka dots! They couldn't have made me look worse."

The young actress had loftier ambitions. Onslow Stevens, who appears briefly in *I Like It That Way*, had costarred with her in a production of Chekhov's *The Seagull* at the Pasadena Playhouse. Now she was caught in the Hollywood studio machine, turning out one potboiler after another. In 1933, her second year in movies, she appeared in nine feature films. One day Universal's production chief Junior Laemmle—they really called him Junior, she says—told her he was going to turn her into a female Tarzan, which prompted a violent reaction.

Of the would-be mogul, she says, "He was a nice little man with no talent; he just had his father behind him. He was not a moviemaker, that's all."

But if acting on-screen didn't give her the satisfaction she craved, political activism did.

"It was Melvyn Douglas who said to me one night here at Universal about 9:00—when we'd been working since dawn—'We're forming a union; would you like to join?' I said, 'What's that?' He said, 'What's what?' I said, 'What's a union?' We were working 10, 12, 14 hours a day and working Saturday into Sunday. For women, we had to be in makeup by 6:00 in the morning, [and] we'd get home by 9 or 10 at night. It was murder."

Gloria became a founding member of the Screen Actors Guild and served on its board for many years.

When I moved to Los Angeles and *Entertainment Tonight* allowed me to do interviews and feature pieces, I invented a story idea just so I could meet Gloria. I stayed in touch with her after that and nearly did a double-take when I saw a vintage photo of her in *Batman & Robin* as the deceased wife of Alfred the butler (Michael Gough). I may have been the only person in the audience who recognized her. She told me she'd gotten a call from someone at Warner Bros. telling her they'd found the still photo and were prepared to pay her for its use.

Meanwhile, she heard a rumor that another movie was seeking out an older woman "who was still breathing and could remember her lines and was not falling down. That's how James Cameron found me."

I kept tabs with Gloria during the endless months that followed. She told me all about her meeting with casting director Mali Finn and the call that finally came with the good news that she'd landed the job. Even though they had no scenes together, Kate Winslet paid a visit one day to meet the woman they both would play on-screen—and won Gloria over by bringing champagne, which she adored. (Her mantra was "Everything in moderation—including moderation.")

She was so excited that she asked the manager of the Village Theater in Westwood if he would show her the trailer when it was first unveiled.

Then the dam burst. *Titanic* was a mega-hit and Gloria Stuart was a "somebody" again in Hollywood. She was approached to write her life story and in time, was nominated for an Academy Award as Best Supporting Actress. She made no attempt to hide her disappointment when she didn't win.

She went on with her life and enjoyed it fully. She made her memorable appearance at my USC class following a screening of John Ford's *Airmail*. I feel fortunate to have known her. If you read her book, you'll learn why she was so much more interesting than most of the women she got to play on-screen.

Getting Close to Walt Disney

I'm often asked whom I'd like to have interviewed if I'd had the chance. My answer is automatic: Walt Disney. He and his work have been a significant part of my life since I was four or five years old. I've written articles and books and hosted TV shows and DVDs about his films and television programs. There are so many facets to the man, as evidenced by the parade of scholarly articles and books that come out every year. I don't think we'll ever run out of topics to research.

For instance, in the 1930s Walt and his brother Roy took up polo as a hobby. Among their fellow players were Spencer Tracy, Will Rogers, 20th Century Fox chief Darryl F. Zanuck, and producer Hal Roach. The friendships they made paid dividends for years to come. Tracy's wife, Louise, remembered meeting Walt and Roy when they were still beginners at the sport and playing with "the wives." When she later started a clinic for deaf children named for her son John, she recruited Walt to be on the board of directors.

According to James Curtis' *Spencer Tracy: A Biography*, "Walt Disney ... was interested in seeing firsthand how the clinic worked. It was when Louise was showing him around a few days later they came upon the kids during nap time. 'Don't they have cots?' he asked. 'No,' Louise told him, 'they just sleep on mats on the floor.'

The next day there were cots and at Christmas time a truckload of gifts—puppets and toys, all Disney-licensed, that could be used in teaching."

When Hal Roach wanted to use the Three Little Pigs as characters in his Laurel and Hardy feature *Babes in Toyland*, he received an exceedingly friendly note from Walt granting permission. "If you would like to use the original girls who did the voices, I would be glad to get them together for you or you may use any piece of the sound track, as well as any models of the characters. In other words, we are more than glad to cooperate with you in every way." Roach was able to return the favor when Disney wanted to use Laurel and Hardy's theme song "Ku Ku" to accompany their caricatured appearances in some of his cartoon shorts.

And when Walt made his first steps into live-action production in the 1940s, the directors he hired (Alfred Werker for *The Reluctant Dragon*, Harold Schuster for *So Dear to My Heart*) were 20th Century Fox veterans who had Darryl Zanuck's seal of approval.

While playing polo at Riviera Country Club, Walt took a shine to a bright, ambitious teenager named Larry Lansburgh and offered him a job. He started as a messenger boy and went on to hold a variety of jobs, eventually becoming a producer and director at the studio. (He even made a film about the John Tracy Clinic under Walt's supervision.)

Reading up on Walt and his extracurricular activities—like railroading—has brought me one step closer to the man. I've also spent time with a number of his colleagues, but my most exciting and meaningful encounter was meeting his daughter Diane and her husband, Ron Miller.

In the late 1990s, with Walt's centenary approaching, Diane felt that her father was fading from public consciousness. Everyone knew Disney as a corporate name, but ordinary people were no longer familiar with her father the way they had been when he hosted a weekly television show. She decided that it was time to celebrate his life and achievements. This was not a casual decision, as Diane was not a public figure and tended to keep a low profile.

Diane and I first met at a panel discussion held at Disneyland in December 1998. It featured a handful of lifelong Disney buffs and experts. Toward the end of a wide-ranging conversation, moderator Tim O'Day asked her what misimpression she would most like to correct in people's minds and she said, "Well, he isn't frozen." Her response was drowned out by audience response to a prior remark by another guest, so I took the initiative of reiterating the question and she repeated her answer. You can imagine how the audience reacted. She elaborated by explaining that he had been cremated and his remains are kept at Forest Lawn Glendale cemetery. Wild rumors and conspiracy theories still abound, but that's the truth. Who better to hear it from than his eldest daughter?

My wife and I got to chat with Diane before and after the formal event, and she kindly signed my copy of the paperback book *The Story of Walt Disney*. I took this as a compliment because, as she explained with some embarrassment, she didn't really write the book at all. It was compiled from conversations Walt had with Pete Martin, who covered the Hollywood beat for *The Saturday Evening Post*. Only after issuing that caveat did she graciously inscribe my copy, which of course I treasure.

The success of that modest event led Diane to accept an invitation from the Montreal Film Festival to attend a tribute to her father in the fall of 1999. Alice, Jessie, and I were invited to join a group that included famed Disney biographer Bob Thomas, studio matte artist Peter Ellenshaw, songwriter Richard M. Sherman and his wife Elizabeth, Diane's husband Ron Miller and their son Walter, authors Katherine and Richard Greene, and our good pal, Disney publicist Howard Green. It was not the best organized event but we all got along famously and enjoyed spending time together.

December 2001 was the next milestone: the hundredth anniversary of Walt's birth. The Academy of Motion Picture Arts and Sciences staged an evening tribute in their Samuel Goldwyn Theater, which was packed for the occasion. I hosted the evening, which included film clips and conversations with three of Walt's "Nine Old Men," Frank Thomas, Ollie Johnston, and Ward Kimball, as well as Diane herself. The surprise hit of the evening was a five-minute excerpt of a promotional piece Walt made with Robert Kintner, then the head of the ABC Television Network. It was never meant to be seen by the public, only ABC affiliates and advertisers. Walt's body language revealed more about him than volumes could speak. As Kintner went into high-power sales mode, Walt raised his eyebrow (a "tell" that everyone who worked for him recognized as a warning sign) and became impatient, distractedly fingering the illustration boards in his hands and losing eye contact. Ellen Harrington, who produced the event, thought we should shorten the film clip when she watched it alone, but I had seen it with a Disney-wise audience and promised her that it would deliver big laughs from a knowing crowd. It did and brought a smile to Diane's face because it was such an honest portrait of her father.

At the end of the Academy tribute to her dad, I asked Diane what made her proudest. She thought for a moment and replied, "I'm proud of his work, I'm proud of what he did, I'm proud of what he built, I'm proud that he was a good man, and I'm his daughter. I'm proud of that." This prompted a lengthy ovation from the crowd.

Over the next few years Diane and Ron started working on a museum that would pay permanent tribute to her father. Planning and executing such an ambitious endeavor was fraught with difficulties, including choosing the right people to make it a reality. There were some stumbles along the way, but once Diane was introduced to Imagineer Bruce Gordon, who was also a lifelong Disney buff, things began to gel.

Alice and I were invited to an early "think tank"-type meeting with a number of other Disneyphiles. We liked some of what we saw and didn't care for other ideas. Alice's main contribution was urging Diane to make sure she had a great gift shop—my wife's measure of the value of any museum. On the gala opening night of the Walt Disney Family Museum in 2009, Diane thanked Alice from the podium and assured her that she had taken her advice to heart.

Diane took any attack on her father as a personal sting and couldn't understand why so many people seemed to thrive on wildly false accusations and name-calling. She knew he wasn't perfect and came to accept the idea that her museum timeline wouldn't be complete without an examination of the Disney Studios' painful labor strike of 1941. (Diane had a child's perspective of that watershed event: she recalled some of her father's leading animators swimming in her family pool on weekends during happier times in the 1930s. That casual camaraderie evaporated after the strike.) No father—or mother, for that matter—ever had a stronger advocate.

Diane's husband, Ron Miller, who worked his way up the ladder and wound up running the Disney studio, was something of an enigma to me. He seldom gave interviews, though he had witnessed so much in his decades at the studio and participated in many key decisions. He was an early supporter of Cal Arts graduate Tim Burton, who made experimental shorts like *Vincent* and *Frankenweenie* at the studio in the early 1980s. He backed some notorious flops but was also instrumental in making *Tron*, the most forward-thinking film to come from Disney in years.

He was completely supportive of Diane and her projects, including the museum, into which they plowed millions of dollars. He was not a talkative fellow and rarely broke into a conversation to volunteer his thoughts or memories, leading me to feel a certain frustration because of his long history with the company. He had gone to work for his father-in-law in the 1950s and even directed him in some of his TV show introductions. He wound up becoming the heir apparent and did in fact run the studio after Walt's death in 1966, until the threat of a takeover by corporate raiders in the 1980s impelled Roy E. Disney to step in with a new management team led by Michael Eisner and Frank Wells. Overnight, Ron Miller was out.

This created an awkward schism within the Disney family. Roy Edward was hardly a stranger to the company that his father Roy O. Disney cofounded, having worked there since his teens. Now he was responsible for ousting his cousin-by-marriage.

A few years after Diane's tragic and untimely death in 2013, I had a rare opportunity to sit with Ron Miller in his office at the Walt Disney Family Museum. He was still shaken by his wife's passing and he began to reminisce. He recounted how unnerving it was the first Monday morning he had no job to go to. He sat on his patio sipping coffee and wondering what life had in store for him. By that time, decades later, he realized that he'd been given a gift—an opportunity to spend time with his wife and their seven children, to travel, to pursue other interests (like the Silverado Winery), and more. He redoubled his dedication to the museum because now it was not only a tribute to his famous father-in-law but an homage to his wife, to whom it meant so much.

At the grand opening of the museum I ran into Roy Patrick Disney, who was pleased that his side of the family was also well represented. That made Alice and me feel good, as we had become friendly with his father, Roy Edward. Our relationship was cemented when he brought his pet project, *Destino*, to the Telluride Film Festival in 2003, where I introduced it with him on two separate occasions.

Destino came about because, in the process of preparing *Fantasia 2000*, Roy viewed the tantalizing footage the great Spanish surrealist Salvador Dali had created for Walt Disney in the 1940s. He also learned that the studio still had three full-sized oil paintings of images intended to be used in the picture. Roy asked the studio lawyers to see if they actually owned these priceless works of art and was told that, contractually, Disney owned the paintings upon completion of the short. That's what fired Roy's interest in doing just that, 58 years after the project had been set aside. He assigned the task to studio producer Baker Bloodworth, who in turn chose Dominique Montféry, a talented artist at Disney Studios Paris, to direct it. He in turn received vital input from Dali's primary collaborator on the Burbank lot, John Hench, who was still reporting for work every day at the age of 93.

When *Destino* was completed, I was among a handful of people invited to a screening at the Disney Animation building in Burbank, hosted by Roy. We also got to view the Dali oil paintings. After watching the mind-boggling seven-minute short, we peppered Roy with questions and at one point I asked, "Could we see it again?" The second showing was even more rewarding than the first. That experience prompted me to do the same when we presented *Destino* at Telluride. No one minded seeing this hypnotic short a second time, understanding more about it having listened to Roy.

Roy and I shot interviews about the history of *Destino* on two separate occasions for documentaries that took years to see the light of day. I came to learn that Roy's pet projects were held at arm's length by other power brokers at the Disney company. It took years for *Destino* to get a perfunctory DVD/Blu-ray release, all but hidden in the bonus content for *Fantasia 2000*. In the years to follow it was available to one and all on YouTube and is now showing on the Disney+ streaming channel.

I also got to interview Roy about his recollection of the studio during World War II for the Walt Disney Treasures DVD set *On the Home Front*. Here was a man who had firsthand recollections of riding his bike on the Burbank lot when it was suddenly occupied by military personnel in the early 1940s. I don't think anyone had asked him about this before. (Roy also encouraged Hollywood biographer Bob Thomas to write a full-length book about his father, who lived his life in his kid brother's shadow. *Building a Company: Roy O. Disney and the Creation of an Entertainment Empire* is a fascinating account that might not have been realized without Roy's encouragement and active participation.)

One day I was thumbing through a hardcover tie-in book for the Disney feature *Perri* and realized that its text was credited to Roy Edward Disney. I brought it along one day we were shooting an interview and asked if he would sign it. He smiled at the sight of the nearly-forgotten volume and wrote, "For Leonard Maltin—with best wishes—and if you read this, please remember that I was only 25 years old—and on my honeymoon—when I wrote it—Roy Disney."

Spending time with this straightforward, unpretentious man was always a pleasure, but one experience stands out in sharp relief.

I had been invited to the Philadelphia International Film Festival on more than one occasion, but the timing was never quite right. Then one day in 2007 I got a call from Thom Cardwell inviting me back with a lure he knew I couldn't resist: Roy E. Disney had said he would attend. He asked if I'd be interested in talking to him onstage before screenings of vintage Disney shorts and features over the course of a long weekend, and of course I said yes.

Then I called my friend, Disney publicist Howard Green, who often accompanied Roy on his travels. I asked if Roy would likely be using his private plane to fly to Philly and if there was any chance Alice and I could hitch a ride. He checked and the answer to both questions was affirmative. That sealed the deal.

Early one Friday morning, we drove to the inconspicuous entrance to Van Nuys Airport, where a guard checked to see that our names were on a guest list. He instructed us to drive toward a hangar where uniformed people were waiting for us. Alice turned the car keys over to a nice fellow who resembled a Disneyland cast member and invited us to relax in a comfortable lounge just inside the hangar. There, coffee and Danish pastries awaited us. Howard Green came shortly afterwards, followed by Roy himself, dressed in one of his characteristic Aloha shirts. After exchanging some small talk, he asked casually, "Shall we get going?" Our luggage had been stowed aboard without our lifting a finger, and there was no security check.

Let me emphasize that this was no Learjet: Roy's Shamrock Airlines (named for his investment company) was a full-sized 727 jet that had been outfitted for complete comfort and convenience. The clean-cut crew included a pilot, copilot, and flight attendant. There were several seating areas and, as we learned, a dining cabin where we would soon have lunch served to us at a table for four. Behind that was a full-sized bedroom.

We landed four-and-a-half hours later at an extension of Philadelphia International Airport, where a giant SUV was waiting to ferry us to our hotel. Again, we didn't have to fuss with our luggage; it was all taken care of. We then embarked on a delightful weekend of screenings, public conversations, communal meals (including a memorable dinner in Little Italy), and a bit of tourism. Our return trip on Sunday was another example of smooth sailing. When we taxied to the hangar in Van Nuys we noticed that Alice's car was already positioned to drive off the property, and in minutes' time our luggage was loaded for us. What an experience! Needless to add, we will never forget it. (p.s. Roy ultimately downsized Shamrock Air to lighten his load and consume less fuel. He sold the 727—for a profit.)

Two years later, Roy succumbed to stomach cancer, just shy of his 80th birthday. It was a blow to the company that bore his family name, but we also took it as a personal loss. After that bonding experience anyone can understand why.

John Wayne's Extended Family

While organizing the "physical media" in my garage I found several unopened DVD sets of old television shows—programs I never watched when I was a kid because all I cared about in those days was comedy. That's how Alice and I spent our time in quarantine, running through complete seasons of *Gunsmoke*, *Have Gun—Will Travel*, *Rawhide*, and *Perry Mason*. They were made in the days when a season routinely meant 39 weekly episodes, providing steady work, especially for character actors and young up-and-comers. Our favorite pastime is trying to identify familiar faces in the cast of each show, but the name we have seen most often in the credits is the director Andrew V. McLaglen.

We look at each other and say, "How lucky were we to meet him?" The son of Oscar-winning actor Victor McLaglen (who turns up late in life in *Rawhide* and *Have Gun—Will Travel* episodes), he was also part of an extended family perpetuated by director John Ford and actor John Wayne.

For instance, Wayne's production company gave Andy McLaglen his first shot at directing a feature film, *Gun the Man Down* (1956). It starred another Wayne protégé, James Arness, just before he became famous playing Matt Dillon on *Gunsmoke*. McLaglen would go on to direct Arness in many episodes of that long-running series. When the producers were casting a new character named Festus to take the place of departing Dennis Weaver, Mc-Laglen recommended someone he knew well, Ken Curtis—who had once been married to John Ford's daughter Barbara.

McLaglen's ties to Wayne and Ford went back a long, long way. His father worked with the director from 1927 on and won an Academy Award for his performance as Gypo Nolan in *The Informer*. By the late 1940s, the younger McLaglen had made a niche for himself as an up-and-coming assistant director, but Ford's regular a.d. was his brother-in-law, Wingate Smith. In order to work on *The Quiet Man*, Andy graciously took a "demotion" to second a.d., even though he wound up doing much of Smith's work.

"I'd been around Mr. Ford since I was, like, 13," Andy told us. "I remember driving to the studio to see my father going on location for *The Lost Patrol* (in 1934). They were all going down to Yuma, Arizona, and I remember Ford coming over and patting me on the head. As he drove away he waved at me. From then on, I'd see Ford from time to time as a boy. Around 1943 and '44 I used to go up to his house quite a bit. That's when John Wayne was getting his divorce from Josephine, his first wife, and he was courting Chata."

The relationship has endured. Andrew's children Mary and Josh McLaglen have carved enviable careers in film production. He was first assistant director on *Titanic*, to name just one of many credits. She enjoyed a long partnership with Sandra Bullock as unit production manager, then producer. John Wayne was Mary's godfather, and she remains friendly with his youngest son, Ethan. Josh's godfather was Duke's brother, Robert Morrison.

No wonder when "Pappy" Ford retired Wayne felt comfortable handing the director's reins to Andy for such late-career vehicles as *Hellfighters*, *The Undefeated*, *Chisum*, and *Cahill U.S. Marshal*. And it makes perfect sense that the casts of those films include such Ford regulars and Wayne cronies as Ben Johnson, Harry Carey, Jr., Paul Fix, Hank Worden, Chuck Roberson, Bruce Cabot,

John Agar, Pedro Gonzales Gonzales, Chris Mitchum, and John Mitchum. They were family.

We became friendly with Harry Carey, Jr. (known to one and all as Dobe) and his wife, Marilyn. One day he told us, "Do you know how Duke got his walk? My wife's father, [character actor] Paul Fix. Back in the 1930s, he coached Duke. Duke said, 'I don't like my walk. I look awkward when I walk.' He was very aware of these things; he was about 29 years old. So Paul said, 'Point your toes when you walk.' He said, 'What?' Paul said, 'When you walk, point your toes in the ground.' When you point your toes like you're going to stab your toes in the ground it makes you do this." He shifted his shoulders back and forth, just like John Wayne. In *The Desert Trail* (1935) there's a scene where Wayne and Paul Fix walk side by side and it is the identical walk.

He also recalled, "In 1968 down in Mexico, Duke sat and told me that he couldn't watch himself on-screen, he didn't know what to do with his hands. 'I have to find a role model, and Harry Carey fit it.'" Film buffs know that Wayne is consciously mimicking Carey in the final shot of John Ford's *The Searchers* (1956) when he holds his arm. It is one of the most touching homages in all of movie history.

We flew to Mesa, Arizona, to talk to Ben Johnson, whose "bedroom eyes" set my wife's heart aflutter. (She discussed this freely with Johnson's loving wife, Carol.) Johnson, the only man to earn an Academy Award (for *The Last Picture Show*) and the National Rodeo Championship, walked away from the Ford troupe after words were exchanged at dinner one night on location for *Rio Grande*. Ford didn't hire him back until 1964 when he made *Cheyenne Autumn*. Johnson couldn't have been more gracious and, thanks to my wife's telephone friendship with his wife, he carved an hour out of his busy schedule for our interview.

Alice and I got to meet Andrew McLaglen when I was hired to host and produce a behind-the-scenes documentary on the making of *The Quiet Man* with my then-partner, Mark Lamberti. One Sunday morning a tall, imposing gentleman wearing a suit and tie walked up our path in Toluca Lake. It was McLaglen, who bore more than a casual resemblance to his famous father. He held us spellbound as he brushed away the years and took us back to Ireland in 1951.

He needed little prodding to summon memories of that shoot and the accommodations. "Ashford Castle is an old Guinness estate which had been transformed into a hotel," he explained. "It was right near a little village called Cong. It doesn't even sound Irish. That's where we all were. One Saturday night we all gathered on a street corner in Cong and the village priest—one of them, there were a lot of them there—pulled a lever and the first electric street light in the history of Cong went on. May of 1951, during our stay there.

"Every day is what we call a soft day over there, meaning there's a little bit of dampness in the air. It was great for Winton Hoch, who was the cameraman and won the Academy Award for it with Archie Stout, who did the second-unit stuff. Those soft days made for that beautiful soft look. And there's no green like the green in Ireland. We were shooting in three-strip Technicolor on those great big blue cameras that took about thirty minutes to reload."

The mercurial John Ford didn't give Andy much trouble—except on the first day of shooting. Ford's older brother, Francis, had a small part in the picture but wasn't scheduled to work that day. Andrew consulted with his colleagues and they agreed that they were safe, even though the boss had instructed them to have "all the actors" on the set.

"Ford arrives, right on schedule, pipe in his mouth, sits down, surveys the scene, and says, 'Frank will be in the first shot.'"

At this, McLaglen went into action. "We had to lay a whole white beard on him, quicker than had ever been laid before, like in 10 minutes, and by the time the camera was set up, Frank was in the first shot. And he was a very nice man, too—a very, very nice man—I won't say 'unlike his brother,' but he was different than Jack."

Because Ford got to shoot his long-gestating pet project in the summertime, John Wayne was able to bring all four of his children along. They were old enough to have clear-eyed memories of the experience, and if you don't blink you can also see them all on-screen. We talked to three of them.

Toni Wayne La Cava remembered it as a grand adventure. "We went across the ocean on an airplane which had beds in it. It was a big thrill to drive up and see a huge castle. We've lived in California all our lives with palm trees and all of a sudden there's a huge castle and a great big river there, and it was absolutely fabulous. It was not so far after the war so it didn't have a lot of the modern conveniences. My father had a bathroom, Uncle Jack had a bathroom, I think Maureen [O'Hara] had a bathroom, but the rest of the crew had to share one big bathroom area and one big shower area. We learned very fast that if we wanted to get up in the morning and take a shower, we should not go in there because it wouldn't do to have the crew waiting for us to get out of the shower room."

Once they arrived "it was like being with your family. Uncle Jack was there—John Ford—that we've known all our lives. Andy McLaglen and Victor, they were all very familiar faces and so it was very nice."

Patrick Wayne elaborated on that point. "Mr. Ford had his son working on the project, Victor McLaglen had his son Andy working on the project, Arthur Shields and Barry Fitzgerald [were brothers], Maureen O'Hara had two brothers working on the film … everybody seemed to be a family. We ate meals together, we worked together, and then we spent time not working together so you had a sense that you were a part of it—at least I did."

Michael Wayne reckoned, "I was either 16 or 17, my sister

Toni would have been 15 then, Patrick would have been about 10, and Melinda would have been 8 or 9. As I recall, Patrick and I worked every day; my sisters Melinda and Toni got to slip away and go to Paris, which was quite a treat for them. Being the star's son, everybody's very nice to you and I got to learn a lot."

Patrick was especially taken with his father's imposing costar. "Victor McLaglen was a larger-than-life character, a fabulous personality with a world of experience. He'd done everything. He was an older man by the time this film came around; he was a grandfatherly type of a person for me, but I couldn't believe all of the things that he had done and the places he had been. He was a fabulous character to talk to."

Patrick also explained, "My brother and I worked on the film from time to time as supernumeraries, but we also had an opportunity to go with local people and travel around the countryside and visit different places which I can still remember like it happened yesterday." But Patrick had one distinction among his siblings. "I was in a special position that not everyone shared. I was his [Ford's] godson and that put me in a different category from just about everybody else. I never had to experience his wrath or his jokes, but I always was waiting for the other shoe to fall." His brother Mike admitted to being jealous of Pat and his special relationship to the Old Man, whom he wryly described as "a genius between 'action' and 'cut.'"

My then-assistant Ben Herndon took the initiative to contact the local newspaper in Cong, which covered the making of *The Quiet Man* as one would a coronation. This was long before the Internet made worldwide communication a snap. Ben got through to a longtime staff member of the paper who reached into a file drawer, found the original negatives of photos they had taken, and made new prints for us with permission to use them in our documentary.

It was exciting pulling all these ingredients together, although I hit one unexpected dead end. Naturally, I wanted to interview

The Quiet Man's feisty leading lady, Maureen O'Hara. I was told the best way to reach her was through her brother, Charles Fitzsimons, a Hollywood-based producer. We had a pleasant-enough telephone chat but when I mentioned that I was making my documentary for Republic Pictures, he became livid. "Those bastards!" he fumed, recalling (correctly) that studio chief Herbert J. Yates got Duke Wayne and Maureen to work for less money than usual on *Rio Grande* in order to help John Ford make his labor of love, *The Quiet Man*. Fitzsimons was so incensed—half a century later—he refused to have anything to do with the project and even intimidated a veteran Irish-American character actor to back out of giving us an interview.

Fortunately, we encountered no such roadblocks with the Wayne family. Moviemaking was in Michael's blood. He was on many of his father's sets and locations. "I'd hang out mostly with the prop men because they had the guns. I was interested—and still am—in pistols, Colts, Winchesters, and in the history ... and of course, the cowboys, the wranglers, the stuntmen."

He accompanied his father to Camargo, Mexico, to shoot *Hondo* in 1953. "I was a gofer but in those days we called it company clerk. My job was to pay the extras; we paid them on a daily basis and we paid them in cash, and paid the horses, so my day was spent following the extras and the horses. It was physically a tough location because of the heat and the terrain, and of course, the heavy 3-D equipment."

By the time his dad made *McLintock!* a decade later, Michael had earned his stripes and was credited as producer. I asked him what it felt like to be the boss. His answer was disarmingly candid. "Well," he said with a smile, "I was the producer; that doesn't necessarily mean the boss. Once the cameras start rolling the producer's kind of a forgotten man. I remember one day walking on the set and they were filming something that wasn't in the script. The script [was] long and I said, 'What's this?' And they said, 'Well,

Above: That's me, age 13, typing away in my bedroom/office. (Photo by Neil Costa) Right: This was my first celebrity photo, taken at a reception for Ginger Rogers at the Huntington Hartford Museum in Manhattan in 1967. Below: My television debut is noted in a local New Jersey newspaper in April of 1967.

YOUTH ON SHOW

Teaneck — Leonard Maltin, the 16 year old son of Mr. and Mrs. Aaron Maltin of 75 Grayson Place was to appear on the Joe Franklin television show (today) at 12:30 P. M. on Channel 9. Maltin, a junior at Teaneck High School, will discuss his publication, "Film Fan Monthly"

Above: Burgess Meredith was very generous to me as a neophyte interviewer in 1968 at his home in Pound Ridge, New York. He was equally gracious when I talked to him again in 1994—in front of the same Alexander Calder mobile, now uprooted to Malibu, California.

Above: Alice still teases me about my jacket; this was long before we met. It was a coup to get booked on *The Mike Douglas Show,* with that week's co-host Ben Vereen, in 1978. Right: Alice asked my friend Al Kilgore to draw me for a surprise 30th birthday party she was throwing, and he came up with this wonderful, ingenious piece, which holds a special place in my heart. Below: *TV Movies* makes its debut in 1969—offering 8,000 movie reviews in miniature.

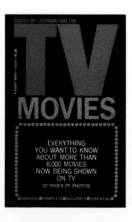

Above: A red-letter day: getting to meet Charles M. Schulz at his studio in Santa Rosa, California, in 1984, more than 20 years after he answered my first fan letter. Below: Standing over Chuck Jones at his drawing board was always a special occasion. When he finished the piece I asked him to sign it to my newborn daughter, so it's easy to date this snapshot: 1986.

Above: It actually looks like I'm directing James Stewart in this candid shot taken on the *Entertainment Tonight* set while we were shooting a tribute to Frank Capra. We were just discussing my script. Below: I first met Gene Siskel and Roger Ebert at the NATPE syndicated TV convention in the early to mid 1980s. The pose seemed a natural choice.

Left: I wish we'd had a professional photographer to commemorate the day in 1988 when I spoke to Katharine Hepburn at her East Side townhouse in Manhattan, but this will do. Below: A command performance: I interview Bette Davis at her request on the *ET* set in December 1988.

Above: Sean Connery was a thorough professional when he was promoting his latest movie, in this case *Family Business* (1989). Below: I spoke to George Lucas at his Skywalker Ranch home base so many times I almost (I stress *almost*) became blasé.

Above: Here is a 1923 Patsy Ruth Miller with Lon Chaney in *The Hunchback of Notre Dame*. (GKB Collection) Sixty-five years later I strolled with her on a remaining set on the Universal Studios back lot for an *ET* interview. What a wonderful experience—and the feedback from viewers was terrific.

Above: This is an all-time favorite photo, taken in 1989 after I interviewed Elizabeth Taylor at the Beverly Hills Hotel. Below: When I asked an intern to snap a picture of me following my interview with Carrie Fisher on the junket for *Postcards from the Edge* (1990), she surprised me by striking this pose.

Three dreamlike experiences in the 1980s: as a guest on the game show *The $25,000 Pyramid*; sitting in the actual Time Machine as Rod Taylor did in the 1960 movie; and being name-checked on *Wheel of Fortune* by Vanna White.

Above: This shot was taken in the Blossom Room at the Hollywood Roosevelt Hotel at the 1990 Cinecon, where we surprised Jackie Cooper by having his award presented to him by his onetime boss, Hal Roach. Below: *ET* reluctantly agreed to let me interview Robert Mitchum in 1991—and he was great.

Above: This courtyard was part of Malpaso Productions headquarters on the Warner Bros. studio lot in Burbank, the longtime home of Clint Eastwood. This shot was taken in 1992 when he was promoting *Unforgiven*. Below: You can't tell from this photo how excited I am to be talking to my childhood heroes Roy Rogers and Dale Evans at their museum in Victorville, California. It was Roy's 82nd birthday in November 1993.

Above: Sheer chutzpah: I play piano with jazz great Benny Carter at his home in 1994.
Below: Another golden opportunity: interviewing Tony Curtis, Jack Lemmon, and Billy Wilder after a 1994 AFI screening of *Some Like It Hot*.

Above: Martin Scorsese signs my copy of his book *A Personal Journey with Martin Scorsese Through American Movies* during the press junket for *Kundun* in 1997. Moments like this made working for *ET* a pleasure. Left: One of the perks of appearing on a hit TV show: a fan crafted this clay sculpture of me. Below: Chatting with Paul Sorvino and William Shatner during a break in a "live" radio recreation of Orson Welles' *War of the Worlds* concocted by KLOS morning-show hosts Mark and Brian in 1997.

Right: Shirley Temple was happy to show off her "grown-up" Oscar when I visited her Northern California home for the second time in 1998. Below: One of our memorable Boxing Day parties in 2006, with Harlan Ellison and Fred Willard. It's hard to acknowledge that they're both gone.

Above: Here is the African Queen as it appeared in the classic 1951 movie (Greenbriar Collection), and here are Alice and I on the meticulously restored vessel, which now resides in Key Largo, Florida. We were there for a Humphrey Bogart Film Festival in 2014. Below: One of my all-time favorite snapshots, taken in Liverpool in 2008. Alice, Jessie, and I took a Magical Mystery Tour of Beatles landmarks and had a ball.

we thought it would be a good idea....' Chill Wills was singing a song at the time and I said, 'I just don't think it's going to be in the picture because we're long and we don't have the rights for the song.' So my father said to Andy McLaglen, 'Well, Andy, let's go home and let Michael finish the picture.' So I realized my position right then and there. I begged them to stay, and we finished Chill's song."

Michael inherited the rights to a handful of films his father co-owned: *Hondo, Island in the Sky, The High and the Mighty*, and *McClintock!* They all enjoyed television exposure at one time and then slipped into limbo, along with other commercial titles that didn't star Wayne (William Wellman's *Track of the Cat*, Budd Boetticher's *Seven Men from Now*, etc.).

Fans and film buffs clamored to see these elusive films. Michael was flooded with offers to license them but repeatedly fended them off. Some people speculated that he was waiting for just the right deal. I think he couldn't bring himself to seal any deal because it would be his last big score. What's more, he was under the impression that the library's value went up every year. That had been true for a while, but times were changing. Wayne's loyal audience was growing older and the star's marketability, while still potent, wasn't what it used to be. (After Michael's untimely death in 2003 his wife, Gretchen, licensed the rights to her father-in-law's movies to Paramount Home Entertainment. I was lucky enough to be hired to host on-camera introductions and conduct interviews for these DVD releases.)

Mike Wayne was notoriously difficult to pin down. When Bill Wellman, Jr., wanted his permission to use footage from *Island in the Sky* and *The High and the Mighty* in a documentary he was making about his father, director William Wellman, he adopted a canny routine. He went to Michael's Batjac Productions business address on Wilshire Boulevard in Beverly Hills and sat patiently in the outer office. In good time Michael showed up and agreed to help Bill because he regarded him as family. Perhaps if other suitors had taken the same approach, they would have gotten further than they did.

Michael was a good guy and fun to talk to. He had deep ties to other show business families, especially Catholic clans. The late Jack Haley, Jr., told me that he and several other second-generationers appointed Michael their representative to negotiate whatever deal he thought fair when the Disney-MGM Studios in Orlando, Florida, wanted permission to use their parents' likenesses at an attraction celebrating the history of Hollywood. Michael returned from his scouting expedition and told them that he'd made the deal for one dollar—and lifetime VIP passes to Disneyland. No one objected.

One night, Alice and I had a dinner party for a number of friends, people we thought would enjoy meeting one another. We sat our gregarious actor friend Jimmy Karen and his wife, Alba Francesca, with Gretchen and Mike Wayne but hadn't had a chance to formally introduce them. Jim was anything but shy and asked Mike about himself. Mike, not one to boast, said he worked with his father, also an actor. "Oh?" said Jimmy, unwittingly taking the bait, "Would I know his work? What was his name?"

"John Wayne," said Mike, obviously accustomed to the reaction he received. It was the only time we ever saw Jimmy Karen at a loss for words.

That night Mike brought along an unusual house gift: a shillelagh he had obtained the summer he and his family spent making *The Quiet Man*. It came from the village of Cong. Alice and I were overwhelmed and Mike said, "I'll get you a letter of authenticity." I told him that wasn't necessary and the subject never came up again. Now I realize that people have to take me at my word when I explain the provenance of this lovely carved wooden piece. Well, that's their worry; I know it's real.

Those Thrilling Days of Yesteryear

As a child of the first television generation, I never understood my parents when they told me that they listened to radio before TV came along. What did they do exactly—look at the console? How could anything possibly take the place of TV?

Even later when friends of mine became fans of Old Time Radio, I remained immune. It never captured my imagination.

I can't believe I am writing those words as in the years that followed, I would become a radio fanatic. I still don't know how I could have missed the boat so completely.

I have my late friend Alan Barbour to thank for getting me started. When he learned that Alice's favorite actor was Ronald Colman, he dubbed several cassettes of *The Jack Benny Show* that featured Colman and his wife, Benita Hume, who supposedly lived next door to Jack. We listened to these episodes while driving and found them hilarious. The more we heard, the more our appetite expanded. From Jack Benny we moved on to *The Halls of Ivy*, a more cerebral but very enjoyable show featuring Mr. and Mrs. Colman. Then it was *Lux Radio Theater*, *Suspense*, *Dragnet*, *Escape*, *Gunsmoke*, *Yours Truly Johnny Dollar*, and so on. (Our daughter became a fan of *The Jack Benny Show* when she was quite young and connected with the silliness of Dennis Day. She still enjoys it today and thinks one reason is that it didn't rely on topical jokes like some other comedy programs.)

When we moved to L.A. we discovered a Sunday night program on public radio station KPCC hosted by two brothers, both blind, named John and Larry Gassman. Their show was followed by another featuring Bobb Lynes and Barbara Watkins. These good people, whom we got to know, not only played vintage shows but interviewed veterans of radio's golden age. It was thanks to them that we discovered a group of dedicated enthusiasts called SPERDVAC: The Society for the Preservation and Encouragement of Radio Drama Variety and Comedy. We attended our first meeting and watched in wonderment as a handful of veteran actors re-created classic shows, complete with music and live sound effects.

That's when we got hooked, and when I get that interested in anything I have the urge to write about it. I started approaching some of the radio veterans to ask if I could interview them, and no one turned me down. It turns out that people who worked in "live" radio loved that medium and were happy to share their memories. Why not? There was plenty of work, real camaraderie, and a chance for character actors to play stalwart leading men and beautiful leading ladies. Looks didn't matter: it all depended on your voice.

I sold an article to *Smithsonian* magazine and used it as a sampler to interest my editor at Penguin in doing a book. He wasn't crazy about the idea but he knew how much it meant to me and ultimately agreed. I will always be grateful for that turn of events.

Every book I had written up to that time was produced on a deadline. *The Great American Broadcast* was an exception. I wrote several chapters but then had to put the project on hold to complete a higher-priority job for Penguin, editing a movie encyclopedia that turned out to be something of a nightmare. It took eleven years for the radio book to come to fruition, but as a result I had the opportunity to reexamine my writing and improve it. I continued doing interviews and happily folded them into the manuscript.

As soon as I embarked on this book, fate smiled on me. My friend John Wirth set up my first official interview, with radio's Renaissance man, Elliott Lewis. Elliott, at the time, was a story supervisor on the *Remington Steele* TV series where, as John explained, he'd been hired to help give the series some old-time style and panache. We all had a wonderful lunch at the Warner Bros. dining room, then I returned with tape recorder in hand to Elliott's office, where he gave me a lengthy and incisive interview about working in radio on both sides of the mike. It may be the best interview I've ever had.

The esteemed actress Jeanette Nolan, whom I met through her friend Tracy Campbell, wanted more than anything to have her husband and partner, John McIntire, talk to me about his early radio career, but John, in failing health, was reluctant to wax nostalgic. (It seems he associated reminiscing with drinking, and he'd given up the latter.) Then, one day, when they were visiting my neck of the woods, Jeanette told me to drop by their motel; she thought John was in the mood to talk. It was true, thank goodness. His memories of early days at KMPC Los Angeles, dating back to the 1920s, were priceless, and his observations along with Jeanette's gave me a real understanding of the territory I was trying so hard to learn about.

William Conrad turned down all requests to attend SPERDVAC gatherings, even those proffered via old friends and colleagues. But my dear friend Jimmy Karen offered to act as go-between to see about an interview. Conrad replied that he'd see me if I could get him a video copy of the 1939 movie *Of Mice and Men*, which he'd been searching for in vain. I had it within a day and had my interview several days later; we spent two glorious hours together, and he sent me a bottle of Dom Perignon to thank me.

Not every interviewee was aware that they were helping me with my book. I seized any opportunity to talk to people whose careers went back to the radio era, even if it was just a casual chat. In the 1980s and '90s *ET* used to send me to the NATPE convention, a trade show for syndicated television producers and distributors. When I spotted Ralph Edwards working the convention floor, I made a beeline for him and engaged him in conversation for a few precious minutes. I asked him about his famously folksy style of delivering commercials (which I'd heard so often on *Vic and Sade*) and got him to reveal the long-held secret of how *Truth or Consequences* always opened with the audience laughing hysterically. The gimmick was having two volunteers from the audience—one male, one female—agree to put on all the clothing in a suitcase, with a time limit. At the moment the man had to don some frilly piece of woman's undergarments, the show went on the air. It was a sure-fire laugh-getter.

Then I saw producer Norman Lear, who seemed approachable (and still is today). I peppered him with questions about writing for Dean Martin and Jerry Lewis' radio show. It was the only medium the red-hot comedy team didn't conquer. Despite this arcane question coming out of the blue, Norman needed no prodding to tackle the subject. He remembered that Dean cared so little about the job that he invariably had cigarettes from another manufacturer in the pocket of his jacket instead of their sponsor's. If you gather enough anecdotes like that you can build a story, and that's what I tried to do.

I also spoke to Ralph Edwards' onetime roommate, veteran announcer André Baruch. The third occupant of their Manhattan apartment was Mel Allen, later to become famous as the voice of the New York Yankees. I got ahold of Allen's home phone number in Connecticut and dropped André's name. Before he knew what was happening, he was spinning stories of their early days working for CBS at 485 Madison Avenue. Ten minutes into our phone call he realized that he had somewhere he had to be and hadn't meant to go on as he had. But I had all I needed to flesh out my word portrait of young announcers who often spelled each other. (Allen succeeded Ralph Edwards as the friendly announcer promoting Crisco on *Vic and Sade*.) I didn't mean to ambush him—I just started asking questions and he responded. I doubt that he even caught my name.

When I had more relaxed interviews I took the opportunity to ask if my subjects had any photos or memorabilia I could borrow. Some of them were uncommonly generous. Fred Foy, the unforgettable announcer on *The Lone Ranger*, sent me a script page with his original markings, indicating where to pause and which words warranted particular emphasis. For a time he and his colleagues at station WXYZ in Detroit had to perform three live shows back-to-back for America's major time zones, with only thirty seconds to breathe in between. (Eventually this was reduced to two live shows, but still...)

Character actor Harry Bartell was a photo hobbyist and offered to send me some samples, including shots inside the studio while Jack Webb was rehearsing a *Dragnet* show. Former child actor Conrad Binyon sent along snapshots of Agnes Moorehead and Lionel Barrymore that he had saved. Best of all, MGM director George Sidney made up new prints from his original negatives of major movie stars rehearsing for the movie studio's weekly radio variety show *Good News*. As the son of Metro executive Louis K. Sidney he had the run of the studio, and as a pack rat he knew how to put his hands on the negs.

Once again, my timing was good. If one made a list of the most significant writers and directors from the golden age of radio, three names would stand out: Arch Oboler, a true innovator and the creator of *Lights Out*; Carleton E. Morse, the incredibly prolific creator and author of the long-running daytime serial *One Man's Family*; and Norman Corwin, often referred to as the poet laureate of the airwaves whose seminal broadcast *On a Note of Triumph* marked the end of World War II. I met all of them and was lucky enough to form a friendship with Norman. Alice and I even co-hosted his 100th birthday party with actress Janet Waldo.

Janet was married to Robert E. Lee, who is best remembered for writing the play *Inherit the Wind* with his longtime partner Jerome Lawrence. It was Lawrence who put me wise to the fact that virtually all the playwrights of his generation did at least some work for radio—even Arthur Miller, who wrote about it in his memoir *Timebends*.

Lawrence and Lee found success on Broadway, but Oboler, Morse, and Corwin functioned at the peak of their powers in the medium of radio. Oboler made a handful of films, most of them endearingly odd. (His cerebral end-of-the-world drama *Five* was shot in and around his Frank Lloyd Wright house overlooking the Pacific Ocean.) He also earned a footnote in movie history by launching Hollywood's 3-D craze with his awful movie *Bwana Devil*.

Corwin earned an Oscar nomination for his adaptation of Irving Stone's *Lust for Life*, but his screen career was sporadic at best. He told me he "blew" his golden opportunity to adapt Robert Penn Warren's *All the King's Men*, turning in a screenplay that was never used. What's more, film is a collaborative medium that never afforded him the autonomy he enjoyed in radio.

As for actors, I asked everyone I met who they thought was the most talented performer they ever worked with, and everyone on the West Coast said Elliott Lewis. Again, I was fortunate to spend time with him. He had no ego about his ability as an actor, because he was more fully engaged as a writer, director, and producer. At one time he had three successive shows on CBS every Sunday night!

Getting to know Peggy Webber was another treat. Peggy, who came to Los Angeles as a teenager and soon earned her stripes as a young character actress, has never forsaken the medium that built her reputation. She still produces audio plays for CART, the

California Artists Radio Theatre, and when there is no one else to handle a small role, plays it herself, using a dialect if required. She was 21 years old when she started playing Sergeant Joe Friday's aged mother on *Dragnet*, and says that Jack Webb had a tough time stifling his laughter when they worked together.

A day I wished I could rewind and redo occurred when a fellow reporter at *Entertainment Tonight*, Scott Osborne, was assigned to interview Orson Welles, who was then holding court at a restaurant called Ma Maison in Beverly Hills. I asked Scott if he would mind asking the Great Man a few radio-related questions for me and he kindly did. I got my quotes—including a great one about how radio encouraged variety because it was run by a great variety of sponsors, instead of three network chairmen. But I missed the opportunity to meet Welles myself. How lazy can you be? I talked to a number of people who worked with him, including his one-time business partner John Houseman, but I blew my chance of having a personal encounter with the one and only Orson Welles.

The last chapter I wrote for *The Great American Broadcast* was about music, and here my luck ran better. I talked to bandleader Les Brown, musician-turned-arranger Billy May, singing star Tony Martin, conductor-arrangers Frank DeVol and Paul Weston, choral director Ray Charles, and directors who worked closely with them.

Two of my favorite anecdotes came not from firsthand interviews but from seminars at SPERDVAC meetings and conventions. I wound up talking to Hal Kanter later on, but I loved his story of preparing for a Bing Crosby show with guest star Fred Allen, whose sardonic sense of humor was famous. The show's producer, Bill Morrow, told Bing and Fred that their studio audience was waiting outside and it was beginning to rain. He wondered if they should let them in early. "Oh Bill," said Allen, "Let 'em in. They're bad enough when they're dry."

The other story came from an especially informative session

featuring veteran director Jack Johnstone, whose career spanned the entirety of network radio. He remembered an incident involving his friend and mentor Carlo D'Angelo and Al Jolson. "They finished a skit and Carlo punched the talk-back and said, 'Al, I think if you accent the word groom in that last gag, it might get a bigger laugh.'"

Jolson, whose ego was as big as all outdoors, said, "Who the hell do you think you are, you little dago son of a bitch, telling Jolson how to read his lines? Look Buster, I've been in show business too many years; I know all about it. And I've got seven million bucks to prove it. What have you got?"

"Friends, Al," Carlo replied.

I still listen to old-time radio on a regular basis and never tire of it. I may be living in the past when I cue up a *Kraft Music Hall* with Al Jolson and Oscar Levant, but I don't care. It brings me joy.

My Friend Freda

When Alice and I settled in Los Angeles we asked friends where they recommended that we observe the Jewish High Holy Days. Taking their advice, we went to the Temple for the Performing Arts, which in 1984 used the auditorium of the Academy of Motion Picture Arts and Sciences. When we saw some familiar faces in the crowd and listened to the sonorous voice of Theodore Bikel praying right behind us, we knew we'd chosen well. It turns out the congregation was about to hire a new rabbi and lose what was known as "Temple Beth Oscar" as its home. All these years later, Rabbi David Baron still presides over services for Temple Shalom for the Arts at our permanent home, the historic Wilshire (now Saban) Theatre in Beverly Hills.

Rabbi David usually asks me to do a reading. Following Rosh Hashanah services in 1995, a little old lady—there is no other way to describe her—came over to compliment me, but in my haziness I didn't pay attention to her name. Alice jabbed me in the side and said, "She said she was Freda Sandrich. Go over to her." Which I did. She turned out to be the widow of Mark Sandrich, the man who directed most of the Fred Astaire-Ginger Rogers musicals of the 1930s. She was there with her proud granddaughter Cathy. We all had a pleasant chat and exchanged contact information. I then sent a signed copy of my book *The Great Movie Shorts* to Freda, as it included a photo of her husband on the set of an RKO comedy.

A short time later I received a note, addressed "My Dear Mr. Maltin." It read: "How to start thanking you for your thoughtfulness and warmth is simple. It requires some well-chosen phrases. But the variety of things for which I'm grateful and which have afforded me special pleasure makes it more complex. So if your busy schedule permits it, please give me the pleasure of being seated opposite Mrs. Maltin and you at breakfast, dinner or lunch so I can list the variety of things that warmed my spirits, enclosed in that big envelope.

"The Bobby Clarks and the Chic Sales were close friends and the thought occurred to me that you might enjoy hearing about the more personal side of them, for to me they were dear people, as was Ben Holmes. (Note how sly I am in trying to lure you to be on the other side of the table.)

"When I walked up to you at temple, I amazed myself, for in all my 95 years I do not recall ever having done such a thing. Now, I realize it was 'bashert.' It was meant to be and I was guided. My vibes were correct about you."

Thus began a warm friendship between Freda and my family. Alice, Jessie, and I loved taking this tiny, sharp-witted senior citizen to brunch and listening to her. She wasn't a particularly anecdotal person; she was just lovable and kind. Mark was the love of her life. He was struck down much too young in 1945 at the age of 44. She never remarried.

Freda told us that Mark dated all her girlfriends before he got around to her because she hadn't shown any interest. That changed rather quickly; she called it an "emotional and chemical" reaction. She moved from Trenton, New Jersey, to Los Angeles with her young husband in the late 1920s, and while she enjoyed California life, she never became part of the Hollywood scene. She said that any time she happened to visit a set, her husband was instantly aware of her presence, so rather than distract him, she willingly stayed home. (One day his secretary asked if she could deliver a script he had left behind and she, of course, obliged. Walking onto a giant set for one of the Astaire-Rogers musicals, she knew to be quiet, but after a few moments an assistant approached her and said, "Mr. Sandrich says come up and kiss him and go home.")

She described her husband as erudite, with a keen ear for music. One day he dared to tell musical director Max Steiner that one of his orchestra members was off-pitch. Steiner was affronted—until he realized it was true.

Of the many stars he directed only a few became personal friends. She shared a wonderful snapshot of her and Mark with Bobby Clark and his wife.

"I have always identified myself with Fred Allen's [character] Tallulah Feeney, 'just a housewife,' and definitely not with celebrities," she wrote.

But she married into a remarkable show business family. Her husband's sister was the celebrated photographer Ruth Harriet Louise, who ran MGM's portrait studio in the late 1920s and married a director, Leigh Jason, who like Mark worked at RKO in the 1930s. Mark's cousin was silent film star Carmel Myers, whose brother Zion was a screenwriter.

Freda's son Jay became one of the most successful comedy directors in the history of television. Her other son, Mark Jr., had a long career as an assistant director in episodic television from the 1950s onward. He directed and produced TV shows as well, and wrote the music for a 1964 Broadway musical, *Ben Franklin in Paris*. He was married to Vanessa Brown, a talented actress who was also one of radio's super-smart Quiz Kids. Her daughter is Cathy Sandrich Gelfond, a successful casting director for films and television. (She has been kind enough to visit my class at USC on more than one occasion.)

My favorite Freda story involves her husband and her son. It was Mark, Sr., who gave Lucille Ball one of her first breaks with screen time in two of the Astaire-Rogers musicals, *The Gay Divorcee* and *Follow the Fleet*. Twenty years later, his son Jay was working as an assistant director on *I Love Lucy*. One day, the star was uncharacteristically late coming back from lunch. When she appeared on the set, she walked over to Jay and said, "Your father would be very proud of me today. We just bought RKO." Indeed, the studio where he had reigned supreme and had given her a boost was to become the home of Desilu Productions.

Just months after we met, Freda suffered a terrible blow. Her son Mark, Jr., died in December 1995. Weeks later, she responded to a condolence letter from Alice, Jessie, and me, saying, "Realist that I am, I still am having problems with acceptance of the tragedy that has befallen us. I'm aware of a variety of techniques one can use to deal with grief but putting them into practice is a different story."

But Freda prevailed. We were thrilled to attend her 100th birthday party, where she showed off by touching her toes. She lived, and lived well, to the age of 103. My life was all the richer for knowing her.

Harlan Ellison: One of a Kind

I suppose it's fitting that I met Harlan Ellison under unusual circumstances. I showed up at the Directors Guild building one morning in 1984 for a screening of a film I knew little about—*The Terminator*. When I gave my name to the publicist who was taking attendance, a man standing a few feet away approached and introduced himself. Naturally I knew who Harlan was, and I'd heard stories of his fractious personality. But he was friendly to me and explained why he was there: to confirm what he'd been told about the movie having stolen ideas that he had created for episodes of *The Outer Limits* years earlier. Filmmaker James Cameron had allegedly acknowledged this in an interview with *Starlog* magazine, which had excised those comments under pressure from Cameron just before it went to press.

Harlan and I were among the handful of people at this morning showing, and I was sitting close enough that throughout the film I could hear his angry mutterings, mostly along the lines of "Jesus!" and "I can't believe it."

Sure enough, Harlan filed suit. The producers of *The Terminator* had to optically insert a credit for him which has appeared in all of that hit movie's sequels and follow-ups. There is no excuse for plagiarism, but if you're going to do it, be smart enough to steer clear of angry authors who are known to be litigious.

The next time we crossed paths was at a video award ceremony in a hotel ballroom. Harlan was there with an agenda. A VHS collection of *The Outer Limits* episodes was slated to win a prize, and he had decided that instead of allowing it to go to the distributor as planned, he would claim it on behalf of the writers—without telling anyone ahead of time. We chanced to be sitting with the nice man from MGM/UA Home Video who was expecting to pick up the trophy. When the man's name was announced, Harlan sped to the stage and made a hurried speech, disrupting the ceremony and leaving the executive slack jawed (and furious).

Harlan was diminutive in size but physically powerful. Our mutual literary agent, Richard Curtis, was eyewitness to an incident in which he pulled a woman across a dining table by the collar! He seemed to have a corner on righteous indignation.

Yet this is the same man who, upon hearing that I was forced to lie on a pillow with my head down after experiencing a detached retina, insisted on coming to my house to read to me. He was especially fond of my wife and daughter and showed infinite patience with Jessie when she was young. When she used the word "like" once too often during dinner chez Ellison, he took her by the hand and led her through the labyrinthine passageways of his house to an office. There he showed her a photocopy of a brief essay on why people shouldn't sprinkle "like" into every sentence. Being shown through the Lewis Carroll-esque byways of the Ellison house made a lifelong impression on her. Later that evening he gently chided Jessie for using the word "awesome." "Sweetie," he said, "the Grand Canyon is awesome; this pizza is good."

He loved telling jokes, especially in a Jewish dialect, and when I heard one that I thought he might like, it gave me inordinate pleasure to pass it along. He won Alice's heart with a spiel he delivered in Erik Nelson's documentary *Dreams with Sharp Teeth*. (It has a life of its own online under the title "Pay the Writer.") In her role as my gatekeeper, Alice pumped her fist in support of Harlan, who was a hard-liner where this was concerned. ("Do you get a paycheck?" he asked the person who was pressuring him do a commentary track for a *Babylon 5* DVD. "Does your boss get a paycheck? Do you pay the teamsters when they schlep your stuff on the trucks?")

Harlan was a man of many parts. Like other individuals with a gruff or bluff personality he was acutely sensitive. I once inadvertently hurt his feelings, and he wrote about it one of his books, granting me the courtesy of warning me about it in advance. The occasion was a surprise party Alice threw for my 50th birthday. Harlan was one of the first ones to greet me as I walked in the front door. A little later I introduced him to another guest and said, "This may be the longest time Harlan's ever been so nice." He said it gave him a frisson (his word) of insult. I'm grateful it didn't cut any deeper.

He was also utterly unpredictable. One night while driving his wife Susan, Alice, and me to dinner in his Geo he impulsively ran it onto the sidewalk and drove an entire block that way, without incident. He had appeared in a TV commercial for the car labeled as a futurist and received one of the vehicles as payment, in part. (We saw our futures quickly evaporating until he returned to the roadway.) He told us that he had once worked as a test driver for an automobile company, to put our fears at rest. He also casually mentioned that he had appeared on Broadway in the chorus of the 1950s musical *Kismet*. Just how many lives had he lived, I began to wonder.

He wrote a fair amount for television and (to a lesser degree) movies. He asked me to write a foreword for a published version of one such screenplay, *None of the Above*, an adaptation of a novel by Norman Spinrad called *Bug Jack Barron*. In his seminal book *Adventures in the Screen Trade*, William Goldman admits that descriptive prose in a script is something of an indulgence, intended more for the gatekeepers who first read it than the people who will actually bring the piece to life. It certainly makes for better reading than a dry list of stage directions.

Ellison, as you might expect, went far beyond the norm. Here's one example: on page 113 of *None of the Above* he introduces a new setting. "A CIRCULAR ROOM empty of anything but white wall that curves fully around a white ceiling and a white floor. If one were to expand an empty hatbox to room size, cast it in flaw-resistant polymer resin, spray it eggshell-white, one would see this room." The description goes on for a generous paragraph.

Here's another: on page 83, the author describes a Greenwich Village street of the future, circa 2005. The detail is six paragraphs long, including this: "Billboards of Venetian slatting with neon writing change in rotations of three, each one advertising a product we've never heard of: STRIP, FLIP & BIP! (A detergent used with wash-once throwaway clothing you strip off, flip into the washer and douse with Bip.) PLEASE YOUR PALATE WITH NEW PLANKTA-FRY! (A plankton-based food substitute pressed to look like steak, fish, chicken. It sizzles!) CHOP AWAY IN A MANCHU GOSHAWK! (The new 200 model Manchu copter, equipped with all-new Data-Logic Auto-Pilot Control, McPherson Sensors and Nose-Cone Jumpseating!)"

I don't know how any filmmaker could illustrate these intricately described billboard ads in what is supposed to be a simple establishing shot, but that's not the point: once Ellison hatched these ideas he couldn't resist sharing them with the reader. That's one reason the finished work is so much longer than a typical screenplay. There's an old Hollywood joke: a script can be any length at all so long as it's 120 pages. Ellison's ran 225.

Obviously, Harlan didn't follow the precepts of Screenwriting 101. He took his cue from an old friend, Robert Bloch (the author of *Psycho*), who told him, "Just close your eyes, run the movie, and write down what you see." To TV and film producers whose eyebrows went up at the heft of his scripts, Ellison would say, "No, it's not too long. Time it out and you'll find that it runs exactly right. All the additional stuff is just to help the director."

His screenplay for *None of the Above* is extremely specific in its indications of camera moves and visual effects. I asked him if he did this in all of his film and television writing (he did) and wondered what directors thought of it. "In the main, they resented it," he admitted. "They either ignored the specificity or they went out of their way to change it, because God forbid I should get in the way of the auteur theory."

Yet *None of the Above*, a pungent satire of American politics, was written by a man who shied away from joining any party—or group, for that matter. "I've always had this deep social conscience, but it's like being the loose cannon on the ship," he said. "Libertarians don't want me, Republicans wouldn't have me, Democrats find me very unhappy as an ally. I'm the last guy on the team, I'm the kid that your mother told you not to play with. And the same in politics. I expect a level of intelligence on the part of the average voter which simply and clearly is not there. There's a great sadness about the screenplay because of that."

Harlan had another avocation: movie critic. He contributed essays to the Writers Guild of America newsletter and other publications for many years. Not bound by the conventions of the trade, he expressed his feelings in ways most critics wouldn't—or couldn't. Only he could get away with saying that "Ali MacGraw can't act for shit" in a review of *The Getaway*.

But he brought something else to his pieces, aside from his dizzying command of the language: firsthand experience in the film and television business. I don't think this is a requirement, any more than a restaurant critic should have the ability to cook a sumptuous meal, but there's no denying that Ellison's exploits in The Business colored his writing. He had no compunction about dropping names, but then they're names of people he actually knew, worked alongside, insulted, had been insulted by, or dealt with in some manner.

He talked me into removing his credit for writing the notoriously ,awful movie *The Oscar* from my *Movie Guide*—an accommodation I have never granted anyone else and which I have often regretted. But it was Harlan. How could I say no and remain in his good graces?

A mutual friend once said it was a shame that Harlan didn't have a signature novel, like his friend Ray Bradbury's *Fahrenheit 451*, because he preferred writing short stories. I'll admit, it's hard to identify Harlan to strangers who aren't old enough to remember the TV series he worked on decades ago.

I would venture to say that his greatest creation was Harlan Ellison, a gifted wordsmith and world-class provocateur whose persona was definitely larger than life. I miss his phone calls and dialect jokes, and I miss him terribly.

Diving for Disney Treasures

If you had told the younger me that I would not only meet the original Mouseketeers from *The Mickey Mouse Club* but be inducted into their group as an honorary member, I wouldn't have believed you. Nor could I have dreamt of getting to know Davy Crockett, Elfego Baca, the man who wielded Zorro's sword, or the voices of Mickey Mouse, Minnie Mouse, Donald Duck, and Goofy.

All that came to pass because I wanted to see these Disney TV shows and movies released on DVD.

The year was 2000. I met the president of The Walt Disney Company, Dick Cook, at several studio screenings and press events. He seemed genuinely nice and friendly, so I asked if I could pitch him an idea. He liked having breakfast meetings so we arranged a get-together near the studio (and my home) in Toluca Lake. Dick was already seated when I arrived right on time. I had brought a one-page "sell sheet" but, as it turns out, I didn't need it.

I suggested that instead of selling a "Best of Donald Duck" cassette or disc with randomly chosen cartoons, as the company had been doing, he might release the contents of the Disney library in an orderly fashion on DVD, which was just then supplanting VHS as the home-video format. This would appeal to Disney buffs and collectors without affecting their core audience of families with kids. I saw it as a win-win situation. What's more, the DVD format would enable us to add behind-the-scenes features and interviews, which would make the releases all the more appealing.

Dick replied, "Let's do it."

That may have been the shortest meeting in Hollywood history—or at least the easiest pitch. Either way, it was followed by some months of processing and negotiating with the company's business affairs people, but it was still a solid green light.

I was introduced to the folks in Home Video (later called Home Entertainment) who would shepherd my ideas to fruition and assigned an independent producer, Jeff Kurtti, who would be Disney's "vendor." (What a cold word—appropriate to the way they treated their content providers.) And so we set to work.

Nine years and 37 DVD sets later, *Walt Disney Treasures* came to an end, coinciding with the firing of Dick Cook. It was an ignominious finale for a man who had started as a jungle cruise operator at Disneyland and risen through the ranks. I wasn't privy to the backroom politics that led to this unhappy turn of events.

At least our series went out with a bang. The folks in Home Video had no enthusiasm whatsoever for issuing *Zorro* on disc; they said that other TV series hadn't been strong sellers.

"This isn't just any TV series," I protested. "This is Walt Disney's *Zorro*!" My plea fell on deaf ears. By this time I'd learned that Dick Cook was not a micromanager and didn't like to interfere with day-to-day business in his departments. I also knew that he was a *Zorro* fan, so I picked up the phone and told him my dilemma. "Oh, I think we can do something about that," he replied.

My home video contact called me in a lather. He and his colleagues knew about my relationship with their boss, so I never felt like I was sneaking behind their backs. "What did you say to Dick Cook? He wants us to restore all 78 episodes of *Zorro*!" I told the truth, and that's how the entire series came to be released in handsome tin cases, just like the rest of the *Treasures*.

Of all the projects I've worked on, the *Walt Disney Treasures* has cut the widest swath. People love those DVDs and over a decade since their demise, continue to ask me if they will ever be released on Blu-ray. The apparent answer is "no," because there is no one to champion them within the Disney company.

Disney never did much in the way of advertising or promotion for the series, but it found its intended audience all the same. The marketing people decided to issue a limited number of each volume with a facsimile of Roy E. Disney's signature on a band ringing the tin case with two discs inside. The first series of four were released in editions of 150,000. The numbers shrank with each passing year.

One of the concepts I'd sold to Dick Cook was that we wouldn't censor or cut any content. Instead, I would provide historical context for sensitive or offensive material, which would appear in a separate section of the DVD. I am unaware of any negative flak that resulted (as opposed to fan response when the studio used a substandard video master—boy, those fans are quick to pounce).

In fact, the biggest seller in nine years was *On the Front Lines*, which highlighted Walt Disney's contribution to World War II through training films, morale-boosting shorts, topical cartoons, and an entire feature film, *Victory Through Air Power*. All of this had landed on the "verboten" list of library titles that were pulled from circulation, which is why there was such keen interest in our collection. Dave Bossert, who worked on special projects in the animation department, had tried to interest the company in doing this kind of release before but never got a commitment. Even so, he devoted a great deal of effort to gathering material from the National Archives in Washington, D.C., and various branches of the military that wasn't already on hand in the studio vault.

Eric Young of Sparkhill Entertainment, who took over from Jeff Kurtti in Year Three, shared Jeff's enthusiasm for all things Disney. He was always willing to go the extra mile to create the best product we could deliver.

Walt Disney Treasures was launched on December 1, 2001, with four two-disc sets: *Mickey Mouse in Living Color, Volume 1*, *Davy Crockett*, *Disneyland USA*, and *Silly Symphonies*. I called on the wonderful Richard Sherman (not for the last time) to provide perspective on the songs introduced in *Silly Symphonies* and he came through as always. Studio archivist Dave Smith gave us a show-and-tell exhibition of *Silly Symphony* collectibles. Disney superfan Paul F. Anderson was the perfect person to interview about "The Davy Crockett Craze" having written a book of the same name.

But the highlight of this venture was the day my family and I spent with Fess Parker at his vineyard and offices in Los Olivos, California. One of my earliest memories is wearing a coonskin cap and singing a stanza of "The Ballad of Davy Crockett" in nursery school at age four. Imagine my delight at getting to spend quality time with the actor who brought that character to life. He was graciousness personified.

He had great recall of his ascent to stardom, from doing bit parts in TV shows and movies to his hiring for the role of Davy. He spoke warmly of colleagues like Crockett costars Bill Bakewell (Major Norton), who introduced him to the charitable Motion Picture and Television Fund, and veteran Basil Ruysdael (Andrew Jackson), who gave him common-sense advice about acting.

While Parker had his share of differences with Walt Disney—early on over a cut of the merchandising rights and later when he was told that Walt stood in the way of his making movies for other studios (including *Bus Stop* and *The Searchers*, according to the actor)—he was sensible enough to realize that there was no point in grinding an axe after so many years. Ultimately, he was grateful for the opportunity Disney gave him. And he was much too polite a man to speak ill of his longtime boss.

After our interview, he invited Alice and me to stay for lunch, which was served on the veranda of his winery. Then he gave us a personal tour of the property, explaining how as a total novice he became involved in the wine business and how his son Eli studied to become a vintner. His wife, Marcy, lined the fence surrounding their property with rosebushes. Running this as a family operation gave him great pride, and while he wasn't one to live in the past, he recognized that everything stemmed from the worldwide fame he achieved as Davy Crockett (and then, a decade later, as Daniel Boone). That's why, if you visit the Fess Parker Winery and purchase some of his delicious wines, you can also buy a unique accessory: a miniature coonskin cap to slide over the bottle.

Every entry in the *Treasures* series was fun to work on, beginning with brainstorming about whom we could interview and what extras we could provide our loyal audience. For the second collection of Mickey Mouse cartoons, we brought legendary animators Frank Thomas and Ollie Johnston to Disney's Animation Research Library, which occupies an entire building in Glendale, not far from the studio lot. The ARL's staff couldn't have been more helpful in digging out original animation drawings for these veterans to examine. We had the actual pencil drawings that Ub Iwerks rendered in 1928 for *Plane Crazy* and *Steamboat Willie*!

What's more, Frank was able to handle pieces of animation paper from *Two Gun Mickey*, which he'd worked on almost 70 years earlier. Both men spoke of their fondness for Mickey, who laid the foundation for everything that followed at the studio.

Ollie said, "I loved saying I worked for Mickey Mouse, not Walt Disney but Mickey Mouse, and to me he was an inspiration."

For *On the Front Lines* Roy Disney personalized the experience of being at the studio during World War II. "I guess I was 11 when the war broke out, so I was in my young teens throughout the war," he said. "I have some pretty distinct memories of coming on the lot and its being filled with guys wearing the uniforms … chain-link fences here and there that kept studio employees out of certain areas … walking up and down the halls and seeing a lot of art work related to defense movies of one kind or another.

"They kind of let me wander around because I was just a kid," Roy explained. "So I did see a lot of the models. In fact, I remember they made a series on aircraft identification, and they had some plastic models of both American and Japanese airplanes that they were shooting silhouette film of. And they gave me a model of a P-38, I remember, that I had for many, many years after that. It was a favorite toy, actually, for a while."

And, being the son of Walt's brother, he had indelible memories of his father complaining about his sibling's inability to stick to a budget, even for Uncle Sam.

"I remember very clearly my dad saying, 'I don't care how much they give him, he'll still spend more than they give him,'" he related with a chuckle. "And, you know Walt; he couldn't help himself."

We were also lucky that two key figures from this time period were not only alive and lucid but still working for the studio: John Hench and Joe Grant.

When we presented the first week of *The Mickey Mouse Club* just as it aired in 1955 we called on Loraine Santoli, the unofficial den mother of the group who wrote the definitive book on that unforgettable TV show. She helped us wrangle the Mouseketeers for a memorable Sunday of shooting. And the studio pitched in by finding—and hanging—the original curtain backdrop that was used for the series! I let out a gasp as I walked onto Stage One and saw that curtain—not only in person but in color, as I'd never seen it on my black-and-white TV set. I was the perfect age to fall under the spell of this daily series, which invited us to identify with one or more of the "regular kids" on-camera. Bobby Burgess, Doreen Tracy, Lonnie Burr, Karen Pendleton, Cubby O'Brien, and Sharon Baird were there that day and enjoyed reminiscing with me and walking around the studio lot they once called home. They hadn't had a lot of contact with Walt Disney, but they remembered him as a benevolent presence on the lot.

Later, we caught up with Cheryl Holdridge, Tommy Cole, Sherry Alberoni, and the stars of two serials that aired on the program: *Spin and Marty* (David Stollery and Tim Considine) and *The Hardy Boys* (Considine and Tommy Kirk). I took a snapshot of Alice standing with David and Tim, and I swear she's three feet off the ground.

On these projects I was merely a stand-in for the aging baby boomers in the audience, expressing my love for the show and the talented kids who made it a "must" every day after school. If the Treasures series had offered me nothing else, meeting the Mouseketeers would have been payment in full. And to top it all off, they re-enacted the ceremony I'd seen so many times in which they issued custom-made Mickey ears to welcome an honorary Mouseketeer—in this case, me!

The one Mouseketeer we couldn't interview was the most popular—and the most ethnic (admittedly not much of a stretch)—Annette Funicello, whose battle with multiple sclerosis had made her a recluse. But her dear friends Sherry Alberoni and Shelley Fabares (who appeared in the Annette serial) were happy to be interviewed along with Annette's husband, Glen Holt, and Richard Sherman, who with his brother Robert wrote so many of her signature songs.

Walt Disney played such a vital role in my life that working on these DVD sets was like reliving my childhood. When we wanted to show samples of two miniseries that were part of the hour-long *Walt Disney Presents* and we called character actor Robert Loggia, he not only agreed to reminisce about *The Nine Lives of Elfego Baca* for us, he brought along his original gun belt, which he proudly told us was given to him by Walt himself after the series wrapped.

Longtime Imagineer Tony Baxter, who fashioned his first homemade version of Sleeping Beauty's castle when he was 12 years old, was more than willing to share his encyclopedic knowledge of Disneyland as we added a commentary track to TV episodes showing off the Anaheim attraction, rare footage of the park under construction, and much, much more.

Walt's first "star," Virginia Davis, who played the little girl who lived in a cartoon world in the *Alice* comedies of the 1920s, was delighted to share her memories of working for Walt and Roy in the earliest days of their enterprise in Kansas City.

Our *Tomorrowland* DVD set inspired us to interview Ray Bradbury, the eminent author and futurist who was one of Walt Disney's greatest admirers. Spending time with Ray was a rarefied experience, and his enthusiasm was positively infectious. It was this quality that created a bond of friendship between him and Walt. Here's how he defined it during our conversation:

"Walt, like myself, is not an optimist but an optimal behaviorist. Which means that every day of your life, if you behave well, you begin to feel well. That's not false, that's real. You get your work done every day and at the end of a week, a month, a year, you turn around and say, 'Hey, look what I did.' So you feel good. That's real optimism—optimal behavior. That's, I think, the way he behaved. And he could look back at the end of each year and see his behavior. And it made him want to go on."

Our crew felt the same electrifying energy in the air as Ray spoke. We didn't want the shoot to come to a close.

The most challenging releases to produce were the cartoon collections, because they filled so many discs. After meeting the voices of Donald Duck (Tony Anselmo), Goofy (Bill Farmer), Mickey and Minnie (the inimitable married couple Wayne Allwine and Russi Taylor), we called on modern-day Disney animators like Andreas Deja and Mark Henn to help us assess and appreciate the work of their predecessors. The ebullient Eric Goldberg was game to act out a Donald Duck cartoon called *Trouble Shooters* that had been fully storyboarded but never produced. I came to appreciate how much depends on the salesmanship of a story man to generate interest in a cartoon like this.

For one Mickey volume I was able to persuade my friend Bernie Shine to allow us to invade his home and get a private tour of his world-class collection of Disneyana, with a special emphasis on Mickey Mouse. Another pal, animator and sculptor Ruben Procopio, was willing to let us show him creating a figurine of Donald Duck out of clay, with no guide except his memory of the character's attitude and dimensions. Played in time-lapse fashion this became one of my favorite segments.

One release came about because of popular demand: *Dr. Syn, Alias the Scarecrow*, also known as *The Scarecrow of Romney Marsh*. We negotiated with a fellow who had already shot an interview with its star, Patrick McGoohan, and had a show-and-tell of original props. Fan interest in this program, which originally aired in three parts on *Walt Disney's Wonderful World of Color*, was so great that it was out of stock within weeks of its release and (like many of the other Treasures) was already commanding scalper prices on eBay. I pleaded with the head of marketing to release more copies but he refused. And so it goes.

For our grand finale, Volumes 1 and 2 of *Zorro*, we enlisted Guy Williams, Jr., whose father brought such brio to the dual role of Don Diego and Zorro. We also lucked out when his stuntman, Buddy van Horn, turned out to be such an amiable interviewee with nothing but positive memories of working on the show.

I don't take that for granted: not every set is a happy place and not every studio engenders loyalty. At one time the Mouseketeers filed suit against Disney for residual payments they felt they were owed. But even that couldn't taint the warm feeling they had for each other and their cast mates Jimmie Dodd and Roy Williams.

If I'd had my druthers, I would have continued producing and hosting *Walt Disney Treasures*, but as it stands I am proud of what we accomplished over nine years. We certainly hit the high spots and were fortunate to interview so many talented people who are no longer alive to share their stories.

40 Years of Telluride

Every year, the buzzy year-end-award contenders show up at the Telluride Film Festival in Colorado. It wasn't always that way, but the festival has evolved from a haven for connoisseurs to a "must" for serious film buffs and journalists.

Telluride was a prosperous mining town in the late nineteenth century. There are postcards from 1880 that show how little the main street has changed since then, thanks in part to the government designating it an official historic district. Merging a prototypical Western street with a touch of Switzerland, it dead-ends at the base of an enormous mountain. No one passes through Telluride: you have to want to be there. For film distributor Bill Pence and his wife, Stella, it seemed like a perfect place to hold a festival, especially after they discovered (and renovated) the jewel box of a theater called the Sheridan Opera House, which opened in 1913. The *Field of Dreams* mantra "if you build it, they will come" proved true of this remote location.

For Alice and me the festival has special significance. It was more than 40 years ago, in 1979, that we made the difficult decision to skip Cinecon—a Labor Day weekend event that I'd attended since I was 14 years old—and make our first trip to Colorado, on the recommendation of the ultimate Cinephile, William K. Everson. It was an adventure for us New Yorkers. We'd had a tough year and we needed to get away and do something different. Little did we know how much that trip would reshape our lives. We flew to Denver and spent four days winding through Colorado before arriving at our destination.

It didn't take long for us to fall in love with the place. The scenery is truly breathtaking, and the festival is one of a kind. At first we alternated years, attending Cinecon and even hosting it (along with Randy Haberkamp) in 1990 and 1991. But the call of Telluride was too strong to ignore and we haven't missed a year since 1992. Over that time we've made wonderful friends, from house managers to volunteer drivers who always make us feel welcome. One of the nice guys scooping popcorn at Telluride, Barry Jenkins, went on to win an Oscar as the director of *Moonlight*.

Our daughter Jessie has grown up there. When she was 10 she sold lemonade with Ken Burns' daughter Lily and Louis Malle and Candice Bergen's daughter Chloe outside one of the screening venues—and turned over their earnings to the festival. That was also the year we allowed her to walk from our hotel to see her first festival film (*Dancing at Lughnasa* with Meryl Streep). We never doubted that she would be safe on her own.

Attending the festival is a pricey proposition, but I've sung for my supper over the decades, introducing films and conducting interviews with Streep, Chuck Jones, Bertrand Tavernier, Richard Widmark, Peter O'Toole, Roger Corman, Alfonso Cuarón, and countless other movie notables. I was privileged to preside over a wildly ambitious 3-D program and a unique salute to Cinerama, arranged by our friend Chapin Cutler and his tireless team at Boston Light and Sound.

Telluride's co-founders Bill and Stella Pence, Tom Luddy, and James Card (who bowed out early on, passing his baton to Bill Everson) prided themselves on keeping their selections and guests a secret. Talk about a leap of faith: they wanted to attract people who loved movies—not just certain movies—and trusted them to put on a good show. In fact, SHOW is the visual symbol of the festival, and appears on the exterior of the Sheridan Opera House.

Although the festival has grown along with the town, it retains the casual vibe that set it apart so many years ago. There are no red carpets and no paparazzi. Stars who attend with their latest work are disarmed by the realization that they can walk the streets and even attend screenings without being hassled. Attendees quickly learn that if they don't get a chance to ask a question of an actor or filmmaker at a panel, they might just as easily speak to the person while waiting in line for coffee. As for us, we wind up talking to strangers all weekend long, asking for opinions on what they've seen and meeting wonderful folks who have no connection to the film industry. They just happen to love movies.

Under the stewardship of Julie Huntsinger and Tom Luddy (and for a time my old friend Gary Meyer), Telluride has become a valued destination. The eclectic mix of silent films, discoveries, and cutting-edge world cinema is as intoxicating as the beauty of the Rocky Mountain setting.

When we spoke to Ken Burns during a hectic trip he made to Los Angeles to promote his *Country Music* PBS series, Jessie realized that she'd never discussed movies with him before, only family matters. That's how we know him, his children, and grandchildren: from our annual reunion in the Rockies.

Our first year, 1979, was capped off by an outdoor showing of British film historian Kevin Brownlow's restored print of *Napoleon* with its 89-year-old director, Abel Gance, in attendance. This was a very ambitious enterprise, as three screens had to be built for the Cinerama-like finale of Gance's epic French silent film. The show couldn't start until 9 p.m., when the sky got dark. Hank Troy played accompaniment on electric piano. It got chilly and damp that night, which made it difficult for everyone, including the pianist. *Napoleon* is quite long and it was being run at proper silent speed. When intermission came, people literally ran to the few coffee shops and bars that were still open to fortify themselves. Not everyone returned.

Alice and I did our best. We were sitting near Kevin Brownlow and the unflappable Bill Everson and wanted to show our like-minded devotion to silent cinema, but at a certain point we were just too cold and had to leave. (We took some razzing the next day from Kevin and Bill.)

Because so many people missed out on the excitement, the festival scheduled a special showing the following night of the last half hour of the film. It began on a single screen and then majestically expanded to fill all three screens for its triptych finale. It was an unforgettable experience for everyone—including, I presume, the Maestro, Abel Gance (despite his age, still very much the Frenchman, he groped my wife).

That same year, Alice and I kept running into director Jacques Demy all weekend—sitting next to him in the theater, in line for coffee, etc. He couldn't have been more charming or more accessible. Then on Sunday night, we attended a midnight showing of his musical *The Young Girls of Rochefort*. We noticed that when Gene Kelly opened his mouth to sing, it clearly wasn't his voice on the soundtrack. My wife, who's got a great ear, said, "That's not George Chakiris' voice, either." In thinking it over we hatched a theory that because the film is so stylized and deliberately artificial, perhaps Demy chose to recast the singing voices of all the actors.

The next day we searched for the director in vain. We asked everyone we ran into, "Have you seen Jacques Demy?" That evening (our last in town) we were having dinner when someone popped into the restaurant and said, "He's right outside." I threw down my fork, ran into the street, found him, and rattled off my theory.

He listened politely and replied, "No, no. Gene Kelly couldn't stay in Paris for the dubbing session, and he told me to use anyone's voice … he didn't care." What about Chakiris? "He could not sing. Danielle Darrieux could not sing. Catherine [Deneuve] could not sing!"

He had a practical, mundane answer for all of it. (I still contend that the result adds to the unique quality of the movie, whether it was intended or not. But maybe I'm being stubborn.)

As we quickly learned, Telluride is a very social festival. One year we were standing on Colorado Street for the Opening Night Feed, with storm clouds rolling in and out, when the power went out. Nothing fazes people in Telluride. They kept on schmoozing and eating and ducking out of the rain showers. At some point we started wondering if the SHOW would go on. Finally Bill Pence appeared on the courthouse steps and announced, "I've talked to the utility company and they promise we'll have power up in 20 minutes." They were good to their word, but if they hadn't been, I have a feeling that everyone would have gone on partying.

Adjusting to the altitude (8,600 feet) has always been a challenge, and I have many memories connected with that. One was seeing Luis Trenker, fabled German "mountain film" actor and director, then 80-something, striding around town without missing a beat. On the other hand, after a showing of Les Blank's documentary *In Heaven There Is No Beer*, there was a polka party at the community center. I, like an idiot, tried to dance, which lasted about 15 seconds, after which I felt I needed a respirator. Lesson learned.

In 1983 I was scheduled to interview Richard Widmark onstage at the Opera House as part of a career tribute, but when the actor arrived in Telluride, he told Tom, Bill, and Stella that he couldn't possibly do that. Despite his screen persona, he was extremely shy. He agreed to meet me at his ski condo so we could get acquainted. He turned out to be a highly intelligent man and a great raconteur. I was disappointed that he wouldn't show this side of himself to an audience, but we bowed to his wishes.

As the film clips came to an end the next night, I stood in the wings of the Opera House with him while he stared intently at the speech he had written, trying to memorize it. I looked over his shoulder and it read, "Thank you very much ladies and gentlemen, I can't tell you what an honor it is." He didn't feel he could face a crowd of people and make a simple speech like that without having a "script." Considering the kind of people he's played on-screen, I guess this means he's an even better actor than we ever realized.

One of the most moving moments Alice and I experienced was in 1987 when Louis Malle flew in from Venice with a print of *Au Revoir les Enfants* for its first U.S. showing at the Sheridan Opera House on a Saturday afternoon. When it was over, the audience was so choked up that there was no applause. We all filed out of the theater onto the lawn, including Malle, and for some reason, nobody left. Everyone stood there, digesting the film. Finally, Bill said, "Louis, we just want to thank you for your film." With that, everyone burst into applause. It was a great release for all of us—and especially for Malle, who was greatly relieved, because he was worried about how this highly personal film would be accepted.

I've met all kinds of people—great people—over the years, but I don't know if I'll ever top the morning I had breakfast with two celebrated directors, Lindsay Anderson (*If....*, *O Lucky Man!*) and Don Siegel (*Invasion of the Body Snatchers*, *Dirty Harry*), and Bill Everson. It doesn't get any better than that.

Another moment I cherish occurred the year Bob Gitt of UCLA Film-Television Archive brought the restored print of Budd Boetticher's long-unseen *Seven Men from Now* starring Randolph Scott. I introduced the showings, and as I was headed to its second presentation I hitched a ride. French filmmaker Barbet Schroeder hopped in too, and I asked him what he was going to see.

"*Seven Men from Now*."

"But I saw you at the screening the other night," I said, to which he replied, "I'm going again. I have so much to learn from it." No wonder he is such a respected filmmaker.

If there is one word that sums up this festival, it is certainly eclectic. You never know who will be attending or what discoveries you will make. One often has to choose between a hot new movie—like *Slumdog Millionaire* or *Parasite*—which will give you bragging rights when you return home, or a rare silent film that you may never have another chance to see.

In 2017 I made the right choice and sampled the silent films, which were presented by my friend, archivist Paolo Cherchi Usai. The National Film Archive in Prague recently restored Carl Junghans' *Such is Life* (1929), written and directed by a man whose career never realized its potential in Europe or America. This brilliant portrait of the underclass, made by a Communist, needs few written titles to tell its simple story. In introducing the film Milos Stehlik, the founder of Facets Video, said it predates Italian neorealism, and he's right, if you add the fact that it is punctuated with wild, dizzying Eisenstein-like montages. I still hold out hope that this little-known film receives the wide exposure it deserves, with the score Donald Sosin composed and played so beautifully inside the Sheridan Opera House.

As I left the theater I drifted toward Elks Park, where film teacher and scholar Annette Insdorf was moderating a panel with a daunting lineup of participants: Mike Leigh, Wim Wenders, Werner Herzog, Walter Murch, Alejandro Gonzáles Iñárritu, Volker Schlöndorff, Francis Ford Coppola, and Ethan Hawke. One topic was film vs. digital capture. Leigh confessed that he fought off digital for years but succumbed for his latest feature, *Mr. Turner*, and thought it turned out fine. Then Hawke told a funny story about working on Sidney Lumet's final film, *Before the Devil Knows You're Dead*. He and Philip Seymour Hoffman were disappointed to learn that Lumet was going to shoot it digitally and told him they were hoping for the gritty feel of *Dog Day Afternoon*. Said Lumet, "You guys want it to look cool and vintage, right?" They said yes, and he responded, "Well, wait 20 years and it will look cool and vintage."

Lumet's remark may well prove to be true, and if there is anyplace his movie is likely to be revived and reassessed, it is Telluride.

Leading Ladies:
Bette Davis, Barbara Stanwyck, Olivia de Havilland

One didn't refuse a command performance from Bette Davis—at least I didn't. Even *Entertainment Tonight*, which had only middling interest in vintage stars, reacted swiftly when she called requesting an interview. She was upset that raggy newspapers and other media outlets were accusing her of walking out on a movie in mid production. She wanted a chance to set the record straight.

I will never forget the sight of Miss Davis, dressed to the nines, looking incredibly thin and frail, yet projecting assurance and strength as she walked onto our soundstage. It was no effort making small talk with her as our director set his camera positions. Somehow we got on the subject of wardrobe, and she remembered director Robert Florey trying to bamboozle her into wearing a gauzy slip for a scene in *Ex-Lady* in 1933. She realized it would result in a see-through effect and refused to wear it. Even then she knew how to stand her ground.

In this case, she had agreed to appear in a Larry Cohen movie called *The Wicked Stepmother* but had to depart after five days for emergency oral surgery back east. She claimed that she left with his consent, but the story got muddy after that.

She made no secret of how she felt about the movie. "I knew if audiences saw this with me in it ... they would have really thought I had lost my mind, and it is very possible I might have. It is very possible," she said with a laugh.

"Mr. Cohen never took anybody's suggestions. He worked completely for the camera. Any ideas I had about performance he just wasn't interested in at all, so that whole first week I was playing scenes, I wasn't comfortable and I was bad. I was bad."

"So with his permission I went off to New York for oral dentistry and all the time I was getting all that work done, I was thinking about the week's rushes I saw. It was a question of taste. Much of it was very vulgar, very vulgar, scenes I was not in. I saw everybody's work for the week and there was no resemblance to the script."

She looked at me and added, "You're nice enough to be the first person that I am talking to about it. I felt I must let people know why I am in only about 15 minutes of finished film. It's quite a comedown for Bette Davis, and I think audiences have a right to know."

I said, "What you're talking about really is keeping faith with your audience, isn't it?"

She answered, "It really is. I've never put anything on film that I felt dishonest about. And I've never been vulgar."

"Let's make something else clear," I added. "You are ready, willing, and able to make another film."

"I'm praying on my knees every day to get a good script in 1989. We have one that we hope will work out; it's *The Aspern Papers* by Henry James. There's a marvelous script on that, and a terrific role. And people are looking into this so let's hope it works."

I told her how good she looked after several health crises and she said she was feeling good. Then I asked, "When somebody calls you a survivor, how do you respond to that?"

"Well, I think it's the truth. I think I am a survivor … then, don't forget I'm a Yankee. New Englanders are apt to be survivors."

"Strong stock," I suggested.

"Strong stock. Not tough—strong. I resent being called tough.

I picture tough as a kind of gum-chewing tough person, and that certainly is not I. Willful? Of course. Determined? Of course, but that doesn't have to be tough."

"It's like the difference between being assertive and aggressive," I said.

She agreed, and said, "I have a little saying at home, 'No guts, no glory,' and that I was given by my mother, father, and ancestors."

As the interview wound down, she referred to a quote from Larry Cohen claiming she was 80 years old and difficult. She laughed and said, "I was difficult when I was 20. There's never been any other way."

She kept thanking me for giving her a forum to say her piece. That was *ET*'s doing, not mine, but she added, "You're fun to talk to," and that's a compliment I was delighted to accept. A few days later an enormous, ornate Christmas wreath was delivered to my house. We kept it for several years, as well as the note that accompanied it. Miss Davis didn't live to see another Christmas, but I will never forget my meeting with her.

There was apparently no love lost between Davis and her contemporary Barbara Stanwyck. Stanwyck nursed a grudge for years about losing the leading role in *Dark Victory* to Davis when it was Stanwyck who had urged the hit radio show *Lux Radio Theatre* to adapt the Broadway play, which director Edmund Goulding happened to hear and then encouraged Warner Bros. to purchase the screen rights to—and give the part to Bette Davis.

It was no simple matter to see, let alone interview, Stanwyck. A friend tipped me to the fact that costume designer Nolan Miller was the best go-between to approach. *ET* was doing a tribute to her favorite director, Frank Capra, and Miller agreed that if anything would get her to say yes, that would be it. He explained she was self-conscious about the way she looked because of the cortisone she was taking for her ailing back. I said we'd be happy just to have her voice; he thought she would agree to that, and she did.

First, I had to pass muster with Miss Stanwyck, which I did over the course of several lively telephone calls. We talked a lot about current movies as well as classics; I knew she was testing me to get a sense of my mindset. On the subject of Capra she expressed "eternal gratitude" for his helping to shape her career-boosting performance in *Ladies of Leisure*. "Nobody would have taken that much time" with a relative newcomer, she insisted. "I thought every director worked like that; I had a very rude awakening."

She soon learned that the success or failure of every movie hinged on the quality of the script. "I can't write the words, I'm not that talented," she said, but she had no hesitation in telling a writer, "I can't say that 'cause I don't believe it, and if I don't believe it, I can't make the audience believe it, and that's my job."

"Honesty—that's the foundation of everything," she said, and it's that very quality that makes her performances so vivid.

Of course, it would have been nice to show Stanwyck on camera. Her face was a bit puffy but she still looked great. It was a bit odd to walk into her home with a camera crew, but that's the way we would record her voice. We made small talk for a while, and then we taped her personal tribute to Frank Capra.

Here's what she said: "I was a newcomer to movies when I got the opportunity to work with Frank Capra, and I can honestly say he taught me everything I know about acting in front of a camera. Now, I've always believed that honesty was the foundation of any good movie, and that was part of Frank's moviemaking bible too. His films appealed to audiences because he loves people. He loves people so much, and that's the wonderful thing about him. He gave me not only the benefit of his wisdom and knowledge, but his friendship. And as we all know, friendship money cannot buy."

After she read her prepared statement she allowed me to interview her to get some more casual remarks about her working relationship with the director.

As we left, Larry Kleno, a longtime fan who was helping her on a day-to-day basis, told us that there had been a fire at the house a little while back, and she had lost a lot of personal memorabilia, including a copy of Capra's book that he'd inscribed to her. That set me to thinking.

I called Jeanine Basinger, who I knew was in regular touch with Capra and his caregivers. "If I got a hardcover copy of his book to him in Two Bunch Palms, do you think he could autograph it for Barbara Stanwyck?" The director had good days and bad, but on a good day she felt certain he would come through, and he did. When the book landed on my desk, I sent it to Miss Stanwyck with one of our drivers. In return I received the following letter:

"Dear Leonard, What a lovely surprise! To think that you and your staff would go to all that trouble to replace my beloved Frank Capra's book—as well as his lovely personal photo—both inscribed—was a gesture of thoughtfulness that I shall remember always.

"As I told [your assistant], my close friends call me Missy—and you are a good friend—so thank you. Fondly, Missy."

What a satisfying conclusion to an altogether pleasant experience.

In 1998 I got to interview Olivia de Havilland, who had flown in from her home in Paris to help promote the theatrical reissue of her most famous film, *Gone With the Wind*. I had about 20 minutes to pack in as many questions as possible, while trying to avoid the most obvious ones. It just shows you how much territory you can cover when you have a subject who is engaged and articulate.

We discussed the glittery opening of *GWTW* in Atlanta, where her date was man-about-town Jock Whitney, and New York, where her escort was James Stewart.

"I met him for the first time at the airport, LaGuardia I think it was. It was a very cold day when I arrived. Irene Selznick, David's wife, thought it was very important to select Melanie Wilkes' escort, and it was decided it should be Jimmy Stewart, who had just done *Mr. Smith Goes to Washington*. He met me at the airport with the longest, blackest limousine you ever saw and was very tall, wearing a long black overcoat and a hat. We were both wildly shy, so I went toward him and we shook hands and said how do you do. I got in the back of the limousine and I sat in one corner and he sat in the other. We tried to make conversation and it was extremely difficult, but then we saw each other several days in a row. I think he introduced me to a bourbon old-fashioned. It was the first I had ever tasted, and that was at the 21 Club. I enjoyed it and we had a happy time together. Then he looked me up when I got back to Los Angeles, and we began to see something of each other."

I asked if he had proposed to her, as I'd read. "No, he didn't. I waited and he didn't. And I waited some more and he didn't, and finally I decided not to wait any longer."

Stories have varied over the years about Miss de Havilland's relationship with Errol Flynn, with whom she costarred eight times, most memorably in *Captain Blood* and *The Adventures of Robin Hood*. She told me, "I thought him extremely attractive, extremely charming, beguiling, touching, moving. I felt a deep attachment toward him, but I suppose I never really knew him well. You can get very attached to someone with whom you play these relationships and scenes, and I felt a profound attachment to that man. When I got the news that he had died, it was in Paris.... I went out and walked, it was in the autumn, and well, I just cried. And I cried a long time. I had a tremendous sense of loss because in an odd way, our destinies had been interwoven. We began at the same time, and we were part of each other's lives through our work."

I was curious about her relationship with the tempestuous director Michael Curtiz, who piloted many of the films she made with Flynn. How did she get along with him?

"Not very well. I thought he disliked me intensely, or that's the impression he gave me. I found him terribly, terribly difficult to work with. But to my great surprise, years after we did the films with Flynn, the telephone rang in Paris and it was Sam Goldwyn, Jr., and he wanted to talk to me about *The Proud Rebel*.

"He said, 'The director insists that you play the feminine role with Alan Ladd.' And I said, 'Who is the director?' He said, 'Well, he's right here beside me.' I said, 'Who could it possibly be?' and he said, 'Mike Curtiz.' I couldn't believe it. But he insisted that I play the part and we got along quite well. There was a slight moment of friction there, but aside from that, we got along very well."

I wondered if she thought the director was tougher on women than men.

"I think he was tough on both. He was awfully tough on Errol," she told me. "I can remember on *Elizabeth and Essex* he had been goading Errol in some way, and Errol couldn't stand it one more minute. He went for Mike and they had to separate them."

She had more positive things to say about William Wyler, who steered her through her Oscar-winning performance in *The Heiress*—despite his penchant for shooting take after take. "I can remember doing 45 with him," she said, "but it didn't bother me. I thought what he's after is perfection, and so am I, so I'm not going to complain, I'll do it 45 times. But the curious thing is, he would often pick take 2."

I asked her what she thought was so appealing about Howard Hughes, whom she got to know in the late 1930s.

"Perhaps it was the shyness," she replied, "the shyness coupled with his extraordinary accomplishments. You sensed a lot of courage and immense ability, and the shyness combined with that is quite a powerful combination."

Hughes consoled her at dinner the day that Victor Fleming replaced George Cukor as the director of *Gone With the Wind*, a turn of events that upset Vivien Leigh as well. Hughes was "very comforting and reassuring. He said, 'Don't worry, between George and Victor it's the same talent, but Victor's is strained through a coarser sieve.' Sure enough, he was a very sensitive man, and after the first rehearsal of [the scene] where you first see Scarlett and Melanie together, I said the line in kind of a social way, polite. And he said, 'Remember, Melanie means everything that she says,' and of course, that meant approaching the meeting in a very different way. Complete sincerity."

Not long ago I revisited *Hold Back the Dawn* (1941), which features one of de Havilland's finest performances as a prim American schoolteacher who falls under the spell of a scheming Charles Boyer during a visit to Mexico. She makes the character vividly real, or to put it another way, sincere. That was always her stock in trade—in costume dramas, romantic films, and comedies alike. What a marvelous career she had, and how lucky I was to meet her, even if only once.

Pursuing My Other Passion: Jazz

When I graduated from NYU I had no idea what I was going to do with my life. I had already published four books with another on the way. These brought me great satisfaction and untold rewards but they wouldn't have paid the rent. (I used to joke that given the amount of time it took to research them, I'd have made out better working at Arby's.) I was still living at home for free and far from eager to set off on my own. In those days I could leave my house in Teaneck and be in midtown Manhattan in 20 minutes.

I pondered the possibility of teaching, but friends told me that even in 1972 the field was so competitive that landing a job without an MA or PhD would be tough. Then someone mentioned the New School for Social Research, where all it took to launch a class was having 10 people enroll in it. I began teaching a course on the history of animation in 1973 and continued doing that for the next nine years. After a few semesters, my department chair suggested that we might attract more students if it was a film series rather than a credit course, which turned out to be true. All sorts of interesting people attended that series at one time or another, including future Disney/Pixar chief Ed Catmull, future IFC Films honcho Jonathan Sehring, and a number of up-and-coming animators, including Tom Sito, Eric Goldberg, and Dan Haskett. Another occasional visitor was Al Goldstein, publisher of *Screw* magazine.

I also made a lifelong friend there: Jerry Beck, who has written a number of books on animation and presides over a terrific website, cartoonresearch.com.

If I hadn't taught that course I couldn't have written *Of Mice and Magic: A History of American Animated Cartoons*. Teaching forced me to articulate and organize my thoughts; it proved to be an invaluable experience. The class also became a gathering place for cartoon junkies and other pop culture followers.

But it, too, did not provide a living wage. I had sold a number of freelance articles over the years and decided to pursue that avenue. I had become an aficionado of mainstream jazz, and I felt compelled to write about it. How, I wondered, do you announce to the world that you have some knowledge of a subject and are worthy of being paid to write about it?

My NYU pal Dennis Fine, who went on to a successful career in the music industry, suggested that I try submitting a piece to *The Village Voice*. I went to the Half Note and so enjoyed hearing Duke Pearson and his big band that I composed a review and sent it to the *Voice* with a cover note. This was in the days of what we now call snail mail. Even fax machines were yet to come.

Imagine my excitement when I received a note from a features editor named Diane Fisher and a check for $70. I immediately called her and she tactfully explained that while she would be open to other submissions, she had more pieces for the Riffs column than she could handle. "Anita O'Day opens tomorrow night at the Half Note," I said, trying not to sound nudgy. "All right," she replied, "Give me 400 words by next Tuesday."

After a few more pieces she commissioned me to write a new article every other week. I met one of my colleagues the night I went to hear Supersax, an extraordinary group led by Med Flory that played Charlie Parker's transcribed solos. (Med held down an alternate career as a supporting actor, mostly on television. He's also the bully in Jerry Lewis' *The Nutty Professor*.) I wouldn't get to review them, however, because another newcomer to the *Voice* roster had dibs: Gary Giddins, who was and remains a brilliant chronicler of jazz music—and film. He was serious about establishing his bona fides as a jazz critic while for me it was a lark. We've remained friendly all these years.

I had another ambition: to appear in the pages of *Down Beat*, the long-established jazz journal which I had read in high school. Although it was headquartered in Chicago, the magazine's editor, Dan Morgenstern, lived in Manhattan. I called several times and left messages but I never heard back from him. Then one day he chanced to pick up the phone himself, and I pitched him a feature story. He took it and also added my name to the roster of contributors who reviewed new record albums.

I was so thrilled that I would now be assigning star ratings to new releases that I didn't ask how much I'd be paid. When my first check arrived, I was stunned that it read $8.00. Had a decimal point been misplaced? No, that was the going rate. At the end of the calendar year I received a form letter from the managing editor declaring that from that point on, I would receive the full $8.00 even if they killed the review! I continued writing those pieces for several years (never having any say about which albums I'd be assigned) and then decided it was time to move on.

A family friend provided an introduction to the dean of jazz critics, Leonard Feather, who lived in Los Angeles and answered my letter with an encouraging note. (He said I was more honest in my review of Anita O'Day than he had dared to be.) I subsequently contributed an index of jazz films available to rent for the second edition of his *Encyclopedia of Jazz*.

When I told my editor and mentor Patrick O'Connor what I had done, he laughed in my face, calling me a fool. "You're already in the lowest-paying type of journalism writing about film, and what do you expand into? Jazz." He was able to chide me with impunity because he wrote and delivered dance reviews for our local public television station for $35 a shot.

The jazz community was tight-knit but informal. I met John S. Wilson of the *New York Times*, Stanley Cowell, Ira Gitler, and other leading lights while covering my "beat," which included concerts at Carnegie Hall and gigs at several nightspots around town. But I doubt if the critics who wrote about classical music also hung out with the musicians, as I sometimes did. If at the end of a set I didn't know the name of a piece that someone had played, I walked over to the bandstand and asked. Everyone was approachable.

My timing was great. I saw so many giants in person: Duke Ellington, Count Basie, Benny Goodman, Buddy Rich, Joe Venuti, Roy Eldridge, Gerry Mulligan, Oscar Peterson, Teddy Wilson, and many others. One night at the Rainbow Room I saw the famous columnist Earl Wilson trudging into the club looking bored, as his B.W. (Beautiful Wife, as he called her in print) walked behind. So much for glamorous nightlife in the big city.

For two-and-a-half years I had a ball. Then Clay Felker purchased the *Voice* and, after proclaiming that he wasn't going to make changes, did exactly that. My new editor was an esteemed rock critic named Robert Christgau. He called me and said he had read my latest article (admittedly not one of my best) and several other recent columns and found them "adequate but mediocre, not up to the level I want to maintain." I asked if I could submit another piece "on spec" and mentioned that the great vibraphonist Red Norvo was making a rare New York appearance at Michael's Pub. He agreed to read whatever I sent in.

This happened to be the first night I took a date to a club—and the date was Alice. The staff at Michael's Pub was unforgivably rude, none more so than its owner Gil Wiest, who turned his back just as John S. Wilson was introducing me. It was one of those nights. Needless to add, Christgau didn't run my review.

A short time later I brought Alice to one of my favorite places, The Cookery on University Place. It was run by Barney Josephson, who decades earlier had showcased the likes of Billie Holiday at a famous club called Café Society. Barney stopped by our table and I introduced him to Alice. Then I explained that I couldn't allow him to put our tab on the cuff because I had lost my gig at the *Village Voice*. He wouldn't hear of it. "You'll have other gigs," he said with a smile. What a gentleman.

When we moved to Los Angeles there were a handful of thriving jazz clubs; it seemed every time one closed down another opened. The sole survivor is Catalina's, which used to be on Cahuenga Boulevard, then expanded to the adjacent storefront, and finally moved to an enormous room on Sunset Boulevard. Vocalist Ruth Price ran The Jazz Bakery for a number of years and still books concerts under that umbrella; she is steadfast in her love and support of the music and offers opportunities to veterans and up-and-comers alike.

Every rare now and then at *Entertainment Tonight* I would manage to get a jazz-related piece onto our weekend show. My ulterior motive in doing these stories was getting to play piano with my interviewees. I have some feeling but not much technique. Still, I got to play with Jack Sheldon, Marian McPartland, and even the great Benny Carter. They were all polite and complimentary. Jack went so far as to let me sit in with his big band on two separate occasions, because he had a chart of "Pennies from Heaven" in the only key I can navigate: C.

I also had the privilege of hosting the annual awards dinner for the Los Angeles Jazz Society on a number of occasions, where I got to meet even more exceptional musicians.

I am lucky that L.A. has a full-time public radio station, KJAZ. Being the only one in any given crowd who loves the music can be lonely—even Alice isn't a fan—but so long as I can get a regular dose of straight-ahead jazz I'm happy. Writing and talking about it hasn't enriched my bank account but it has nourished my life.

Lena Horne: In a Class by Herself

I grew up listening to the albums and old 78 rpm records my parents owned. I played some of them over and over again, and one I especially liked was called "Lena Horne at the Waldorf Astoria." It had the excitement of a live performance by a woman who knew how to get the most out of every song she performed. The bonus was a glamorous shot of the singer on the cover. I subsequently got to see her on a number of TV variety shows.

When decades later I had the chance to come with an *ET* camera crew to watch her film segments for *That's Entertainment III* in 1993, I jumped, even though I knew our time together would be limited. She was going to shoot her intros on the soundstage where she had recorded vocal tracks for all her MGM movies. Never mind that Sony now owned the Culver City studio lot; the soundstage was intact, a soundproof room within a room lined with padding. The wooden floorboards were well-worn. I'd never seen anything like it.

Making the day even more special was the presence of legendary MGM hairstylist Sydney Guilaroff, a silver fox who came to supervise Ms. Horne's coiffure, and fellow MGM survivor Roddy McDowall, who snapped candid photos.

My crew and I set up inside an unused control room right near the action. We watched the filming from a safe distance until they called a lunch break. That was our cue. I was introduced to Ms. Horne and we made small talk as the *ET* crew prepared to shoot our interview. By the time they were ready to roll, I think she felt relaxed talking to me.

I started by asking her about *Boogie Woogie Dream*, an early short subject that spotlights three great jazz pianists: Teddy Wilson (with his band) and those exponents of boogie-woogie piano, Albert Ammons and Pete Johnson.

"That's when I worked at Café Society in 1940 [most sources say 1941 - Ed.], I guess, before I came out here. Billie Holiday worked around the corner; I went around there and I said, 'Billie, they're trying to make me sing boogie-woogie and blues and even want me to sing "Fine and Mellow," which was [really] her song. She said, 'Listen, you have two babies and you have to pay your rent. Sing any of them they want you to sing.'

"I laugh because I knew nothing about singing the blues, but the people there were great; I learned a lot from them. Nobody talks now about boogie-woogie; they talk about scat and bebop but boogie-woogie came first."

Somewhat awed by being on that historic soundstage, I asked what it felt like to come back to her old stomping ground.

She replied, "I would have felt stranger than I did but [for] Sydney Guilaroff, who's my friend for many years and who used to do our hair. I called him before I came out here and said, 'Will you come to MGM with me?' He said yes. So already I was pacified, and actually the set itself, the soundstage, was very familiar. I liked my director and the crew. I don't pay attention to anybody else but them and I felt good. I didn't feel like I had returned home or anything, but it was a working element that I can deal with."

As for the memories of recording on that stage, Ms. Horne said, "I think part of what I am is the security I always felt with musicians. As long as I hear that good sound then I don't worry. It's when I'm with amateurs that I get nervous. I worked with a lot of great musicians besides my husband." That would be the well-respected arranger and conductor Lennie Hayton.

I asked if she met him on the MGM lot. "Yes," she said, "we were doing *Thousands Cheer* with Vincente Minnelli and I saw him around the set for about a year and disliked him intensely. He had disliked me because everybody came and said, 'You got to go hear this girl singing at the Little Troc, she's great.' He says, 'Nobody can be that great.' Besides, he didn't like vocalists anyway—no musician does—but when we finally faced each other, we hit it off. And it was very good for me because he made me stretch.

"You know who really was great? Kay Thompson. The best vocal coach I ever worked with, beside the one that's married to Nancy Walker...."

"David Craig?" I offered.

"David Craig. Anyway, Kay said, 'Well now, we have to do what we can with what you've got.' Which is great; you get tired of people saying, 'Well, she's cute but she can't...' Kay said, 'You got something; we got to work with that.' And she did it."

Thompson earned the respect of everyone she worked with, including Judy Garland, before launching her own highly successful nightclub act and appearing (memorably) in the musical *Funny Face*.

I told Ms. Horne I had the impression that working at MGM was like being at a university.

"It was; it was a training [ground] for me and I worked with the best.... I didn't do any acting, but I had the best vocal help and best orchestrations."

Except for the all-black production *Cabin in the Sky* and *Stormy Weather*, the musical she made on loan-out to 20th Century Fox, Horne's appearances in MGM movies were solo numbers where she was beautifully showcased but disconnected to the plot and characters, so her segments could be snipped out by Southern theater owners without affecting the film's continuity.

I said I realized her feelings about her time in Hollywood were bittersweet, and she said, "Yes, very." I added that she didn't strike me as a nostalgic person.

"Oh, heaven forbid," she responded. "I can remember some funny stories of things that went on. And a good friend named Ava Gardner. She was younger than I, but we hit it off 'cause she was what I call a really reconstructed Southerner. I mean she was born good, and we understood everything. And she had problems too; that was nice for me to find that other women did have the same problems I did."

At this point I asked if she would tell me about her famous meeting with Hattie McDaniel, the first African-American to win an Academy Award. She readily obliged.

"They didn't quite know what to do with me. My father had told them—I had a very feisty, marvelous father—and he came with me to meet Mr. Mayer and he said, 'You know, I can hire a maid for my daughter. I don't want her playing somebody's maid out here.' Nothing against maids but there were so many of that and none of the other. They were a little angry with me here, and then my own people were a little teed off because the Urban League and the NAACP were trying at that time to get blacks behind the camera or in any kind of position other than menial. I had to appear before them and explain my feelings about that. I finally said 'I'm so unhappy' to someone.

"They called Hattie and came back to me and said, 'You call this number.' I called her and I heard her voice. She said, 'Would you mind coming and having tea with me?' I went to her house, which was absolutely beautiful, beautifully furnished, and the tea was a real English tea with tiny sandwiches and tiny cakes and she said, 'You know, I've had to wear two hats all my life.' She said, 'The bandanna I wear for making my money and taking care of my family. And here you see me in my hat which is my home and niceties of life that I like. I want you not to let them make you unhappy.'

"It was so much like what Billie [Holiday] had said, but here was this great genius lady who was untapped still, even though she had got the Oscar. I was ready to go home every month, back to New York, to work in some cabaret, get out of this, but she made it bearable.

"I had a great support group," she concluded.

We had gotten a signal to wrap the interview, so when I asked what young people could learn from her experiences, she said, "The thing that I think is important is that they know a great deal more about their history than they feel they should. Only because when the time comes—and at one time in your life a slap can come to you—but if you know what had come before and how people dealt with it, it kind of strengthens you. I was strong because I knew what my grandmother had gone through and my father and my grandfather."

Her work ethic: "Know the lines, know where you're going to stand and trust the pros that are behind you. If the hairdresser is great, I don't worry about the hair once I get working, and if my costume designer is brilliant I don't worry about the way I look. All I worry about is getting that stuff across to the audience."

Lena Horne always came across—in any medium she tackled. She influenced countless singers who followed, and although my meeting with her was brief, she made a lasting impression on me. She posed for a photo and signed my copy of her autobiography. As we chatted, she told me that she enjoyed watching old cartoons. That Monday I prepared a VHS tape of vintage animation and sent it off to her; it was the least I could do for someone who had been part of my life for so many years.

Inside the Playboy Mansion

The last place I thought I'd ever find myself was the Playboy Mansion. As my wife and daughter will tell you, I am nothing if not a square. Yet I found myself on a permanent guest list in the early 1990s because Hugh Hefner and I had one thing in common: a love of old movies.

Hef, as everyone called him, was no dilettante. He grew up during Hollywood's golden age and never tired of watching films of that era. He also supported their preservation. His all-time favorite movie (like mine) was *Casablanca*, and while his critics berated him for his exploitation of women, he always thought of himself as a romantic.

My old friend Dick Bann, with whom I wrote a book about Our Gang (aka The Little Rascals), was perhaps the second unlikeliest man to find a home away from home chez Hef, but over time he became an intimate and confidant of the Playboy founder.

Other people I knew had attended Hef's screenings, but I didn't feel right forcing my way onto a guest list. It was only when I received a bona fide invitation for Alice and me to attend a showing of the silent film *It* with Clara Bow (featuring live accompaniment by Robert Israel) that I felt comfortable going there.

To be admitted, one turned off Sunset Boulevard onto Charing Cross Road, up to a rock in front of an imposing iron gate. Embedded in the rock was a security system, and before long a voice asked for identification. That's when the gate slowly swung open and you drove up a winding path, past a yellow traffic sign that read "Children at Play." Hef's two sons, Cooper and Marston, were thus acknowledged. At the top of the ramp was a courtyard with a fountain in the middle and several valets ready to take your car.

The Tudor-style mansion was built in 1927 and was impressive in old-school fashion: a heavy front door, a formal entryway, a dining room to the right, a majestic staircase to the left, and a passage underneath that led to the screening room. Straight ahead was a well-tended bar. And outside was a private zoo, where primates and peacocks held forth.

Hef was the most gracious and generous host I ever met. Friends who pumped me for stories about our first visit were disappointed when I told them that there were no Playmates cavorting around the premises. Alice and I didn't know what to expect, but somehow it wasn't the den of iniquity we had vaguely pictured in our minds.

On Fridays and Saturdays, which were ritualistic Old Movie Nights, the crowd was what you would call mature. (Read: old.) Gathered here were longtime friends and cronies, many of whom came almost every night of the week, led by Hef's likable brother Keith. Other members of the extended clan included trumpeter and bandleader Ray Anthony, comedian Chuck McCann and his wife Betty, actor Robert Culp, singer Mel Tormé, Tony Martin, Jr., athlete-turned-actor Fred Dreyer, filmmaker Leon Isaac Kennedy, former child actor Johnny Crawford, pinup artist Olivia De Beradinis and her husband Joel Beren, and other congenial folks. They were very welcoming to Alice and me, and we cultivated some lasting friendships.

A delicious buffet dinner was served, requiring guests to vie for seating in the main dining hall or one of several adjacent rooms. At precisely 7:00, Hef would sing out, "Showtime! Showtime!" The improvised screening room held two sofas, where Hef would sit up front, and a number of folding chairs. His right-hand woman, Mary O'Connor, always made a special effort to save us two good seats. Bowls of popcorn dotted with M&Ms were never far away.

I sent Hef a thank-you note and he sent a kind reply saying that we were always welcome. I learned that Sunday nights were when he screened brand-new movies, evidence of the fabled "Bel-Air Circuit" of VIPs who were given access to the latest studio releases. When we first appeared on the scene, Hef had a professional projectionist to run these 35mm prints. Eventually he gave way to the practicality of showing everything in digital form, especially the older movies.

Monday was Manly Night, when females were excluded from the fun. Over the course of dinner, the evening's entertainment was subject to a vote, although Hef exercised veto power as often as not. I only attended a few of these, as my nights were often taken up by press screenings, but the one evening I'll never forget is when I sat next to Mel Tormé and asked him to tell me the process of recording a record album in the "good old days." He was happy to oblige.

When Alice and I received a formal invitation to Hef's New Year's Eve party, we could barely contain our enthusiasm. Ray Anthony's big band entertained, and when they took a periodic break they were spelled by Johnny Crawford's band, which specialized in music of the 1920s and '30s. I was in heaven.

Food and drink were plentiful, and so were beautiful people—men and women alike. Everyone was dressed in formal wear, and on the stroke of midnight, balloons were released for a traditional welcoming of the new year. Alice happens to love shrimp, and a gigantic serving bowl filled with cracked ice was restocked on a regular basis. She and Bill Dana (the comedy writer who portrayed Jose Jimenez way back when) compared notes while enjoying the delicacies.

The atmosphere was completely different at Hef's Midsummer Night's Dream party (which required guests to come in sleepwear) and on Halloween. Those occasions resembled a bacchanal, at least on the surface. None of it was accidental, we came to learn. These gatherings were carefully orchestrated and stocked with attractive young people of both sexes. I was taught never to stare, but it took tremendous restraint when nearly naked women walked by. At our first Halloween, Alice and I were determined to find our host and say hello. We located him in the center of the tented back yard wearing his characteristic smoking jacket. Alice asked who he was supposed to be. He fished in his pocket and pulled out a pipe to complete the picture: he was Hugh Hefner.

An official videographer wandered around the party, which I learned was standard operating procedure: a highlight reel was released for television use on local newscasts. Monday morning several colleagues said, with some envy, that they saw me talking to Hef at the Mansion and I realized why: I hadn't covered my face with a mask or makeup like so many others in attendance.

There was another annual event that became a family tradition: the Easter Egg hunt on Easter Sunday. This was the only time children under 18 were welcome, and Jessie had her fair share of adventures over the years, from recognizing famous actors and musicians to having an overly ambitious Playmate slap an egg out of her hand. The eggs were beautifully hand-painted by the Mansion staff over the course of the year, and there were substantial prizes at stake for the fullest baskets turned in (for several age groups). I think Jessie inherited my aversion to heated competition, but one year Alice's mother was with us and complained to Hef's wife, Kimberly, that some kids had an unfair advantage. Mrs. Hefner responded by giving Jessie a special prize. No one left unhappy. (A favorite memory was the year Alice and I got to chat with master comedy writer Larry Gelbart, who speculated that the older guests were hunting for egg whites.)

The Mansion became a haven for us. Once Jessie turned 18 we would all go there for Super Bowl Sunday and the Academy Awards. (Ultimately, Jessie got to bring her husband, Scott, the zoo animals making a particular impression on him.) The atmosphere was friendly and low-key. I developed a routine on Oscar night when I was working for *Entertainment Tonight*, thanks again to Mary O'Connor. I'd arrive at the Mansion in my tuxedo and watch the show in the dining room, where we all felt free to exchange reactions and wisecracks. Then I needed a place to write my commentary piece for *ET*, and house photographer Elaine would show me to an empty office in a wing of the Mansion where I was free to use the computer and phone. I'd read my finished piece to one of my producers and once it was approved, an *ET* town car was waiting outside to take me to the Shrine Auditorium or the Kodak (now Dolby) Theater where I'd deliver it on camera. Then it was time to go home.

One day in 1998 I received a telephone call from an editor at *Playboy* magazine in Chicago wondering if I would be interested in filling the job of film critic, which had been held for 31 years by Bruce Williamson. (Apparently I was recommended by Chicago's own Roger Ebert.) Of course I said yes and spent the next six years happily filling two pages of the monthly magazine: a handful of reviews, a feature story, and a mini-profile of a current film personality (preferably female). I also got to assign bunny heads, Playboy's version of a star rating system.

In lieu of a contract I received a gentlemanly letter of agreement from the publication's longtime editor, Arthur Kretchmer, explaining my responsibilities and confirming what I had always read about the magazine—that it paid its writers well. The next time we were at the Mansion, Alice told Hef how impressed she was with this classy way of doing business. He appreciated the compliment and said he wouldn't have it any other way.

My editor, John Rezek, was a classics scholar who joined the magazine right out of college on the recommendation of a friend and was a 25-year veteran when I began working with him. He was genial and erudite, and I've never enjoyed a better relationship with an editor. Hef was largely an absentee landlord by this time, but every now and then he would make his feelings known if he strongly disagreed with a review—never directly, but through John or Arthur. He blinded himself to the simple fact that with a three-month lead time it wasn't possible for us to cover the current box-office fare. I generally filled my column with indie films, foreign imports, and documentaries. They were the only movies that had early press screenings.

My dad had subscribed to *Playboy*, and I often peered at the centerfolds when I was growing up (never mind the articles). In those days it was a thick magazine bursting with advertising. By 1998 it had lost its cachet and much of its readership, although it still sold more than three million copies a month (as opposed to *The New Yorker*, which had infinitely more prestige but a quarter the circulation). One telling fact: in my six years I never once received any feedback about my column.

I prided myself that one October I had articles in *Disney Magazine*, AARP's *The Journal*, and *Playboy*—not that anyone but me noticed or cared.

The atmosphere at the Playboy Mansion changed more than once over the years. After Hef and Kimberly divorced and she moved out with her sons, the sign on the roadway was changed back to read "Playmates at Play," and it was more common to find would-be Playboy models on the prowl. A friend of mine dated one such beauty and said he and she had just one thing in common: they were both interested in her looks.

A talented TV producer named Kevin Burns joined the merry band of regulars and earned his stripes by screening rare film clips from the 20th Century Fox vault on the Fox lot. This required hiring out a high-end bus to transport everyone to and from the studio, but everyone agreed it was well worth the effort. Kevin wound up producing a two-hour profile of Hef and then introduced him to a younger generation of viewers with a cable TV series called *The Girls Next Door*. It was wildly successful, although like most "reality" shows it involved more planning and contrivance than the average viewer would recognize.

With three young women competing for Hef's affections, there was seldom a dull moment at the Playboy Mansion from that time on. But after proposing to a woman named Crystal, Hef was publicly humiliated when she ran off during the week leading up to the wedding, taking a car and his dogs, and trash-talked about him on Howard Stern's radio show. That Saturday night all of the regulars made it a point to attend and show support. Hef responded with a grateful speech and screened the Julia Roberts movie *Runaway Bride*. (p.s. Crystal found reasons to change her mind and Hef took her back.)

His last years were difficult, not the least because he was nearly deaf, which made it almost impossible to hold a conversation with him when there were people around. The man who lived a fantasy life had no way of avoiding the reality of fading health.

In recent years Hef has received belated recognition for his championing of civil rights and free speech. The guests on his TV series, *Playboy's Penthouse* and *Playboy After Dark*, included major black artists who not only performed but were seen mingling with white guests. He shut down franchises of his Playboy Clubs that refused membership to African-Americans.

He put his money where it mattered when it came to loving movies: he was a major contributor to the UCLA Film and Television Archive and spent untold thousands of dollars saving films he cared about. He funded documentaries on pioneering women in film, such as screenwriter Frances Marion, filmmaker Alice Guy Blaché, and actresses Clara Bow and Olive Thomas. He also endowed teaching chairs at UCLA as well as USC in Los Angeles.

His ultimate gesture was saving not just the Hollywood sign but the land it occupied. When no one else stepped forward to purchase the threatened plot of real estate he wrote a check for $900,000 to protect the world-famous symbol of the moviemaking capital.

That's why Alice and I find ourselves defending Hef when people who didn't know him cast aspersions. He was no saint, and we weren't around in the earlier days of the Playboy Mansion, so we can't comment on what went on. All we know is that we feel fortunate to have gotten in on the last of the good times there.

My Night at Sammy's House

Alice and I moved to Los Angeles toward the end of 1983. Six years later, I was invited to go to Las Vegas for a book signing. The proprietor of a huge video store had arranged for a special printing of my *Movie Guide* with his logo on the cover. I couldn't turn him down when he asked if I'd make a personal appearance.

Then it hit me: Vegas! This would be my first visit to Sin City. As a kid, I pored over my father's weekly edition of *Variety* and scanned the reviews of headliners who played the showrooms in Las Vegas. Talk about excitement! Times had changed, and I despaired of whom I might have to settle for, but I was in luck: Jerry Lewis and Sammy Davis Jr. were playing on the same bill at Bally's. This was old-school show business at its best.

The year was 1989, and Vince Calandra was on the *ET* staff. Vince was something of a legend in the TV business. He worked on *The Ed Sullivan Show* when the Beatles made their first historic appearance. He went on to produce *The Mike Douglas Show* with another good guy, Erni Di Massa. They had been very nice to me when I made two appearances on that popular daytime show in the early 1970s.

I knocked on Vince's office door and explained that I was heading to Vegas on Friday night and wanted to see Jerry and Sammy. I wasn't trying to score free tickets; I wanted to make sure I had a great seat. Vince told me he'd take care of it, and a short time later called to say that I and a guest were set for the late show Friday— and Sammy was "comping" us. I asked why and he said Sammy's music director, George Rhodes, was an old friend. Clearly, I had asked the right guy for a favor.

On Friday my companion and I showed up on time at Bally's and were shown to a banquette in the dead center of the show-room. It was perfect. Just before the lights went down a light bulb went off in my brain. If we were Sammy's guests, shouldn't we see him after the show and thank him? I approached a security guard at one of the exit doors who, luckily, recognized me and instructed me to wait till the crowd thinned out a bit after the show and then come to his station. He would arrange for us to take the backstage elevator, which we did.

Before we knew it, we were standing in Sammy Davis Jr.'s dressing room, being welcomed like old friends. Sammy was waif-like in appearance; so very, very thin but so very, very talented. After exchanging some small talk he said, "Come, I'll take you to meet Jerry." We followed him next door where Jerry was relaxing with his wife and a couple of tiny pooches. He was wearing a regulation smoking jacket and couldn't have been more gracious.

"What brings you to my hometown?" he asked, and I took the opportunity to introduce my host and explain that he'd arranged for a special run of my book.

"What book?" Jerry asked.

"You don't know his book?" Sammy exclaimed, going into a completely unexpected advertisement for my *Movie Guide*.

"Well, I'll be buying a copy tomorrow," said Jerry.

I stopped him in his tracks. "No, I'll be sending you and Sammy the latest edition when I'm back home on Monday."

(Jerry became one of my biggest boosters. He had his longtime secretary, Penny, call every year to see when the new edition would be ready. Considering some of the reviews of his movies in the book, I was pleasantly surprised. Incidentally, after watching his act I called Alice late that night and reported that, to my amazement, he was still incorporating a "record bit" where he pantomimed to Mario Lanza's recording of "Be My Love." Alice responded, "Did he hold his crotch on the high note?" "Yes," I answered. "How did you know?" "Because that's what he did when I saw him at the Palace Theatre back in 1957!")

Weeks later, *ET* bought a table at a fundraising dinner honoring producer Aaron Spelling at the Four Seasons Hotel. During the cocktail hour I saw Sammy Davis and his wife, Altovise, and made a beeline so Alice could meet them. We exchanged pleasantries, then Sammy said, "Listen, we never last to the end of these affairs, but here is my phone number. It's a direct line. Call me when you're leaving and come by the house for drinks."

It was a weeknight and we had a babysitter watching Jessie, but Alice said, "We're not missing out on this."

As soon as the dinner adjourned I went to the pay telephone in the Four Seasons lobby and called the number Sammy had written out for me. A man answered and said Sammy and Altovise weren't home yet but they were expecting us, and offered directions to their home in Bel-Air. We drove to a gated entrance where the same gentleman waved us in, told us where to park, and said, "They're not here yet, but you can go right in."

Go right in? As in, open the front door?

It felt strange but that's just what we did. Before us was a spacious living room. I could see where the projection booth was hidden. The walls of Sammy's wet bar were covered with photos of him with every famous person you could think of. There was also a Pac-Man game alongside a comfortable chair.

So we waited. And waited. At one point we heard shuffling, and an older woman in a housedress walked by, murmuring hello along the way.

The hour grew late, and we just couldn't stay, so I wrote a note on my business card and left it on the Pac-Man console where I thought Sammy would be sure to see it. And home we went.

That was our evening at Sammy's house. It was an unforgettable experience. All that was missing was Sammy.

About six months later, *ET* sent me to Vegas to do an interview with Jerry Lewis, who once again was sharing the bill with Sammy. This time, Alice joined me and we both enjoyed watching these old pros at work.

Afterwards, I found myself on the same freight elevator I'd ridden before, standing right next to Sammy. There was a moment of silence. Then he turned to me and said, "I owe you and your lady a dinner." I said, truthfully, "You don't owe me a thing, but we'd love to have dinner with you."

It never came to pass, and within a year Sammy was dead. I had one brief phone conversation with him to tell him how much I loved seeing him on the big screen in *Tap* with Gregory Hines. He seemed genuinely pleased. I hope he knew I really meant it.

The Most Famous Little Girl in the World

I feel very lucky to have met Shirley Temple, arguably the most famous child in the world during her heyday—and long afterwards. My appetite was further piqued after attending a tribute to her at the Academy of Motion Picture Arts and Sciences and reading her autobiography, *Child Star*. It was written over a period of eight years, a sign of the determination and discipline that characterized Shirley's work ethic.

She was born in 1928, the same year as Mickey Mouse, and was equally popular around the globe. During the worst years of the Great Depression the little girl with the golden curls brought sunshine into people's lives just when they needed it most.

Acting came naturally to Shirley. "I thought it was normal," she said at our first meeting. "When you start something at age three, you think everyone does that." And even though people around her tried to make it feel like play, she knew she was working. "Any child who works in the entertainment business knows that it's work."

She took pride in being a professional, even at the age of six, and had little patience with anyone who talked down to her instead of treating her like the seasoned actress she was.

Not only did she memorize everyone's lines, she kept a sharp eye out for continuity errors, nominally the job of the script girl (as script supervisors were known back then). She even corrected her distinguished costar in *The Little Colonel*, daring to say, "Put your hand back up there, Mr. Barrymore."

"He didn't care for that," she related with a sly grin more than half a century later.

Playing opposite famous people like Lionel Barrymore didn't mean much to a child, but fostering an ongoing relationship with the electricians, wardrobe people, and other crew members on the set was another matter.

"I liked the guys I worked with, my extended family," she told me. "When I saw work shoes I knew that person worked. I was very worried about people with shiny, pointy shoes." The crew tended to be the same on all her Fox movies and that created a sense of camaraderie.

In the 1930s she had brass badges made that bore the legend "Junior G-Man," referring to J. Edgar Hoover's government agents at the FBI. She bestowed these upon colleagues and visitors. I found one of those badges at an antique show and had it authenticated by Shirley herself. Needless to say, I prize it, as I do the subsequent badge she made for members of the Shirley Temple Police Force.

"I would have all of the crew and various celebrities join my force. I was very careful that they kept their badges polished and if they lost them there was a big fine. If they gave them away, there was a bigger fine."

On February 27, 1935, the Academy of Motion Picture Arts and Sciences gave seven-year-old Shirley Temple a special Juvenile Award "in grateful recognition of her outstanding contribution to screen entertainment during the year 1934." (It was four years before they revived the category.) Shirley was canny enough to be gracious and grateful while the newsreel cameras were running, but in truth she resented the fact that she was given a miniature Oscar. Wasn't she good enough to rate a full-sized gold statue?

The Academy made up for the perceived slight half a century later, and Shirley showed off her gleaming gold statuette with pride. She also confessed that she didn't volunteer to give back the miniature.

It's difficult for adults to fully understand how a child views the world, especially an observant one. "I was so short I became an expert in belts and shoes, people's hands and handbags," she recalled.

During the Academy tribute she provided a running narrative for the silent home movies she donated to their archive. When Jean Hersholt appeared on-screen in makeup for *Heidi* her immediate thought was how she hated the smell of the glue that held his whiskers in place. What a perfect childhood memory.

In a similar vein, she told me that her favorite film was *Wee Willie Winkie* "because I got to march. I wore the kilts and the uniform and [got to be with] Victor McLaglen, John Ford, and all those super people. I was a tomboy; it didn't come across on the screen that much, I guess, but I was a tomboy at heart, so I liked anything with marching."

She had little contact with her fellow actors except for the girl who served as her stand-in; they had lunch together all the time. The one exception was her memorable song-and-dance partner Bill "Bojangles" Robinson, whom she adored. He and his wife were frequent Sunday dinner guests at the Temple home in Brentwood.

I came to the conclusion that Shirley was a diplomat long before she assumed that kind of work by presidential appointment. Everyone who visited Hollywood in the 1930s wanted to meet the world's most famous moppet and be photographed with her sitting on their lap. Some of those laps were bony and some of the grown-ups who possessed them weren't paragons of charm. Shirley smiled all the same and endured their interruptions with the poise and patience of a true diplomat. Along the way she met Eleanor Roosevelt, Amelia Earhart, Albert Einstein, and J. Edgar Hoover, who became a lifelong friend.

I asked if there was a moment in her youth when she realized she was not like other girls. Her response was immediate and vivid. "There was a crowd in Boston in 1938. I was ten years old, and that particular crowd had been waiting for me for about three days because I was sick. I had a high temperature and I'd been in bed. I could hear the crowd on the street calling, 'Shirley... Shirley...' and 'we love you' and things like that. When I came out of the hotel finally, the crowd suddenly started to rush us. I think there were about ten police, some on horseback. It was a big crowd of maybe 20,000 people. It was a different kind of feeling—it was an anger and a growl and a hysteria. The people in front were getting knocked down and I was worried about the children in front.

"I'd had a lot of crowds before but my mother always said, at a premiere, 'They've come to see all of the stars.' And I said, 'Well, why are they saying "Shirley, Shirley, Shirley"?' She said, 'Because your films make them happy.' So I didn't really feel that it was for me until this particular crowd. They were clawing at my legs and pulling on my curls and taking pieces of my dress. It was a wild scene." Shirley had a smile on her face as she related this story; after all, it happened a long time ago.

Her "people skills" were refined when her mother enrolled her in the prestigious Westlake School for Girls at the age of 12. She had never set foot in a school before or had daily interactions with girls her age. Can you imagine being Shirley Temple and having to deal with a peer group on the cusp of puberty? That she survived and was grateful for the experience says a lot about her.

"I think for the first year I sat and studied people's hairdos," she told me. "I studied pimples—I'd never had any. You know, movie stars don't have pimples; it's not allowed. I learned about boys, a lot of neat things, and it was a terrific transition."

It's been my observation that the child actors who made it through the difficult years of adolescence came from solid family backgrounds. Shirley's mother doted on her, it's true, but she had dinner with both parents and her two brothers every night at home. Her upbringing may have been unique, but it's the only kind she knew and somehow it didn't spoil her.

She faced the ultimate test of maturity when she learned, at age 18, that her father had squandered the fortune she'd earned on crackpot investments. Instead of $3.2 million she was left with a mere $44,000. The Coogan Law, named for silent film star Jackie Coogan, should have protected her, but the courts that might have kept an eye out for her presumably felt she was in good hands, as her father worked at a bank.

The revelation that she had a trifling nest egg was shattering. Friends urged that she sue her father but this she could not do, any more than he could have repaid her from his own meager savings. Here is another true test of character. Not unlike the optimistic characters she portrayed on-screen, she took a deep breath and got on with her life.

What must it be like to watch yourself after so many years? "It's like a relative. I know what she's going to do and I know what she's going to say. It's not like I'm watching her objectively. I found when I was writing [my book], I would think about Little Shirley. I'd refer to myself as Little Shirley, as compared to Big Shirley."

And how does Big Shirley feel about Little Shirley? "She's my best friend," Shirley Temple Black replied without a moment's hesitation. "She opens doors for me, still, around the world, and that's been very useful."

I flew to San Francisco and drove to suburban Woodside, California, where I met up with a local crew for *Entertainment Tonight* to interview Mrs. Shirley Temple Black in 1988 and then returned a decade later. Both times she answered the door herself and invited us to partake of sandwiches she'd prepared for us. On one of our visits she even did a time-step with her young granddaughter.

She struck me as a straight shooter. She knew who she was and what she meant to people around the world, but she didn't expect that enduring fame to feed her ego—or her family—on a daily basis.

Weeks before I conducted my second interview in the spring of 1998, Shirley was one of many former Academy Award winners who were saluted during a segment of the Oscar telecast. Alphabetically she followed Rod Steiger, who like most of the famous figures got a respectful round of applause. But when the announcer read Shirley's name the crowd went wild—to her surprise and delight.

"It was really a thrill," she told me. I felt that thrill vicariously, along with everyone in the audience who still holds a special place in their hearts for Shirley Temple.

The Golden Boot Awards and One Thorny Star

The first time I attended the Golden Boot Awards I met Roy Rogers and Gene Autry within five minutes—with photos to prove it. Afterwards I said to Alice, "Now I can die happy." I was surrounded by famous, familiar faces and it was nearly overwhelming.

The annual ceremony was the brainchild of the late Western humorist and sidekick Pat Buttram, who realized that no one ever paid tribute to the Western folk in Hollywood. Cowboy fare was B-movie territory and the genre itself was seldom considered at the Academy Awards (*High Noon* being a notable exception). He also knew that a number of Western performers had spent their final years at the Motion Picture Country Home and Hospital and proposed to the Home's fundraising honcho Bill Campbell (a former actor himself) that the dinner become a benefit for this worthy cause. Everyone agreed that it was a perfect marriage.

Alice and I cherish our memories of the Boot. We even acquired some Western duds (and in Alice's case, jewelry) so we would fit in. In time, I wound up on the advisory board.

Our first year was unforgettable for a variety of reasons. We sat at a table just behind Jackie and Gene Autry. She had a transistor radio pressed to her ear so she could tell her husband how his baseball team, the Angels, was doing throughout the night. Midway through the proceedings, veteran Western star Bob Steele arrived and was taken to his place. He was suffering from emphysema but wanted to be there. Gene got up from his seat and walked over to Bob, put his hand on his shoulder, and paid his respects to a man that he and every Western movie veteran seemed to look up to.

At the end of the evening, Western balladeer and B-movie veteran Eddie Dean serenaded the crowd, his voice still strong and clear. He urged Gene to join in when he sang the Autry anthem "Back in the Saddle," and we saw Jackie shake her head, as her husband no longer sang in public. But Gene got caught up in the spirit of the moment and began to sing along. It was a thrilling moment, and no one was more surprised (or delighted) than his wife.

The crowd cheered and stamped when Clayton Moore recited the Lone Ranger Creed, and when he presented a posthumous award to his friend and colleague Jay Silverheels, the immortal Tonto.

Over time, virtually every living actor and actress associated with Westerns attended the Golden Boot, from stars like Clint Eastwood, James Stewart, Charlton Heston, and Charles Bronson to singer Frankie Laine, who sang so many memorable theme songs (including those for *High Noon*, *Gunfight at the O.K. Corral*, *Rawhide*, and even *Blazing Saddles*). Herb Jeffries earned his Boot as the first black singing cowboy. We honored producers, directors, stuntmen, and stuntwomen. Burt Lancaster politely turned down the award but was willing to present one to Katharine Ross, who costarred in *Butch Cassidy and the Sundance Kid*. Unlikely honorees included Bob Hope (who made three hit Western comedies) and singer-dancer Ann Miller (who gave Gene Autry his first screen kiss). All six of John Wayne's children were present for a posthumous salute. Three siblings were honorees: Robert, Keith, and David Carradine. Others spanned generations, like Jane Fonda, Harry Carey, Jr., Lloyd Bridges, and his sons Jeff and Beau.

Representing the television generation were such stars as James Arness, Guy Madison, Gene Barry, Dale Robertson, Hugh

O'Brian, Jock Mahoney, Dick Jones, and Amanda Blake, to name just a few.

At one time almost every actor made at least one or two Westerns over the course of a career. Fred MacMurray, who did his share, confessed, "I would have enjoyed Westerns a lot more if horses hadn't entered into it. I never felt at one with the horse."

No one could top Pat Buttram as master of ceremonies; his delivery was incomparable. "I had a good dinner tonight," he began matter-of-factly after guests had finished their meal. "Then I came over here...."

He told a story of how he became Gene Autry's sidekick, stepping into the shoes of Smiley Burnette. His agent told him to meet his prospective new boss at the Vine Street Brown Derby at noon. He didn't spot Autry right away so he asked the bartender if he'd seen the singing cowboy. "You're standing on him," came the reply. Gene had given up booze by then and was long accustomed to Pat's needling.

I invited two friends to join my wife and me one year; they were movie buffs, but they weren't particularly Western fans and didn't know what to expect. As veterans of the Hollywood banquet circuit, they figured they would endure yet another rubber-chicken affair with a lot of speechifying. Instead, they were wowed by the friendliness and sincerity of the evening and came away believers.

The evenings got long and a little ragged at times. This was not a highly produced, pre-fab event. It was planned, organized, and staffed largely by volunteers, along with the hard-working folks from the Motion Picture and Television Fund. The fund now operates a number of facilities beyond its fabled home and provides health services to working members of the film and TV industry, not just the aged. Its sense of tradition is perfectly in keeping with the atmosphere of the Golden Boot Awards, where Dale Evans wouldn't let a stroke keep her from delivering her traditional invocation.

Veteran character actor Denver Pyle (best known to latter-day audiences from *The Dukes of Hazzard*) conducted a somewhat distended live auction every year which the board wanted to cancel but couldn't because it raised so much money, largely from bids placed by John Wayne's son Michael. Besides that, no one had the heart to take it away from Denver.

Buddy Ebsen was a welcome presence at an early ceremony, an ideal choice to present an award to one of the last of the singing cowboys, Rex Allen. Ebsen had been hired to work as Rex's sidekick in a series of B Westerns for Republic Pictures in the early 1950s. He and Rex got along well, and it was a good job.

Then, one night Republic chief Herbert Yates went to a local nightclub and saw Pinky Lee perform. The next morning he told Ebsen he was fired because "you're not as funny as Pinky Lee."

"I've had to live with that all these years," said Buddy with a straight face. Then he explained that he'd just been hired to costar in a new television series that fall called *Matt Houston*.

"And now, every night, before I go to bed," Ebsen said, "I pray, 'Please, don't let Aaron Spelling see Pinky Lee!'"

After Pat Buttram passed away, a number of people hosted the Golden Boot, including Ben Cooper, Dale Robertson, John Schneider, and even Patrick Swayze. One year I was selected, and while I was nervous I think I did a pretty fair job. Midway through the evening I ceded the stage to George Montgomery, who presented his own award—a beautiful bronze sculpture—that was not an official part of the Golden Boot roster.

George's speech went on and on. The audience was becoming notably restless. Someone backstage said, "You've got to go out there and cut him off!" I was petrified, never having dealt with anything like that before. After several more minutes and considerable nudging I worked up the courage to saunter onstage, getting closer and closer to the podium. When George finally spotted me out of the corner of his eye, he said, "I've been waiting for you, Leonard."

He needed someone to help him finish gracefully.

That was as nervous as I've ever been onstage. Thank goodness the episode ended well.

Another evening began on quite a different note. As usual, I was covering the ceremony for *Entertainment Tonight* as well as attending it. Seeing Burt Reynolds in the green room, I approached him for a quick interview, which he agreed to. As my cameraman hoisted his equipment to his shoulder, Burt said, "I'd love to slug ya, but there are ladies present."

I knew he harbored a deep but mysterious resentment toward me, but I'd never faced him before. Determined to keep my cool, I told him, "I have never said an unkind word about you. About some of your films, yes, but never about you."

"Oh," he said mockingly, "so then it wasn't personal." (No, it wasn't.)

At that point my cameraman was ready to go and Reynolds gave me a wonderful interview about the legacy of the Western, as his then-wife Loni Anderson looked on approvingly.

Somehow, in the early 1980s the actor had been led to believe that I was gunning for him, and he had gone on at least two national television shows calling me names. He said things like, "When he came out of the womb I bet his parents rated him zero," echoing the number-rating system I used for movie reviews on *ET*. If anything, I thought I was kind when he made a string of back-to-back bombs like *Cannonball Run 3* and *Stroker Ace*, choosing not to take potshots at him but only criticizing the poor quality of the movies themselves.

One of the shows where he went off on a tear was a pilot for an hour-long interview program hosted by comedian David Steinberg. I heard about this secondhand from the *ET* cameraman who shot the conversation.

At that year's TV syndication convention I asked a vice-president of Paramount Television if it made sense to have Burt denounce me on a Paramount show. He said, "Are you kidding? It makes him look like a jerk and you like a million bucks." I said, "Really?" and he repeated his opinion. I decided to leave it at that.

When the show aired months later I blithely ignored it. Unfortunately, my parents saw it and my father wanted to kick in the television set. Other friends were similarly offended. I never gave it a second thought.

Years went by and I faithfully attended meetings of the Golden Boot advisory board, which convened early on weekday mornings in a meeting room that was only available before business hours. One day, to my surprise Burt Reynolds showed up and claimed the seat right next to mine. As the meeting adjourned, he said we should have lunch to talk about Old Hollywood.

From that day onward, I felt like Charlie Chaplin in *City Lights*, dealing with the millionaire who loved him when he was drunk at night and ignored him in daylight hours, except I never knew which version of Burt I was going to encounter.

One day Alice and I attended a charity luncheon that Burt co-hosted, and he gave me a warm introduction. Another time his lady friend of the moment told him I had just published a *Classic Movie Guide* and he snapped, "Don't mention that name to me!"

Little did I dream that this glimpse of his temper and quirky personality was an indication of deeper issues that dogged him and the women he was with for many years. He was openly and gleefully hostile toward critics; his wisecracks got a guaranteed round of applause from studio audiences on the *Tonight Show* and other outlets.

But one day I overheard my office mate Jeanne Wolf talking to someone about Reynolds' upcoming Bill Forsyth film *Breaking In*, which had been selected to play the New York Film Festival. I gathered that he wasn't doing any publicity to support the picture. When Jeanne hung up the phone she told me I had intuited the situation correctly.

"Hold on," I said. "You mean he's finally going to get critical acclaim for playing a character role in a movie that's been selected for a major film festival, and this one he's not going to promote?" Jeanne picked up the phone and followed up with his rep, encouraging her to get Burt to participate.

The same thing happened when *Boogie Nights* opened. He reluctantly attended the premiere of Paul Thomas Anderson's knockout of a movie and didn't linger, annoyed that the director hadn't used what he considered his best takes. In spite of this, he earned his first and only Academy Award nomination for the picture.

Burt was a good actor and a dazzling personality, especially on talk shows. He displayed a rare sense of humor about himself that won him even more fans. In the 1970s when he was America's number-one box-office star, he boasted that he was following a game plan: he'd make one film for the critics, then one for the mass audience. Alternating *The End* and *Starting Over* with *Smokey and the Bandit II* and *The Cannonball Run* made it seem like he had a sure-fire formula for enduring success. But he made some notoriously bad choices and wore out his welcome in the process. He retreated to television, where he remained a star.

I wish he had derived more satisfaction from his work. He was justly proud of *Deliverance* and participated in a 40th anniversary promotion with his talented costars. My daughter told him she had attended school with his son Quinton, but he was unresponsive.

From all evidence he became his own worst enemy, drowning in debt and no longer able to play the lighthearted lothario as he neared the 80-year mark. He deserved better. One thing he never lacked was talent. Even in the minor film *The Last Movie Star* he delivered a solid, knowing performance.

I was a Burt Reynolds fan in spite of our many odd encounters over the years. He was a man of many parts, full of contradictions, but he was the very essence of a movie star, and no one can ever take that away from him.

Meeting Modern Masters

Clint Eastwood made the most unusual and attention-grabbing entrance I've ever witnessed when he arrived at the Santa Barbara Film Festival in 2009. Fans were clustered behind stanchions outside the Arlington Theatre on State Street, craning their necks to see who would emerge from the occasional limousine that pulled up. What they couldn't see was Clint Eastwood striding up the sidewalk behind them, cutting a path through the crowd and climbing over the metal barrier to take his place at the official arrivals line! Most of them never got to take the picture or selfie they'd waited for because they were caught so completely off-guard.

It turns out that Clint's driver didn't know the territory and couldn't figure out how to pull his vehicle up to the Arlington on a street that was blocked off. Mr. Eastwood believes in getting the job done with a minimum of fuss, so he stepped out of the car and walked the half-block. He was cool and collected onstage, as well. I've interviewed him many times but he seemed especially relaxed and open that evening. His (then-) wife Dina agreed with me.

At the end of the evening, after Sean Penn presented his award, Clint told the audience, "I've still got a couple of rabbits left in the hat...." That was in 2009; he's made nine films since then and starred in two of them: *Trouble with the Curve* and *The Mule*. Don't ever count him out.

The Santa Barbara International Film Festival was founded in 1986 by Phyllis di Picciotto, a local movie lover who also programmed thematic film series for Laemmle Theaters in Los Angeles. She persuaded local resident Robert Mitchum to participate in a tribute evening, and the festival was off and running.

The following year she honored James Stewart. "Jimmy Stewart made it all worthwhile," she later told the *Ventura County Star* newspaper. "He came and he said, 'I'll do anything you want.' And he really meant it. He did every interview—not just two or five. He loved everything about the small-town aspects of the festival. We had an orchestra performance, and he brought his family and sat there through every note.

"We also figured out how important the celebrity factor was to the festival. We still wanted the quality U.S. and foreign films, but celebrity was key."

Truer words were never spoken. Santa Barbara is home to many people in the entertainment industry, but it also has a constituency that supports the showing of documentaries and foreign-language and independent films. But without the glitter of movie stars, the festival wouldn't be the same. That's why Roger Durling, who succeeded di Picciotto as executive director in 2004, moved the event to the midst of Oscar season, when stars, screenwriters, directors, and producers are out and about and willing to make the short trip from Los Angeles to meet enthusiastic audiences.

In 1988 I interviewed Ann Sothern for *Entertainment Tonight* following a festival salute to the underrated actress and singer. (For some reason my *ET* segment is posted on YouTube, which is fine with me.) A few years later I shared a stage with the luminous Kim Novak, who was refreshingly candid and free of movie-star airs. Luckily, we spoke before the screening of her newest film, *The Children* (1990), a mediocre European import based on an Edith Wharton story. I wish I had a recording of that conversation, which is now lost to the mist of memory. Ditto for a brief chat with the charming Fay Wray following a showing of Erich von Stroheim's *The Wedding March* (1928) at the Santa Barbara Public Library.

It was in 2000 that I was formally invited to interview Anthony Hopkins onstage as part of a career tribute. What I remember most vividly is how he described his approach to a new part: reading the script over and over again. "As long as I know the text so well and can be relaxed in that then hopefully the 'acting' will come out," he explained.

As to what inspired him to be an actor, he said, "I came from the same town as Richard Burton and I was an admirer of his because he had escaped from his own inadequacies. I have to explain that I was such a poor student, I knew that my first day in school that I was on the wrong planet. And I was a constant source of worry to my father, who said there was something incredibly wrong with me. I just wanted to be rich and famous, that's all I ever wanted. I had no grounding and I had no cultural background at all."

There were not one but two high-profile costars to help present Hopkins with his award: Jodie Foster and Edward Norton. Jessie will never forget the after-party at a local restaurant. She was about to perform a scene from Shakespeare's *Romeo and Juliet* at school and wondered if she should attempt an accent as she played the nurse. I encouraged her to ask Sir Anthony for his opinion, which he was happy to give. "Oh no," he said. "If you use an accent you put a layer between you and the role. Do it in your own voice." She still treasures that moment.

I didn't know what to expect when I was told I'd be interviewing Sean Penn in 2002. I was a great admirer of his work but didn't have a handle on what he was like out of character. We wound up having a good rapport and the evening was a success—with one near interruption. The actor insisted on smoking onstage, and when it became apparent that he had run out of cigarettes, a man in the audience approached the stage and started to climb onto the apron. A security guard hauled him away. While this was happening Sean got up from his seat, approached the interloper, and grabbed a smoke. He never stopped talking during this episode, yet afterwards he complimented me on not losing my cool. He was the cool one, believe me.

Every year brings new experiences for me. I'd never spoken to Kate Winslet before and enjoyed our conversation. She explained that she was busy making a sandwich at a delicatessen when she got the phone call telling her that Peter Jackson had cast her in *Heavenly Creatures.* Two years later her *Titanic* costar Leonardo Di Caprio was honored and wowed the audience with his impression of Robert De Niro, who called him personally to ask if he'd appear in *Marvin's Room.* There were issues with the projector that night, and someone on staff asked me to vamp for time, which Leo did most entertainingly. The lesson he learned that night: don't drink too much water in between film clips; when the program was over his bladder was about to burst.

When George Clooney walked into the green room backstage at the Arlington Theatre in 2006, I witnessed something I'd never seen before: every woman in that room, regardless of age, simply melted. It's a feeling I (and millions of other men) will never know firsthand. We showed film clips from early, cheesy films he had made and he took it all in good humor.

Will Smith may be the most likable man on the planet, as he proved when he received the Modern Master Award in 2007. He impressed me as he told the story of how he was raised, which explains his work ethic and his humility in spite of worldwide fame. As icing on the cake, his friend Tom Cruise flew himself to Santa Barbara Airport in order to present Will with his award. Now, that was a memorable green room.

Two days later I met Smith again at the Oscar Nominees Lunch, where I shared a table with him and his wife. As is tradition, each nominee's name is read aloud, and the person is invited to join the others for a group photo. Bleachers had been set up in the Beverly Hilton ballroom just for that purpose. That year, I recall, 120 nominees attended and after each name was read, Will Smith led a whooping round of applause like a high-school cheerleader. He was as vigorous at the end of the list as he had been at the start.

Cate Blanchett was quite pregnant with her third child when she appeared on the red carpet for her tribute in 2008. She had already struck me as a modern-day Superwoman, able to juggle a busy career on several continents as well as marriage and motherhood. Nothing I saw that evening dissuaded me from that opinion. In fact, she enjoyed teasing me onstage. As I introduced an excerpt from *The Aviator*, in which she played Katharine Hepburn, I mentioned that I had interviewed the veteran actress.

She immediately asked, "How was that experience?" I answered, "One of the greatest experiences of my life."

"As good as this?" she taunted, to great laughter. I replied, "About on a par. Just about on a par, yes." We had fun talking.

She vividly recalled "the last thing that was said to us when we left drama school: 'In ten years' time…out of twenty-four of you, only two of you will be working.' And you don't believe it's going to be you. I mean, you can see everybody in the room thinking, 'It'll be her and him that'll give up, it won't be me.' But I was very pragmatic. I gave myself five years. I just said, 'There's too many great actors out there who are not working and frankly, I don't think I can stand the rejection…. I just thought 'If I don't find a groove, then I'll find something else to do.'"

I said it seemed as though she connected fairly quickly, to which she replied, "I suppose so, it didn't feel quick at the time."

James Cameron was honored in 2010, which threw our schedule off-kilter as Arnold Schwarzenegger, then serving as governor of California, had agreed to present his award as a surprise to the man who had changed his life by casting him as *The Terminator*. Normally this came at the conclusion of our tribute, but we were told that he would have to speak as soon as he arrived—whenever that turned out to be. I was having a good talk with Cameron while looking out the corner of my eye for signals from the staff. These tributes are carefully planned and cover our guest's career in chronological order. All of a sudden I saw frantic hand signals, which impelled me to interrupt Jim's flow of conversation—and my concentration to boot. But The Governator came prepared with a terrific speech, alternately amusing and sincere, and Cameron appreciated the gesture. (Jessie, who likes to watch the ceremony backstage in the green room, was intimidated by Schwarzenegger, who made neither eye contact nor small talk as he sat awaiting his cue to go onstage.)

When the presentation was over, Jim and I did our best to pick up where we had left off, and the evening was counted a success, thank goodness.

As a small entourage entered the green room in 2012, I said loudly above the din, "Immediate seating in the mezzanine" and Martin Scorsese said, "It's in the Bag," identifying the 1945 Fred Allen comedy where that announcement is part of a sequence inside a movie theater. It's so much fun to talk movies with Scorsese that it ought to be against the law, but I had the pleasure and privilege of spending almost two hours onstage with him doing just that.

Roger Durling, who plans this ceremony months in advance, has razor-sharp antennae and in early autumn selects the recipient of the Modern Master Award based on who he thinks will be nominated for an Oscar. He slipped up just once with Robert Redford, who seemed a shoo-in for his performance in *All Is Lost*, and we wondered if he would honor the commitment despite the lack of a nomination—and he did. I had never had more than a brief conversation with Redford before and genuinely enjoyed talking to him onstage. I didn't reckon with his sense of humor. When I told him that I'd be talking to his *Great Gatsby* costar Bruce Dern the following night, he said, "See if he remembers me."

I made one tactical error that evening that I hope never to repeat. As a good defense attorney knows the answer to any question he asks a client, I should have known better than to query Redford about his experience doing voice work for the animated film *Charlotte's Web* without knowing if he enjoyed it. He did not.

Speaking of Oscars, I thought Michael Keaton got robbed of an award he truly deserved for *Birdman* in 2015. But he was a great guest, naturally funny and outgoing. What's more, he answered a question I'd always wondered about. Was he aware of the kerfuffle that followed news of his casting as Batman in Tim Burton's movie of the same name? This was long before the Internet or the rise of social media, yet somehow angry fans made their feelings known. He explained that because of a custody issue with his son, he flew from the London location to L.A. every weekend on the Concorde. One evening he picked up the *Wall Street Journal* and saw one of their distinctive line drawings—of himself! That's when he learned about the fan uproar, which undermined his confidence on the set. Fortunately, he persevered and delivered a first-rate performance.

Michael was the first recipient of the newly named Maltin Modern Master Award. Roger Durling sprung this idea on Alice and Jessie when we saw him at the Telluride Film Festival over Labor Day Weekend in 2014. My pals Pete and Madelyn Hammond also knew—and somehow managed to keep it to themselves through the end of January 2015. What a lovely gesture on the part of Roger and the festival, which we always enjoy—in part because we love spending a leisurely weekend in Santa Barbara.

The following year's honoree was Johnny Depp, whom I hadn't seen or spoken to since 2001. I had read that he doesn't like watching himself on-screen and it turned out to be true. At Santa Barbara tributes there is a television monitor positioned at our feet so we don't have to look over our shoulders at the giant movie screen to watch the film clips. The moment I saw Johnny averting his eyes I started chatting with him and continued doing that through the entire evening, with our microphones silenced. Afterwards, people asked me what we had discussed. "Nothing," I said truthfully. "We were just making small talk."

Before the program began we said hello backstage and he told me, "I tend to be rather irreverent at events like this," and I told him that was fine with me. As a result, he felt free to answer the occasional catcall or outburst from members of the audience, and I kept my cool—until it was time to rope him in and get on with the show (which he understood perfectly). We had a good time, and while he wouldn't pose for pictures with festival sponsors, he spent the better part of an hour behind the Arlington Theatre signing autographs and posing for selfies with fans.

Since then Denzel Washington, Gary Oldman, and Glenn Close have accepted the Maltin Modern Master Award. In 2020 the honoree was Brad Pitt. I have never seen anything quite like the reaction of Santa Barbarans to this mega-movie star. If George Clooney made the women swoon, Brad Pitt knocked them senseless. Even men fell under his spell. Truth be told, I was more nervous doing this interview than I'd ever been before, for the simple reason that Brad keeps to himself. He's not a fixture on talk shows and has worked hard to keep his life private. As he began collecting awards for his work in Quentin Tarantino's *Once Upon a Time…In Hollywood*, we all got to see how unpretentious he appears to be and what a good sense of humor he has.

That came through the minute I introduced him onstage, following a montage of memorable moments from his career. I usually do this at a podium on the right side of the stage, then walk to our interview area at the other end. This gives the star of the night a chance to take a bow and accept the audience response, but Brad ran behind me and followed me closely, step by step, like a gag from a Buster Keaton comedy. I had no idea why everyone was laughing until I saw a video later on.

We had a good rapport, although my nervousness made me a bit stiffer than usual. The hardest part of the presentation was deciding which films we could afford to leave out. He's been working in Hollywood for more than 30 years and amassed a huge list of credits. But our event producer Mike McGee did a good job of representing Brad's range and I think the crowd enjoyed the clips we showed.

When I look back at my decades of interviews in Santa Barbara the word that comes to mind is gratitude. I am grateful for the chance to spend "quality time" with so many significant actors and filmmakers, and I'm grateful to Santa Barbara for its hospitality. Alice, Jessie, Scott, and I have a wonderful time every year and get to stay at some truly beautiful hotels. Roger Durling has gone out of his way to make us feel valued and welcome.

I'm also grateful to the people I meet every year. If Alice and I have brunch the day after my evening program, people will stop me on State Street to pay me compliments. It's very much like being in a small town where everybody knows everybody—and they just happen to love movies. Who could ask for anything more?

Off-the-Cuff Interviews and Encounters

I can't remember why, but at some point in my young life I decided it was tacky to ask actors to autograph movie stills. I think I was affected by some of the people I met at Cinecon and other such gatherings. You could almost see the drool forming in the corner of their mouths, and I didn't want to be considered one of those people. That's when I hatched an idea: instead of autographs I would collect quotes.

My first success was at the Cinecon held in Hollywood in 1975, and my subject was Jack Oakie. The veteran comic actor had just attended a panel and there was a small crush of people surrounding him in the hallway at the Hollywood Roosevelt Hotel. I sidled up to him and asked, "How did Charlie Chaplin cast you in *The Great Dictator*?" He replied without hesitation, "Chaplin called me and asked how I'd like to play Mussolini. I said 'Charlie, I'm Scotch-Irish and Mussolini is Eye-talian.' And Charlie said, 'What's funny about an Eye-talian playing Mussolini?'" Score!

Sometimes the results boiled down to just a few words. When I saw Benny Goodman at a reception during the Santa Fe Film Festival I blurted out, "Whose idea was it for you to sing 'Paducah' in *The Gang's All Here*?" He looked at me and snapped, "Well, it wasn't mine." Only now, looking back, do I understand the absurdity of someone you don't know hurling a question at you about something you did decades earlier. I'm lucky I didn't get decked.

In the same vein, I followed bandleader Stan Kenton backstage up a flight of steps when he appeared at a local school in New Jersey and asked, "Do you have a favorite of all the short subjects you made?" Having again brought up a topic he considered dead and buried, I'm lucky he was as nice as he was, calling back over his shoulder, "I thought they were all pretty bad."

Actor John Howard made an appearance at a screening of Frank Capra's *Lost Horizon* in the 1980s, and I followed him out of the theater afterwards. All I wanted to know was what it was like to work with John Barrymore on the Bulldog Drummond series—after the great Barrymore had lost his memory. His answer: "My arm was black and blue from him grabbing me and saying, 'What's my next line?'"

Alice and I used to host Saturday night screenings at our home, which being on Whipple Street we called Loews Whipple. One evening in 1994 we screened a 16mm print of a 1931 film called *Politics*, starring Marie Dressler and Polly Moran. Dressler's daughter was played by Karen Morley. The next morning we went to a local antique show and ran into our friends Claire and Frank Thompson, who were there in the company of Karen Morley! The same woman, 61 years later.

This, as my wife often reminds me, is the reason we moved to Hollywood. It's a virtual playground for movie buffs like us. Miss Morley had little interest in her former life as an actress and re-garded all that as ancient history. All she remembered of Marie Dressler is that she gave good advice, which Miss Morley admitted she didn't take: "Save your money."

Frank said with a smile, "She doesn't even think anything of the fact that she knew Greta Garbo or worked with a director like Michael Curtiz."

Miss Morley shook her head in agreement. Then she added, "They had one thing in common: perfect teeth. So did King Vidor.

Those three people never visited a dentist in their life, never heard the sound of a drill. Can you imagine that?" The young actress marveled at this and tried to learn their secret. All Curtiz could tell her is that his family was so poor that when he was growing up in Hungary, he ate nothing but herring until he was 12.

My greatest challenges came when I met an actor unexpectedly. This was long before the invention of cell phones and the Internet. One day after appearing on *The Joe Franklin Show*, I spent a long elevator ride descending from a high floor standing right next to Anne Baxter—and I couldn't think of a movie she'd been in aside from *All About Eve*, which she'd just discussed with Joe. Not wanting to completely waste the opportunity, I said something about how much I loved that film. She graciously replied that Joe Mankiewicz had done a great job with it. When we reached the lobby she smiled and took off down the street. Within moments a torrent of movies sprang into my mind: *The Magnificent Ambersons*! *The Razor's Edge*! *The Ten Commandments*! But it was too late. I was so frustrated that when I got home I called a number of first-class Manhattan hotels inquiring if she was staying there. No such luck.

(Years later I got to meet Joseph L. Mankiewicz when he made a rare visit to Los Angeles and was able to tell him—as I suspect few people did—how much I enjoyed *Diplomaniacs*, the nonsense comedy he wrote for Wheeler and Woolsey in 1933. He looked up from the book he was signing and said, "You know, Henry Myers and I wrote a pretty good script, but then they added all those musical numbers and ruined it." I was delighted to get a definitive reaction to a film that was such a small part of his long career.)

Over the years I made small talk with a number of celebrities in talk-show green rooms. I was almost always unprepared, but at least I had a chance to speak to and shake hands with Vincent Price, Gina Lollobrigida, Joanne Woodward, Walter Cronkite, Jane Goodall, and Nadia Comaneci.

At the same Cinecon where I met Jack Oakie, I attended a

screening of Charlie Chaplin's *The Kid*, followed by a Q&A with its costar, Jackie Coogan. I raised my hand and said, "Here we are at the Hollywood Roosevelt, just around the corner from Chaplin's studio, where you made the movie. You have your family with you, even your grandson. As you watch the film again, I wonder what goes through your mind?"

Without a moment's hesitation he said, "I think about the money."

A simple answer that explained a lifetime of resentment and regret. There was no need to ask a follow-up question.

The first time I met Ginger Rogers I was attending a reception in her honor at the Huntington Hartford Museum in Manhattan (no longer there). She was clutching a telegram from Fred Astaire that read, "Another great night for Gin..." Her then-husband, William Marshall, was roaming through the crowd. She was kind enough to pose for a picture with me, which is my first bona fide celebrity photo. It was taken by my friend Barry Gottlieb, who was then working with me on our *Profile* fanzine.

We returned to the scene of the crime a short time later for a similar reception honoring Groucho Marx. We were there with flimsy press credentials thanks to the kindness of Raymond Rohauer, the mention of whose name usually elicits foul language and spit-takes. (A notorious film pirate, he later acquired the rights to Buster Keaton's films and made trouble for good people, to put it mildly.) I had unwittingly found the way to his heart: mention of his name in print. As a result, I was on his permanent guest list.

For this evening I had brought my brand-new copy of *The Groucho Letters*, which had just been published. Barry and I were there early and got the lay of the land. The elevators opened right into the room, and over on the extreme left-hand side reporter Cindy Adams was waiting with a TV crew from WABC. Aha! That meant that Groucho had to follow the path to her; if we positioned ourselves midway along that path we couldn't miss him.

A short time later Barry asked me, "Why didn't you say something?" I told him I didn't understand, and he pointed out that Groucho had just walked by, joined by his brother Zeppo. It took a few minutes to understand what had happened. I was awaiting the arrival of GROUCHO MARX, a larger-than-life comic figure in my mind, so I didn't recognize the little old man who passed me in the company of another "little old man" who looked just like him. Fortunately, I was able to recover in time to thrust my book in his face when he returned along the same route. We barely said hello, but I can attest that he signed the book in my presence. The inscription reads, "Love, Groucho."

The next time I saw Ginger Rogers was decades later at a short-lived Santa Fe Film Festival launched by Telluride's co-founders, Stella and Bill Pence. Knowing she would be there I brought along a portrait still that I hoped she would sign. Alice and I were still New Yorkers when we made this trip and didn't anticipate how the elevation would affect us when we arrived in New Mexico. That's the only reason she wasn't with me at the cocktail party for Miss Rogers.

At an opportune moment I asked the gracious, still-glamorous star if she would mind autographing my photo. She took pen in hand and asked to whom she should sign it. "To Leonard," I said, quickly adding "and Alice." Having already written my name, she looked up at me sharply and said, "It should be to Alice and Leonard." I replied sheepishly, "I know. I'll be hearing about this later." She fixed her gaze on me and said, "You're hearing about it now."

That was in 1982. I had one last encounter with Ginger Rogers nine years later at her home in Medford, Oregon. She had just published her autobiography and agreed to do an interview to promote it on *Entertainment Tonight*. She was in good spirits, and in the good care of her longtime assistant, Roberta Olden. The one thing she couldn't do was walk. She had broken her hip and, being a practicing Christian Scientist like her mother, refused to have an operation. As a result she was in a wheelchair, although she stood next to me on her back porch for the duration of a shot for us to use on the air.

Jessie was five years old but had already become a fan of Fred Astaire and Ginger Rogers, so I brought along an 8x10 still and asked for an autograph on her behalf. Midway through signing the picture, Ginger looked up and said to me, "Since this is for your daughter…" and added the word "love" to her inscription. It meant the world to me and Jessie.

When I worked for *Entertainment Tonight* and had a chance to interview Hollywood veterans, I was always mindful of what the show was interested in. So long as I brought back a handful of sound bites for them, I could take advantage of the situation and talk about things that interested me.

One weekend in 1993 *ET* sent me to Wilmington, North Carolina, to take part in a set visit and mini-junket for the Coen Brothers' *The Hudsucker Proxy*. I had only 10 minutes to talk to its star, Paul Newman—a ridiculously short time. He had no idea who I was, so I tried to make an impression right away by saying, "I think you're the only actor who could be sitting here talking to me who has worked for Michael Curtiz, Leo McCarey, Robert Altman, Joel Coen, Martin Scorsese, and Alfred Hitchcock. That's a pretty wide spectrum."

Newman turned to his longtime publicist, Warren Cowan, who was standing just off-camera, and said "I'm very impressed by all this. Who is this guy?"

Then he gave me a thoughtful response about his career. "I've never thought of it in those terms. God, I think that was Leo Mc-Carey's last film, wasn't it? And Hitchcock's … he did one more picture after that … [it's been] a long, rocky road."

I asked him about Curtiz in particular. "Well," said Newman, "He had a lot of definition. He knew pretty much what he wanted. I don't always think that it was the right thing but he was very determined, and of course I kidded him unmercifully, which he couldn't handle. I had a lot of guts in those days; I've slowed down a lot."

"Were you cocky?" I asked.

"Pretty cocky. Then I go back and look at the old films and I'm not so cocky anymore. In those days they simply handed you the script and you either did it or you were put on suspension. It was smart to be recalcitrant and difficult in those days 'cause at least they knew that there wouldn't be much sense in giving you the bad scripts 'cause you'd just screw them up out of perversity."

Before they gave me the hook I squeezed in one more question the guys on the *ET* stage crew had begged me to ask. "Did you really eat a lot of hard-boiled eggs for that famous scene in *Cool Hand Luke*?"

Newman replied with a smile, "I never swallowed an egg. The magic of film."

Our time together was maddeningly short, but I consoled myself with the knowledge that I came away with a few nuggets. I'm still grateful for that.

Mel Brooks and Me

My first meeting with Mel Brooks was not what you would call auspicious. AFI had screened *The Miracle Worker* for its premium contributors and asked me to moderate a Q&A session with its star Anne Bancroft following a celebratory dinner. Alice and I were very excited to sit at the same table with Mr. and Mrs. Brooks. (Bancroft, née Anna Italiano, and my wife shared an alma mater, Christopher Columbus High School in the Bronx.)

Mel was in good spirits, proud as ever of his wife, but he gave me a hard time when we chatted during the cocktail hour. He chided me about my reviews of his films, which his son Max had shown him. "You're tough on me," he said. "No, I'm not," I protested. "I'm a fan. I love *The Producers. Blazing Saddles* and *Young Franken-stein* are two of my all-time favorite comedies." He heard me out but he wasn't buying it.

The next day I photocopied reviews of his best work from my *Movie Guide* and used a yellow highlighter to emphasize the high ratings and praiseworthy reviews. I attached a note and had an *ET* driver deliver the package to Brooks' office. He called a few hours later and said, "You're clever—you only sent me the good notices." Flustered, I said, "I like most of your movies. In fact, I daresay I've given your films better reviews than many other critics. The harshest word I use in the review of *High Anxiety* is 'uneven.'"

"Uneven?" he replied dramatically. "That's the most even movie I ever made." There was no way to win this debate, so I retreated and we continued chatting.

"You know the film I'm going to be remembered for?" he asked rhetorically. "*Life Stinks*."

I tried to hide my shock at this absurd statement and asked him if he truly believed that to be the case.

"Absolutely," he insisted. "What do people remember Chaplin for? *City Lights*, because of its pathos." That's why he felt that *Life Stinks* would be his lasting contribution to movie comedy.

It's important to remember that this conversation took place in 1996. *Life Stinks* had been a box-office flop, as had *Dracula: Dead and Loving It*. He was several years away from the extraordinary success of the musical version of *The Producers* on Broadway—and around the world. The Mel Brooks renaissance was still to come. It brightened his outlook considerably, to say the least.

In the years since, I've had wonderful opportunities to spend time with Mel. The Academy of Motion Picture Arts and Sciences asked me to host a tribute evening, and in preparation for that we had a long, chatty lunch. (I wish I had a recording of our conversation.) I returned to the Academy stage with him and several of his colleagues to celebrate the anniversary of *Young Frankenstein*.

But the pièce de résistance came one afternoon in 2016 when he agreed to allow Jessie and me to come to his office at the Culver Studios to record an episode of our podcast. We clustered together close to the microphones to help blot out the ambient sounds of a workplace, and Mel held Jessie's hand as we talked. He told his assistant that we had 45 minutes, but she never interrupted and we talked for well over an hour.

When we wrapped, he happily posed for photos and wished us well. As we stepped out of his office into the hallway I sank back against the wall and began hyperventilating.

I hastened to explain my reaction to Jessie. When I was 12

years old and saw *Dr. Strangelove* at the Teaneck Theater in my hometown, it was accompanied by a three-minute animated short called *The Critic*. It consisted of abstract art accompanied by classical music played on a harpsichord. Just at the moment when I was thinking, "What is all this?" the voice of an old Jewish man on the soundtrack muttered, "Vat the hell is this?"

That was my introduction to Mel Brooks, whose reactions to the images got funnier and funnier. I so loved this short that I sat through *Dr. Strangelove* again in order to watch *The Critic* a second time. It went on to win an Academy Award and years later I got to meet its director, the very talented Ernie Pintoff.

Around the same time, Mel and Carl Reiner began performing their "2,000 Year Old Man" routine on television and released their first comedy albums, which I devoured and committed to memory.

In other words, I had been following Mel Brooks most of my life, so spending quality time with him in such an intimate setting was positively overwhelming.

Like most artists he is a man of many parts. He is bombastic, with an outsized ego, but he is easily hurt, especially by criticism. He once told me, "I'll never forget the worst review I ever got in my life. The *New York Times*, Renata Adler. That put a knife through my heart. I thought I was finished and I didn't want to make another movie. I said, 'Well, the *New York Times* didn't like it…. I always believed in these Bibles like the *New York Times*. Now I know that time, not the audience—no, it's time, time is everything."

I asked him if he ever came up with something he felt sure was funny but the audience disagreed. "We did a movie called *Silent Movie* with Dom DeLuise and the late, great Marty Feldman. It was a funny movie, a very funny movie. But there's something you never saw in it. We made a scene: Sid Caesar was a studio boss and he was screening dailies for movies he was making. He sat there, he had two cigars all the time, and we the audience watched it: it was called *Lobsters in New York*. Fade in: Chez Lobster. Go through the door, a lobster is wearing a tuxedo. He invites you in, he's got menus. Lobsters come in tuxedos and tails, nice-looking lobsters. There's a waiter lobster that takes the lobsters, they sit down at a nice table, and the waiter takes their order. They give their order and the lobster waiter takes them over to a huge tank and in the tank there are people swimming, there are human beings swimming around. Then the lobster is lifting and the people are screaming and the lobsters are trying to get them. It never got a laugh. I mean, people were so fascinated by the insanity of the idea of lobsters wearing tails and waiters' costumes that they never bothered to laugh. Anyway, we cut it out of the picture."

He even admits that he didn't like Gene Wilder's idea of him and the monster doing a song and dance to "Puttin' on the Ritz" in *Young Frankenstein*. "You won't believe this: I fought Gene. I said, 'This is stupid. Gene, we're talking stupid here. Nobody's going to buy the monster doing this tap dance. This is beyond me; it's too silly.' He said, 'Well, let's film it and try it once in front of an audience.' It's true. So we did and it was always the hit of the night. I can guess wrong as well as studio chiefs."

And where did all this come from? "I was the baby of my family: three older brothers and I was the baby. I amused my family and I thought that was my mandate, to amuse my older brothers and my mother; my father died when I was a little kid. I was only two, so they literally needed somebody to keep the spirit of happiness in the household. I was the house tummler."

Melvin Kaminsky grew up in the Williamsburg section of Brooklyn. "So I was in high school in Brooklyn and these Army recruiters came around and said, 'You can go to college at 17½. We can accelerate your high school graduation and you can go to college. So I took this test and I passed, and they said, 'You can go to Harvard, you can go to MIT, you can go to Princeton … or you can go to Virginia Military Institute in Lexington.' So, I went down there, and I went to VMI for about six months and it was great. I saw trees, grass, you know? I rode a horse, I threw up a lot. I learned a lot; it was a great school, and for a kid from Brooklyn, the juxtaposition of being at VMI was incredible."

Mel told me he had a happy childhood, which flies in the face of the belief that comedy comes out of anguish. "It does," he replied. "That's one aspect of comedy. There are two basic pillars that support comedy. One of them is anger—anger at the system, anger at the inequity, anger at the greedy, anger at the people who won't share. The other one is completely opposite; it's celebration: it's the joy of life and sharing those incandescent, glorious moments of joy being alive. That's why my movies are often a strange pastiche of intellectualism, philosophy, and primitive—a lot of primitive stuff.

"The Ritz Brothers were for me gods, because as a kid I watched their movies over and over and learned how to cross my eyes. When I met Sid Caesar and wrote for *The Show of Shows*, I said, 'I don't have to do that; he can do it better than I can.' If Sid Caesar wasn't so damn funny, I would have been performing 20 years ago." That was in 1992. Thank goodness he's made up for lost time.

Incidentally, staying through a movie twice in order to hear Mel Brooks as *The Critic* echoes the experience Mel had on a regular basis when he was a kid watching a Saturday matinee. "My mother had to come and grab me by the hair and take me.... Especially if it was a musical, I wouldn't leave, so she literally grabbed me by the hair and yanked me out of the movie house so I would go home and have dinner."

Those movies he watched made a lasting impression and fueled much of the great comedy he's given the world ever since. Who ever said moviegoing was a frivolous way to spend your time?

Remembering Jimmy Karen

Several years ago I got the kind of phone call no one ever wants to receive: it appeared that my longtime friend Jimmy Karen was at death's door. He wanted a "proper" obit and asked me to write one. Jimmy had a wide circle of friends, so I wasn't surprised when his wife, Alba, put me in touch with George Clooney, Morgan Freeman, and Oliver Stone for quotes. Then a miracle occurred: Jimmy rebounded and regained his health! He had been misdiagnosed. George Clooney even referred to this false alarm in his thank-you speech at that year's AFI Awards dinner.

Although his energy was limited in those last years, Jimmy was not the type of person to stay home when something fun was happening. He was happy to attend screenings, lunches, and parties. He was in good humor the last time I saw him, but breathing was difficult and he died peacefully in his sleep. He was 94 years old, just one month shy of his next birthday.

I grew up watching him on New York television as the pitchman for Pathmark supermarkets and never dreamt that one day my wife, daughter, and I would regard him as family. (He even attended Jessie's baby-naming ceremony.) Here is the remembrance I wrote when we had our "scare" several years earlier. I wanted to do him justice, but part of me hoped I would never have to use it. I still can't believe he's gone.

He was born Jacob Karnofsky but changed his name to James Karen when he set out to become a professional actor in 1940 and worked in the theater, television, and movies for the next 70 years. Jimmy was also one of the most social animals on the planet and had a rare gift for acquiring (and keeping) friends. My family and I felt lucky to have been among them.

"His friends have been there for the long haul," says Morgan Freeman. "It's one of the things you notice."

George Clooney adds, "I met him when I was 21 and I was already too old for him. Old was not something Jimmy believed in. Age, yes. Old, no. He was filthy and raunchy and loving and kind and everything you could draw up if your job was to draw up a perfect life."

If his name isn't familiar to you, his face probably is; he appeared in countless TV shows and had some memorable movie roles as well. He's the realtor who sells Craig T. Nelson and family their ghost-ridden house in *Poltergeist*, Jane Fonda's boss at the TV station in *The China Syndrome*, the man who gives newcomer Charlie Sheen an office tour in *Wall Street*, and one of Will Smith's first benefactors in *The Pursuit of Happyness*. He worked with everyone from Marlon Brando to Arnold Schwarzenegger (in his first American movie), for directors ranging from Elia Kazan to David Lynch, and needed little prodding to tell stories about any or all of them.

If you lived in New York or the Northeast, you knew him as the Pathmark man, a friendly fellow who touted the current price of chicken fryers and produce at that giant supermarket chain for nearly 30 years. At one time, market research revealed that he was the most familiar figure on New York television. After all, local newscasters only appeared on one channel, while Mr. Pathmark was on every station in town.

Fortunately, West Coast casting directors didn't know of this familiarity when they started giving him guest shots on TV series in the 1970s, so it never proved to be a hindrance. After he and his devoted wife, Alba, picked up stakes and moved to Los Angeles, Jimmy commuted back to New York on a regular basis to continue shooting those commercials. He accumulated a zillion frequent flyer miles.

He was born and raised in Wilkes-Barre, Pennsylvania, and to hear him tell it, couldn't wait to get out. He started acting with a local theater group and, he claimed, was encouraged to leave after an angry husband learned that Jimmy was having an affair with his wife. Arriving in New York in 1940, he went to see his cousin, the celebrated actor Morris Carnovsky. Jimmy had seen ads for the American Academy of Dramatic Arts in a theater magazine, but Carnovsky dissuaded him from going there. Instead, he picked up the phone and called Sanford Meisner at the Neighborhood Playhouse. That was all it took for Jimmy to be welcomed there. When he explained that he had no money, one of the company's benefactresses covered his tuition and gave him a weekly allowance.

On his first day in Manhattan he met Bill Darrid, a fellow acting student who became his closest friend. (Bill later married Kirk Douglas' first wife Diana; as a result, Jimmy has known her son Michael Douglas his whole life.) When they heard of the Pearl Harbor attack in December 1941, they both decided to enlist, Jimmy choosing the Army Air Corps because of all the aviation movies he had seen and loved while growing up. After his discharge at the end of the war, he picked up where he had left off at the Neighborhood Playhouse. He made his Broadway debut in Elia Kazan's production of *A Streetcar Named Desire* in 1947, taking over the role of the Young Collector after the original actor left the cast.

When the play came to Los Angeles two years later, Jimmy was summoned to a meeting with Louis B. Mayer at MGM, but turned down the opportunity to sign a long-term contract; he thought of himself as a theater man, and that's where he worked most often for the next two decades.

Like many other performers at that time, he thrived on the seasonal employment that summer stock provided. In 1957 he prevailed on playwright Marc Connelly to allow him to rewrite the old stage chestnut *Merton of the Movies* as a vehicle for Buster Keaton, and Connelly readily agreed. Jimmy toured with Keaton that year and called the experience "the most glorious time I've ever had in the theater. The most creative. Buster worked all summer improving the play. It was a creaky piece and it just got better and better and better.

"He was my boyhood idol who turned out to be everything you want a boyhood idol to be: kind, a great teacher. Great teacher."

Jimmy remained friendly with Buster and appeared in one of the comedian's last pictures, the Samuel Beckett short *Film* (1965). He was devoted to Buster's widow, Eleanor, for the rest of her life. In later years it gave him great pleasure to participate in the annual Keaton Festival in Iola, Kansas, near Buster's birthplace. He also hosted a 2004 documentary, *So Funny It Hurt: Buster Keaton and MGM*, for his friend Kevin Brownlow.

He appeared in 20 Broadway plays and formed long-term friendships with fellow actors Barry Nelson and Jason Robards.

He had recurring roles in two daytime soap operas, *As the World Turns* and *All My Children*, but worked most often in guest spots on a staggering number of series over the decades: *The Waltons*, *The Streets of San Francisco*, *Hawaii Five-O*, *The Rockford Files*, *The Jeffersons*, *Dallas*, *M*A*S*H*, *Cheers*, *Magnum P.I.*, *The Golden Girls*, *Murphy Brown*, *L.A. Law*, *Designing Women*, *The Larry Sanders Show*, *Coach*, *Seinfeld*, and *Cold Case*, to name just a few. He enjoyed being cast in the Supreme Court series *First Monday* (2002) and reveled in spending his days in the company of costars James Garner, Joe Mantegna, and Charles Durning.

Jimmy never disdained work of any kind. He and Alba happily accepted roles in *Hardbodies 2* because it meant a free trip to Greece. He made himself available to appear in student films and took a liking to one fledgling filmmaker from USC, going so far as to write a letter to the director's parents to assure them that their son was on the right path. Bryan Singer repaid Jimmy by casting him in *Apt Pupil* and *Superman Returns*, although his scenes were cut from the latter film when it had to be drastically shortened.

Another film, *Return of the Living Dead*, unexpectedly gave Jimmy a certain notoriety among horror-film fans. Decades after making this low-budget film he fielded invitations to fan conventions around the globe. (The hardcore aficionados also appreciated the fact that he costarred in *Frankenstein Meets the Spacemonster* in 1965 and *Invaders from Mars* in 1986.)

It seems as if every gig inspired at least one great anecdote—about John Carradine leaving a shelf of prosthetic noses in Jimmy's refrigerator or Arnold Schwarzenegger struggling with his English in a movie called *Hercules in New York*, where he was billed as Arnold Strong, alongside comic actor Arnold Stang.

It also seemed to me that he knew everybody in the world; six degrees of separation were too many for Jim. My wife's father was a window cleaner who spent years zipping around Manhattan on a motor scooter. Imagine Alice's reaction when Jimmy remembered him—because her father cleaned Jimmy's windows when he ran an antique shop in Greenwich Village!

Like so many character actors, Jimmy endured the indignity of seeing some of his roles cut or nearly eliminated in the editing room. Alice and I were with him when he discovered this at a screening of the Kennedy-era drama *Thirteen Days*. He played President Kennedy's Undersecretary of State, George Ball. Despite his working on the picture for several months, all that was left on-screen was a series of shots of Jimmy looking thoughtful while seated at a long conference table. His only utterance was the last line of the film, "Thank you, Mr. President." Still, I was struck by the fact that in every casual cutaway he was actively participating in the scene, listening intently. It was a brief but memorable lesson in acting for me.

Whenever I mentioned Jimmy's name to directors who'd worked with him, they would smile. Michael Landon, who employed him many times, said what a blessing it was to have a thinking actor on his set who could help solve problems—especially under the pressure of a television schedule. Mark Ruffalo, making his directorial debut with *Sympathy for Delicious*, expressed the same gratitude when Jimmy helped him work out a scene that didn't read well on the page.

On the day Jimmy was to shoot his key scene in *Wall Street*, he arrived on the set with an elegant, silver-topped walking stick, which he intended to use for emphasis. Oliver Stone knew better than to take it away from him. The director used Jimmy again in *Nixon* and *Any Given Sunday*. Stone said, "Through the course of our three films together, James became a valued friend. His human qualities, a combination of warmth, professionalism, and depth of life experience, come through in each of his performances. He was a true gentleman, and very few of his generation remain with us. I will miss him deeply."

Jimmy, in turn, was generous to younger actors, taking them under his wing and offering a variety of life lessons. Campbell Scott once told me that Jimmy staked him for $300 when he needed it desperately, and he never forgot the gesture. (Jimmy, in turn, said Campbell was the only person who ever paid him back!) A young man who appeared with him in *Hardbodies 2* told a story at Jimmy's 80th birthday party about accepting an invitation to join Jim and Alba for dinner. When Jimmy stopped in the actor's dressing room and saw that he'd tossed his wardrobe on the floor, he closed the door behind him and gently explained that the costumer had arrived early in the morning, long before the actors, and would probably be there cleaning up while they were having dinner. The least he could do, Jim advised, was to hang up his clothing.

But Jimmy's greatest alliance was with his wife, Alba Francesca, whom he first met when she was a girl in East Hampton, New York. They were great partners who loved acting, traveling, and living well, an art they perfected years ago. Their age difference never seemed to be an issue, all the more so as Jim enjoyed good health up to his 91st birthday.

"They were quite a couple—they are quite a couple," said Morgan Freeman, who was introduced by a mutual friend more than 25 years ago. He has fond memories of their dinner parties. "The people you would meet there: eclectic without being eclectic. They were all somehow involved in some artistic endeavor."

What attracted him to Jimmy in the first place? "We spoke the same language," he explained. "I always found him very warm and ingratiating…totally likable. I think of somebody who's very alive."

Who else would have thrown a rooftop champagne party for the neighbors in his apartment building the morning of the Northridge earthquake in 1994?

I believe Freeman speaks for many of us who refuse to accept a world without Jimmy Karen in it. George Clooney wrote his feelings in a kind of blank verse, and it seems fitting to give him the last word.

So they tell me James Karen is gone. OK. Maybe. But Jimmy? He's still holding court
Asking me what I think of Uranus as a whole?
That man … that 13-year-old boy means everything to me.
To all of us
He lowered the bar to exactly where we all really exist.
12 years old.

Jimmy … please stay.
You made everything better.
I love you my friend.
George

Meeting the Jedi Master

I'd only been teaching my class at USC a short time when during our weekly break, one of my students came over to introduce herself. She said her name was Katie and that I might know her father. "What does he do?" I asked. "He's a filmmaker," she replied. "What's his name?" "George Lucas," she responded.

"Yes, I know him," was my reply. Incidentally, the warmest smiles I ever saw from George came when he was with Katie.

This man transformed his alma mater by writing a check for $175 million and commissioning an architectural model of his vision of the new School of Cinematic Arts. The first order of business was demolishing its former headquarters, which he sarcastically referred to as the Van Nuys Savings and Loan. The new larger, much improved campus is classically beautiful and its dual lobbies feature some of Lucas' prized European movie posters.

I first met George when I received a cold call from someone at 20th Century Fox Home Entertainment asking if I'd be interested in interviewing Lucas for the first VHS release of the Star Wars Trilogy. There was a nice fee attached to the invitation so there was no reason to turn it down. The people in charge set a date and a location: Raleigh Studios, an old but still-active rental lot just across the street from Paramount, where I worked at the time.

I'd seen each of the *Star Wars* films on its original release, and while I enjoyed them all I was not a fanatic. But my natural curiosity, aided by a bit of research, gave me plenty of questions to ask. When I arrived at Raleigh in mid afternoon, I discovered a huge RV that was set aside for my use as a green room. It was well stocked with refreshments.

George was running a bit late, so there was no time to linger in my oversized dressing room when he arrived. We said hello and with few other preliminaries dove into conversation with two cameras rolling. Midway through our talk, a bank of decorative lights went off behind him but I figured there was a way to cut around that and continued asking questions.

At this time there was little literature relating to *Star Wars*. George hadn't yet been quoted on many key topics regarding the films, nor had he tampered with the theatrical releases as he did later. That's why many fans have clung to their VHS tapes as they are the only unadulterated versions of the trilogy that legally exist.

I found George easy to talk to and was genuinely interested in what he had to say regarding his influences and his approach to telling this epic saga. But when we finished one tape (yes, I said tape), his assistant said we'd have to cut the interview short in order for him to get back to the Bay Area on time that day. There was also a bit of fuss regarding those lights that had blacked out. Off he went, and I returned to my RV to cadge another bottle of water to take home.

Within days I had a call from Fox asking if I'd be available to fly to San Rafael and complete the interview—or rather, start all over again—in the next week. They offered another fee and to get me there and back on a private jet. Again, how could I say no?

This time we had a new director and the shoot was planned with a greater sense of purpose. George had no "hard out," meaning that he was prepared to spend as much time as it would take to get the job done. We set up in a studio buried inside the Industrial Light and Magic building.

I took a deep breath and started from the beginning.

Months later when the trilogy was released as a boxed set, I was told that Fox sold 25 million units. To this day people approach me to say that they grew up watching me interview George Lucas; for some, it is the only credential on my résumé that matters.

The response was so extraordinary that I called my contact at Fox to suggest that they release a separate tape of the interview in its entirety. I found everything George said interesting and I was sure fans would too. (They had extracted seven minutes for each film's introduction.) No one seemed terribly interested and the moment passed.

Following my first ride on a private jet, a town car brought me to Skywalker Ranch on Lucas Valley Road in San Rafael. After a tour of the main house I called Alice and warned her that I might not come home that night. The place encompassed everything I love: a Victorian mansion with a beautiful wood-paneled library (featuring a spiral staircase and skylight), the walls decorated with prized examples of American illustration art. All the wood was milled there on the spot. Wow!

On my second visit, I arrived an hour early, and a publicist was leading me to a place I could wait. George happened to be in the front room and asked if I'd like to have lunch with him. The publicist was more than slightly surprised and I happily had a sandwich in the casual commissary on the ground floor. All I remember discussing with George that day was his fondness for British actors (beginning with Alec Guinness), whom he admired because of their theatrical training and superior work ethic.

Since that time I've talked to George on many occasions at the ranch, in Los Angeles and New York, on the USC campus, in Maui (where we were both on vacation), at the Playboy Mansion, and on one unforgettable day at Disneyland. *ET* gave me the plum assignment of taking the Indiana Jones ride with George on its opening day, with a camera crew in the front seat capturing our reaction. This led to my all-time greatest performance, as I am extremely uncomfortable on thrill rides and tried my best to hide it. (How well I did, I can't honestly say.)

When I marked my 20th anniversary at *Entertainment Tonight*, the show gathered tributes from a number of celebrities they happened to get on camera in the weeks leading up to my special day. George Lucas actually requested that they send a crew to Skywalker Ranch so he could say something nice about me. That meant a lot—and still does.

Not long ago I was invited to host an onstage conversation between George and Robert Redford at the Sundance Film Festival. Redford and I had hit it off, and George knew me pretty well by this time. I eagerly accepted. Jessie came with me and can vouch for the following: for almost an hour prior to going onstage, the two men exchanged stories and made jokes. They were completely relaxed and in high spirits; Jessie and I were in very heady company. George was even kind enough to sign a *Star Wars* poster for Jessie's then-fiancé. Just before the onlookers and entourage were swept away, George's wife, Mellody Hobson, looked him in the eye and warned him about talking too much. It was the kind of moment that only occurs between a husband and wife who are completely honest with each other.

The Egyptian Theater on the main street of Park City was packed and the event was live-streamed around the globe. I had no reason to expect it to be anything less than terrific. But somehow, the two stars lost the easy camaraderie they'd shared backstage and began to speechify, never actually addressing each other or picking up cues to create a conversation. George is an extremely bright man but he can be guilty of pontification, especially when he's recounting his early battles with Hollywood. I'm sure the audience found everything he and Redford had to say of interest, but I viewed it as a missed opportunity.

Inside (and Outside) the Oscars

My daughter, Jessie, has never forgotten the morning we drove to downtown Los Angeles so I could do a live TV interview on the morning of the Academy Awards. She was nine years old, and that year the ceremony was taking place at the massive Shrine Auditorium. Security was not as great an issue as it is now; I was able to borrow a colleague's ID badge to walk her onto the red carpet. It was early in the morning, and we took a photo alongside one of the oversized Oscar statues. The bleachers were filled with fans who had camped out for days awaiting the big night. There was almost a carnival atmosphere that Jessie has never forgotten.

More recently, we bolted onto the carpet after the ceremony at the Dolby Theatre on Hollywood Boulevard to congratulate Barry Jenkins, whom we had met at the Telluride Film Festival when he was a volunteer. Now, he was holding a golden statuette for co-writing *Moonlight*. This is a privilege not afforded many people.

There are other facets of the Academy Awards that few civilians get to see. For many years one of the highlights of Oscar season was the announcement of the year's nominees. I never drew this assignment at *ET*, but as soon as that job came to an end, I realized I shouldn't miss out on this industry gathering. That meant Jessie and I had to set our alarms for 4 a.m., get up in the dark, and drive to Academy headquarters on Wilshire Boulevard in Beverly Hills. The sun wasn't up yet and the normally bustling street was eerily quiet; we could stand in the middle and never have to dodge a car. It's a two-block walk from the parking structure to the Academy building, and the contrast between the tranquility outside and the cacophony inside was always startling. The moment we opened the double doors it looked like a New Year's Eve party inside with friends, colleagues, and publicists galore. It was even catered, and the Academy never stinted on setting out a generous breakfast buffet. I'd usually grab a bagel and look for my pal Pete Hammond. Some crews had been there since 4 a.m. setting up, as had many reporters. Eventually, they let us all into the Samuel Goldwyn Theater upstairs, a plush auditorium that seats 1,000 and features two enormous Oscar statues on opposite sides of the stage.

At precisely 5:30 and 30 seconds the Academy president and a well-known actor would step up to a podium and read the major nominees, eliciting squeals of approval from publicists in the audience. Their 90-second roll call was carried "live" on the three network morning shows, which originate in New York. The minute they finished, the current president (and that year's Oscar show producers) were hustled in front of camera crews for follow-up interviews. That's when Jessie and I went to work.

We would have already touched base with media friends like Sam Rubin at KTLA Television and George Pennachio from KABC. As soon as other outlets saw me functioning as an on-the-spot expert, they approached Jessie to see if I'd be willing to do the same for them. In a half-hour's time I would talk to a dozen or more television crews from the Far East, South America, and various points in between—many of them clueless as to who I was but convinced that I must be credible because other TV reporters sought me out.

With each chat my line of patter got smoother. Inevitably, I'd have to repeat the reason I reject the word "snub" when discussing who was left out of the nominations. "Snub" implies that the whole membership of the Academy gathered in a giant tent and purpose-fully omitted Ms. A or Mr. B. What nonsense.

The experience exhilarated and adrenaline flowed up until the moment Jessie and I returned to our car and realized that it was just 7 a.m. We felt like we'd already put in a full day. But as my friend Jeanne Wolf said, there wasn't any place on earth she'd rather be that morning. If I had other radio interviews to do by phone, I would take cat naps throughout the day.

Then one year the Academy president mispronounced a nom-inee's name. It may have been the same year that Kevin Hart stepped down as the Oscar show host in a flurry of controversy. With that, the Academy decided to discontinue its annual morning ceremony, and I must admit I miss it. It was also good for business.

Several weeks later, we would go to Oscar Central, a nest of offices in the Loews Hotel adjacent to the Hollywood and High-land Center, which houses the Dolby Theater. We would have our pictures taken for our ID badges and use them the rest of the week. The Academy used to gather the foreign film nominees on Friday morning on the red carpet for a photo op. Again, I found myself being interviewed by correspondents from around the world, sim-ply because I was there and could provide sound bites. I also got to meet some celebrated filmmakers and actors. For reasons un-known the Academy eliminated this tradition from the calendar as well. They don't seem to want to give me any free air time!

During that week we have an opportunity to witness one of the world's most-watched events being put together, piece by piece. Whether it's a guy in a forklift setting lights or Wolfgang Puck showing off the delicacies he'll be serving at the Governors Ball, everything about the week leading up to Oscar is compelling.

For most of the 30 years I worked for *Entertainment Tonight*, my assignment on Oscar night was the same: watch the show on TV, then put on my tuxedo, go to the site of the show, and deliver a commentary on the proceedings. Some friends have said what a shame it was that I missed out on all the hoopla. I tell them that I have experiences of my own. I get to see what few others do: when the show is over, winners and losers alike share a look of enormous relief. They can finally relax.

I've been watching the Oscarcast since I was 10 or 11 years old. In New Jersey that meant staying up late on a school night. The first adjustment I had to make when Alice and I moved to the West Coast was how much earlier everything took place. People started getting dressed in broad daylight and the ceremony was over by 8:30 or 9:00. It still throws me a curve.

My most unforgettable Oscar night occurred in 1991 when, at the last minute, I was told I would be working the arrivals for *ET*. Leeza Gibbons, who was an old pro at this, had come down with strep throat, and I was recruited because the show needed a recognizable face that movie stars would respond to. "In other words," I said, "I'm being used as bait." "Exactly," my producer responded.

It may be hard to believe but there weren't that many TV crews working outside the Shrine back then. When celebrities arrived they were greeted by a swarm of "fotogs." Next to them was CNN, and then *ET*. That gave me time to see who was working their way down the arrivals line. Segment producers from our show were allowed to roam the carpet and try to convince stars to come over to me, as I was in a fixed spot and not permitted to move. I'd seen Roger Ebert do this kind of on-the-spot coverage before, but somehow I lost all my composure that evening. I was reduced to babbling phrases like "Some night, huh?" I was so easily confused that when I got Anthony Hopkins on camera, I started asking him about *The Silence of the Lambs*, which had just opened to great acclaim, forgetting that it wouldn't qualify for Academy Awards until the following year.

I was excited to land an interview with Francis Ford Coppola, who was nominated that year for *The Godfather: Part III*, when out of the corner of my eye I spotted Julia Roberts starting down the carpet. I knew which one *ET* wanted more, so I desperately tried to finish my Coppola chat without cutting him off. Fortunately, she spent a little time with CNN, and that gave me just enough of a buffer to send Mr. Coppola on his way without being rude.

Then Kevin Costner arrived. His *Dances with Wolves* was nominated for nine Oscars, including Best Actor and Best Picture. Everybody wanted his photo and an interview, so I found myself among a throng of people yelling, "Kevin! Kevin! Kevin! Kevin!" When he stopped in front of me I had nothing coherent to ask, and that's when I reached my lowest moment as a journalist. "This is quite a night for you, isn't it" may be the most lucid thing I said.

I was relieved when it was all over, to put it mildly, though I'm grateful I had the experience—once. Writing a commentary was easy by comparison, but delivering it on location was another matter. The first year I did it at the Shrine, the show forgot to instruct the teleprompter operator to remain in place, and I had to memorize my minute-and-a-half script. I kept flubbing right near the end, so our director figured out a way to change the camera setup to enable me to memorize it in two pieces. Another year our makeup and hair people had been dismissed before my arrival.

I have an indelible memory of another year at the Shrine when we thought we had everything under control (except for the biggest moths I've ever seen, who dive-bombed us outside). *ET* had arranged for backstage access to the auditorium for several days leading up to the show. Our production manager had plenty of cash on hand to help grease the wheels. The Oscar show producer had agreed to let us into the Shrine after the telecast had finished—a "party's over" look the public had never seen. We set up our camera position in the middle of the enormous hall and I was ready to deliver my speech when a wizened old buzzard of a man walked in and ordered us off the premises. We protested that we had obtained permission to do this, but nothing would dissuade him, not even a healthy bribe. We trudged outside only to find that they had turned off all the lights. With the equivalent of a home-movie sun-gun I recorded my piece and went home.

When my *ET* tenure came to a close, I was hired by KTLA and Tribune Broadcasting to do color commentary for arrivals, perched on a metal catwalk the Academy had constructed high above Hollywood Boulevard. Jessie, now my assistant, came along to help and observe. Sam Rubin and Jessica Holmes were on the sidewalk interviewing stars as they arrived. Gillian Barberie and I were to take cues in our earpieces anytime there was a lull in the proceedings. She was to weigh in on the stars' wardrobe and I was to contribute background information. We had done a run-through and knew what was expected of us.

What an amazing perch we had, overlooking the entire block of Hollywood Boulevard that had been cordoned off for Oscars. We could pick out a variety of Academy members as well as stars dressed in their finery. We took pictures and waved. It was great fun.

The live two-hour presentation went smoothly and I was happy to be an active participant in the show. Being on and around Hollywood Boulevard that day is exciting, and being on the inside gets my juices going. I see friends and colleagues and they, in turn, see me—still plying my trade even without the *ET* credential. Then the Academy raised the rental fee on the catwalk so high that KTLA bowed out and I lost a welcome gig.

My most unusual assignment came out of the blue in 2006, when veteran show producer Gil Cates and his associate Dennis Doty asked if I would be interested in appearing on the official Oscar pre-show, along with *Good Morning America*'s resident film critic Joel Siegel (may he rest in peace) and my journalist friend and colleague Anne Thompson. Who could say no to that? We were even paid for the appearance.

The concept—not scrupulously thought through, I fear—was to have the three of us make predictions about the outcome of the awards right on the red carpet! I won't speak for my comrades, but seeing the nominees walk right past us as we were doing this made me extremely uncomfortable. We had two fast-paced spots, one about an hour before the ceremony began and another with just minutes to spare. We were treated extremely well and each had a trailer parked on Hollywood Boulevard as our dressing room.

As everyone knows, the Oscar telecast is seen by millions of people around the globe. I presume at least some of those people also watch the Academy's official pre-show, yet I never received any feedback about my appearance. Not a peep. In any case, it was a one-time idea that no one chose to repeat. Still, it got me my own clearly labeled parking space in the official Oscars garage. I have a picture to prove it.

When I worked for KTLA, Jessie and I had access to the room at the Loews Hotel that their hosts had used for getting camera-ready. That's where we stayed to watch the three-and-a-half-hour program. The year I appeared on the Oscar pre-show, I tried to line up another viewing spot. It wasn't easy but I finally gained access to a room at the Hollywood Roosevelt Hotel just down the street. I walked as fast as I could so I wouldn't miss any more than I had to.

It's crucially important for me to see the show, just as I have for most of my life. That's the way I want to experience it. One year, Jessie persuaded me to try sitting in the official press room backstage, where we paid for a hardwire line so we could post and comment about the awards in real time. My son-in-law Scott joined us. While it was a new experience and we were well-fed, I didn't find it satisfying because I couldn't hear the broadcast through the din and the ever-so-brief interviews with the winners.

But if we had to pick a year to have chosen that vantage point, this was a good one: it was when Warren Beatty and Faye Dunaway read the card they'd been given and announced *La La Land* as the Best Picture winner, only to be contradicted moments later when *Moonlight* won the ultimate prize. For that alone, it became a year to remember in Oscar history.

There is one other amusing aspect of Oscar season I want to share: Alice and I call it fast-fading familiarity. Every year, the actors' branch of the Academy welcomes relative newcomers into the ranks of nominees. Suddenly, talented performers like Octavia Spencer, Mahershala Ali, Alicia Vikander, Eddie Redmayne, and others are propelled into the spotlight, and just as suddenly we become passing acquaintances because we see each other at the same events: a variety of screenings and panels, the Oscar nominee luncheon, the AFI luncheon, the Independent Spirit Awards, et al. (Alice and I aren't even major players on this party circuit. Our friends Pete and Madelyn Hammond are champs, and Pete does a great job covering the season for *Deadline*.)

As a result, we come to recognize each other and adopt a friendly relationship. Jessie likes to say that for two whole months Gary Oldman knew her name. We know this will come to an end the minute the Oscars are handed out, for the simple reason that the actors go back to work and so do we. But for a month or two we have the pleasant experience of "knowing" men and women who have just given great performances on the world stage. (Years ago, Alice and Martin Landau made a mutual agreement to acknowledge each other with a simple nod.) It's not so different from Cinderella's coach turning back into a pumpkin at midnight, but it's fun while it lasts.

Festival Hopping Around the World

If it weren't for film festivals, I might never have gone to Karlovy Vary in the Czech Republic or, for that matter, Lone Pine, California, or Jackson Hole, Wyoming. Some people don't understand the purpose of festivals, but for me and my family they are an impetus to travel. When I survey my yearly calendar, the milestones are almost all connected to festivals. The coronavirus pandemic in 2020 robbed us of South by Southwest in Austin, Texas, Telluride in Colorado, Fantastic Fest in Austin, not to mention several local events in Los Angeles. We were even counting on attending the New York Film Festival.

For a filmmaker, a festival often serves as a launch pad—a place to showcase a new short subject or feature, get reviews, stimulate word of mouth, and seek distribution. Yet even festivals that aren't marketplaces where films are bought and sold can be valuable in spreading the word about work from new and promising writers, directors, and actors. They also celebrate the careers of notable filmmakers.

For a journalist or critic, festivals are an important hub where one can make discoveries and compare notes with colleagues. Seminars and panels enable a writer to hear what filmmakers have to say.

My most ambitious festival jaunt occurred right after I'd met

Alice—but before we became close—in June 1974. I traveled by myself to the Zagreb Animation Festival in what was then Yugoslavia. (I remember seeing pictures of President Tito on the walls.) I stopped off in Paris on my way and made the mistake of eating steak tartare on Day One. Eating raw meat overseas has got to rank as one of my all-time dumbest moves, and I wound up moaning in my bed for the next couple of days. There's nothing worse than being sick away from home with no one to nurse or encourage you.

Using my high school knowledge of French I got around on the metro surprisingly well and made my way to the legendary Cinémathèque Française. There I fell into conversation with a nice young man who was a habitué and knew me because of my *Movie Guide*. This was my first indication that the book traveled the world and would serve as my calling card.

The Cinémathèque was in the midst of a Cecil B. DeMille retrospective, showing 35mm prints that in many cases had been loaned to them by the George Eastman House. I remember seeing *The Warrens of Virginia*, from 1915, starring Mary Pickford. My new friend told me the local legend, that in spite of honoring Lon Chaney and director Tod Browning the institution had never run *The Unknown*—because when they were scanning titles in their vault all they saw was *L'Inconnu* and concluded that the contents were, well, unknown.

I will never forget landing at Zagreb International Airport and hearing Sammy Davis, Jr., singing "What Kind of Fool Am I?" on the public-address system. That was the first time I learned how American pop culture blanketed the world. The local movie theater was showing a new film starring Djon Vehn. (Say it out loud: John Wayne.)

The staff at the Hotel International spoke very good English, so language was never an issue during my week in Zagreb, although I realized that when my room phone rang at a given time and a voice said something unintelligible, I assumed it was my wakeup call, when in fact the voice could have been telling me the place was on fire.

I had one amazing encounter after another. I met such notables as animator John Hubley, Disney legend Frank Thomas, voice artist June Foray, British animation historian Denis Gifford, and a young Terry Gilliam, who'd brought along some of his inspired work for *Monty Python*. I saw some great animated films as well, including editorial cartoonist and designer Gerald Scarfe's *Long, Drawn-Out Trip: Sketches of Los Angeles*. Midweek we were all herded onto buses and taken to an idyllic spot in the countryside for a picnic. There was a giant pig roasting on a spit, while girls in peasant dresses served slivovic, which I dared not try. As I marveled at the lavish presentation, animator Lee Mishkin said, "You think this is good? You ought to see the picnic at Annecy."

It turned out that this international festival alternated years between Zagreb and Annecy in France. When I showed no sign of recognition Lee asked, "Have you seen Eric Rohmer's *Claire's Knee*? That's where it was shot." I said, "I saw *Claire's Knee* twice. Now I have to go!"

A year later Alice and I spent week one of our honeymoon in London and week two in Annecy, which almost ended the marriage. All the rudeness I'd read about France and hadn't experienced in Paris was clustered in this vacation town just across the border from Switzerland. Example: as a member of the press I had food vouchers for certain restaurants, and when we learned that the fondue was invented there in the Savoyard region of France, we knew we had to try one. Our waiter told us sourly, "No fondues during the festival." We've used that phrase ever since.

Back home, Alice and I made our first trip to the Telluride Film Festival in Colorado in 1979. We came to refer to it as "the spoiler." Some years later when Jessie was a teenager, the three of us went home for one day, then turned around and flew to Toronto, as many of my colleagues are obliged to do.

The Toronto International Film Festival—TIFF as it's known—is a huge festival where scores of films are unveiled. We didn't know the lay of the land, and having just left the cocoon of Telluride, it came as quite a shock. I was also a participant in the festival, as they had asked me to present a classic film in their Critic's Choice series, but you wouldn't know it from the blank stares we received as we checked in. In fairness, I went back on my own several years later and had a much more productive visit as I knew how things operated. (Alice loves telling the story of waiting for me before a public screening of a film, where press credentials don't count. She ran into Chaz Ebert, Roger's wife, just as I met up with Roger at a nearby record store. We walked one more block together, took our spouses' hands in ours and Alice and I followed Roger and Chaz right into the theater, no questions asked. It pays to hang out with the right people.)

My first taste of Sundance came when *ET* had me cover the opening weekend of the film festival two years in a row to get some camera time with its founder, Robert Redford. He held a press conference on Saturday morning after a splashy opening night in Salt Lake City. When the crew and I arrived early at the ski lodge where we were to meet up with Redford, we were the only ones in the room. Other local crews and a few journalists with notepads drifted in. We had a clear shot of Mr. Redford, and as a result, I had the equivalent of a one-on-one interview with him that morning. When it aired on our show Monday, the talent bookers at the *Today* show called the star's publicist in a fury, demanding to know how we had obtained the interview. My boss explained that it wasn't a personal interview; it just looked that way because the press conference was so sparsely attended. Nevertheless, I scored something of a coup.

My first trip to the festival proper came when I was invited to appear on a panel about film preservation. I managed to stretch that one-day event into a three-and-a-half-day stay along with Jessie, who was then 19. I didn't have press credentials, but when we arrived late Friday afternoon, we wandered into the press/media room and spoke to some friendly people behind the desk, wondering if "the word" was out about any films and if there were leftover tickets. Someone recommended the Danish film *Brothers* at the Egyptian Theatre and offered us two passes. We arrived on time, marched into the theater, and were knocked off our feet by the emotional intensity and brilliance of Susanne Bier's film. Having just shown up at the festival we figured we were ahead of the game. (*Brothers* was given indifferent release in the United States by Universal, then remade by the talented Jim Sheridan. The American version can't hold a candle to the original.)

Fortunately, we stayed at the headquarters hotel for the festival and ran into friends and colleagues throughout the weekend. On the last day, Jessie goaded me into surrendering control and allowing her to guide us to a handful of gifting suites, which dotted the town: storefronts, private residences, or wings of hotels and ski lodges where celebrities were welcomed and given all sorts of products in the hope that they would use (and in so doing promote) them. I didn't know if I would rate as the right kind of celebrity, but in a surprising number of places I did, and we came away with boots, headsets, and skin care products, so many that we had to buy a duffel bag to schlep them all home. I felt guilty taking anything at all.

My best Sundance experience occurred in 2014 when I was selected as a member of the U.S. Dramatic Jury, which was chaired by Bryan Singer. Whatever his faults, he's a whip-smart guy whom I'd met before; he is a proud USC Cinema alumnus who came to my class on several occasions. Our jury also included film blogger Dana Stevens, independent producer Peter Saraf, and talented Danish director Lone Scherfig. We hit it off uncommonly well, and a driver transported us to and from every screening. That would be lovely at any festival, but in Park City, Utah, where miles separated the screening venues and the January weather can turn frightful, it's a godsend. (I recall standing all alone one late afternoon at a shuttle bus stop, the winter wind whipping through my clothes, praying for that bus to turn up.)

We saw most of the 16 juried features together, averaging 3 a day, which was just the right number to engage me and still allow for power naps and note taking. (We ran into director Edgar Wright, who saw something like 30 movies in the same amount of time!) Our trips to and from screenings enabled us to share our opinions, and we found ourselves remarkably like-minded. That Saturday night I had the privilege of presenting our Best Dramatic Feature prize to Damien Chazelle for *Whiplash*, which went on to win three Academy Awards. (Damien was also kind enough to come to my USC class.)

When Jessie was in the fourth grade we took her out of school and flew to Venice, then on by car to Le Giornate del Cinema Muto—the Silent Film Festival, which takes place every year in Pordenone, Italy. I wish we could attend this event every year, not only to see rare films in the best available prints, but to meet film archivists and experts from around the world.

Pordenone is not a tourist town, which is why so few people outside of the film community know of it, but it's a beautiful and prosperous town. The residents are well turned out, and we felt downright sloppy by comparison. The hub of the festival is the Cinema Verdi, a vintage movie theater that was damaged in an earthquake decades ago and finally had to close temporarily for long-deferred repairs.

William K. Everson spoke of this festival in glowing terms, but not because of the programming: he fell in love with the gelato. Sure enough, we indulged on our first day there and quickly became addicted. Everyone who attends the festival has a favorite outlet, and there are many from which to choose. Jessie's teacher asked her to draw a picture to commemorate her journey and she turned in a crayon-colored image of the Queen's Bar, her favorite gelato stand.

Pordenone gave us our first experience with simultaneous translation. The year we attended, in 1997, there was a cache of Chinese silent films that had never been seen outside their country, so we all donned headsets to follow the story lines and saw some fascinating movies. (China continued shooting silent films through the mid 1930s.) The closing night featured Charlie Chaplin's *The Gold Rush*, accompanied by an orchestra from nearby Slovenia (just over the border). Twelve hundred people packed the Cinema Verdi, and Jessie marveled at the idea that, although we spoke many languages, we all laughed at the same things in the Chaplin classic. Because this wonderful gathering takes place in October—and involves extensive travel and powerful jet lag—we haven't been back, but we still hope to return someday.

Every festival experience is individual. If you have lodging or transportation issues, it can be taxing and miserable. If fate smiles on you, it can be a journey of discovery that enables you to watch films you might not see otherwise and to meet interesting people. I find myself much more adventurous in my choices when I'm away from home and immersed in a festival.

For Alice, Jessie, and me film festivals became a fixture in our lives. When Jessie got married, we were nervous how Scott would embrace the experience—and anxious that he pass muster with our festival families. We needn't have worried.

The idea of staging a festival of our own came up regularly in our dinner-table conversation. We didn't want to mirror or compete with existing events and knew we had to devise something unique to us. It didn't take long to land on a premise. Promoting underrated films, or hidden gems, has been a recurring theme in my work. I wrote a book called *The 151 Best Movies You've Never Seen* and even hosted a weekly TV show called *Secret's Out* on ReelzChannel based on the same idea. Showing some of my favorite unsung movies here in Los Angeles would mean access to actors and filmmakers, not to mention archives. We began to make concrete plans in 2019 for what we called MaltinFest.

Jessie refers to our family enterprise as The Maltin Empire and our roles in it are clear. Alice is the brains of the outfit; she runs the business. Jessie is the idea person who connects with people. They refer to me as the talent (a term used in television, sometimes condescendingly, for the folks who appear on camera) because if everything goes right, all I have to do is show up—without thinking about any of the details. I'm a worrier, but Jessie didn't allow me to dwell on problems she knew how to solve. She hired a very capable woman named Stacy Howard and put her organizational skills to perfect use.

Time and again Jessie reminded me that this was our festival and we could do whatever we want. We wanted a comfortable and convenient venue—the historic Grauman's Egyptian Theatre on Hollywood Boulevard the obvious choice. It's one of my favorite places to watch a movie. I thrilled at seeing our MaltinFest logo projected on that enormous screen for the first time. What's more, the theater's good-sized lobby and spacious courtyard would allow people to hang out and talk, a crucial element toward attaining our goal: building a sense of community.

Movie lovers who attended our three-day festival were surprised—even astonished—to be greeted at our check-in desk by Alice and Jessie. That was no accident. We wanted everyone to feel welcome and to know that this was a personal endeavor. We kept ticket prices reasonable, especially for students, many of whom we walked in for free. Alice took on the daunting task of finding sponsors so we wouldn't have to rely on our box-office take to break even. Turning a profit was never discussed.

My contacts at Paramount, Warner Bros., and Universal studios made it possible for us to show 35mm prints of cartoons and short subjects along with our feature films. This required more time and money than it should have, but it was a key component of the festival I'd always dreamed about. Mike Pogorzelski, archivist at the Academy of Motion Picture Arts and Sciences, opened the doors to their collection, cut through red tape, and did it all with a smile.

Lining up films and guests was the next order of business. We agreed that our opening night movie had to be *Sing Street*. John Carney created the living definition of a feel-good movie and a great way to kick off our three-day weekend. (Sure enough, the audience loved it so much they stayed through the closing credits so they could hear a medley of the songs one more time. Then, to our delight, they lingered in the lobby and courtyard. Scores of people didn't want the magic they'd just experienced to end. I felt the same way.)

Alexander Payne is one of my favorite writers and directors, as well as a dedicated movie buff. When I asked if he would come to a showing of his debut feature, the little-seen *Citizen Ruth*, he not only said yes but volunteered to "round up the troops." Good to his word, he showed up with his star, Laura Dern, costar Mary Kay Place, composer Rolfe Kent, editor Kevin Tent, and production designer Jane Ann Stewart. They enjoyed seeing each other so much that I'm told they had a long get-together following the screening and panel at Musso & Frank's, right across the street.

Scott Alexander and Larry Karaszewski had brought *Big Eyes* to my USC class and told the incredible story of how they spent their own money to keep the project alive for 11 years. I knew they'd be willing to do their spiel again at MaltinFest, just as I knew our festival goers would enjoy watching Amy Adams and Christoph Waltz in this terrific film.

I first saw the hilarious documentary *Exporting Raymond* when it was booked for my class. That's also how I met Phil Rosenthal, who made the film to chronicle the experience of bringing his hit TV comedy *Everybody Loves Raymond* to Russia. The film was a labor of love for Phil—who has since become a friend—and he enjoyed showing it to a brand-new audience. (Since that time, people have come to know him thanks to his delightful Netflix series *Somebody Feed Phil*.)

A friend provided an introduction to Nicole Holofcener, whose work I love. She agreed to come to a screening of one of my favorites, *Please Give*, and even brought along her leading actress, Catherine Keener. It was our first show late Friday afternoon and I sat near the back of the auditorium with our friend Stephen Tobolowsky behind me. When the final scene played out, I turned to him with tears in my eyes and said, "How does she do that?" He confessed that he didn't know but agreed it was magical.

Another of my favorite unseen/unsung films is *Songcatcher*, written and directed by the gifted Maggie Greenwald. It earned praise at Sundance back in 2000 but never got a proper theatrical release. Maggie lives back East but she generously shipped us her personal 35mm print so we could show the movie as it was meant to be seen. Janet McTiernan, Aidan Quinn, Pat Carroll, and Emmy Rossum star in this feminist tale about a musicologist who ventures into the backwoods of Appalachia to find authentic folk songs.

I couldn't resist watching it with our audience. When it was over, a woman walked up to me and asked, "How could I not have known about this wonderful film?" That kind of response made the whole weekend worthwhile. And it happened over and over.

Los Angeles is a tough city to penetrate when you're promoting an event, but loyal friends came through for us. Susan King wrote a glowing article for the *Los Angeles Times*, which was accompanied by a huge photo of all three Maltins and one of our dogs. On opening day the paper's senior film critic, Kenny Turan, made us one of his weekly picks and paid me the nicest possible compliment: "Los Angeles has no lack of film critics," he wrote, "but there isn't one who is more respected and admired than author and

Entertainment Tonight veteran Leonard Maltin, and he now has his very own film festival to prove it." I was blown away.

KABC entertainment reporter George Pennachio is a big-hearted guy and gave us valuable airtime, as did the all-news radio station KNX.

We ended on a high note Sunday night with one of my favorite bad movies, *Bela Lugosi Meets a Brooklyn Gorilla*, featuring the man who played Dracula and a nightclub duo named Duke Mitchell and Sammy Petrillo—the poor man's Dean Martin and Jerry Lewis. This low-rent B movie has a coterie of followers, one of whom even flew in from New Jersey for our screening. The families of the film's producer, Jack Broder, and the star duo's manager, Maurice Duke, were there along with an enthusiastic crowd. The coup de grâce was learning, at the last minute, that the 35mm print we were showing had been donated to the Academy by the family of Bela Lugosi!

We can't say enough about our friends, who came through in a variety of ways, from providing snacks to guarding the cash box. On Saturday Alice was heard to say, "We really ought to have a gorilla." Sure enough, on less than 24 hours' notice, Grae Drake arrived with her hubby, Steve Gelder, in a gorilla suit. He may still be posing for pictures in the lobby for all I know. It was a hell of a finale.

We had finalized our lineup for MaltinFest 2020 when the world went spinning off its axis. Doing this event virtually didn't make sense to us, but rest assured, MaltinFest will return.

My Adventures in Podcasting

For some time Jessie has worked as a volunteer at the annual Independent Spirit Awards, a massive event that takes place the day before the Oscars. Because she knows so many publicists who are there with clients, she usually winds up wrangling celebrity guests, helping them navigate the red carpet, or escorting them backstage. At the 2014 event I spotted stand-up comic Marc Maron and told her, "I want to be on his podcast. Try and get his contact information." She scanned the room as the ceremony was about to get under way and made a beeline for Maron, planting herself in his path and saying, "Hi I'm Jessie Maltin Leonard Maltin's daughter he'd love to be on your show." He said he was a fan of mine and gave her an e-mail address.

Marc was good to his word. I sent an e-mail and was booked on his highly popular podcast. I drove to his house and had an enjoyable conversation in his garage, where he originally broadcast his show. (I was in the chair where President Barack Obama later sat). I learned that he had actually studied film in college with the estimable Roger Manvell. Some weeks later when our episode aired, I got feedback from all sorts of people confirming what I'd heard, that he had built the biggest audience in the new world of communication called podcasting.

A short time later, performer and entrepreneur Paul Scheer

called me and asked if I'd be willing to meet with him and his partners at Earwolf, a podcast network. They'd heard the Maron episode, as they were about to launch a new cache of shows about popular culture called Wolfpop, and wanted to gauge my interest in joining them. Paul also asked how I'd feel about working with a comedian. I told him I loved the idea: the right person could youthify and energize our show. He recommended Baron Vaughn, who is both a comic and an actor; he plays one of Lily Tomlin's sons on *Grace and Frankie* and is the voice of Servo on the recent reboot of *Mystery Science Theater 3000*. We met, clicked right away, and were off and running.

I had what I considered an original idea for our show: choose a subject, then pick one good movie in that category, one stinker, and one sleeper. For instance, for biopics our good choice was *Capote*, our stinker was *J. Edgar*, and our sleeper was *The Runaways*, with Kristen Stewart as Joan Jett. It was a good idea. The hitch was the huge amount of time involved. I thought I could get by using my memory, along with notes or reviews of the movies, but I soon discovered that I had to watch them again to carry on an intelligent conversation. It was a big investment of time, and some weeks Baron and I were running on fumes.

That's when we started inviting guests to join our discussions, calling on friends and people we knew: Fred Willard, Joe Dante, Stephen Tobolowsky, Phil Rosenthal, John Landis, Greg Proops, Doug Benson, Samm Levine. I got terribly ill during the summer of 2015 and Jessie filled in for me. She had no experience doing this but proved to be a natural. She was traveling in the UK at this time and Skyped in at a pre-arranged time with Baron. When she came home she joined Baron and me for an unforgettable episode recorded in front of an audience at South by Southwest in Austin, Texas, with comedian-turned-filmmaker Mike Birbiglia and his producer, Ira Glass, of *This American Life*. What a great day that was.

Then Baron started getting work—that is to say, paying gigs—and confessed that he couldn't maintain a weekly recording schedule. Our show never shot into the profit column so there was no argument. We parted as friends, and I continued interviewing guests including John Sayles, Lenny Abrahamson, Jeff Nichols, Kevin Pollak, and Alec Baldwin. Eventually Jessie and I started working as a team and we've never looked back. We also left Wolfpop for so-called greener pastures at the Nerdist network, encouraged by its founder, Chris Hardwick, and did our first show from a baseball stadium in San Diego during Comic-Con. Our kickoff guest was our pal Doug Benson, whose *Doug Loves Movies* podcast is a longtime favorite.

I called in favors everywhere I could to get in touch with actors, comedians, and filmmakers who were willing to spend an hour in a recording studio with us. Sometimes all it took was knowing a friend who knew a friend who knew how to reach our target. That's how we wound up with the wonderful Hayley Mills. Just before our engineer began recording she admitted that she felt funny because she had nothing to plug.

"You don't need to plug anything," Jessie and I said almost in unison. "You're Hayley Mills!"

Publicists started to approach us, offering potential guests who did have something to promote. That's what led to a surreal moment we will never forget. For several years we did our show in a recording booth overlooking Los Angeles' enormous Meltdown Comics on Sunset Boulevard. It was a colorful place to hang out and the last place one would expect to find Al Pacino. Yet there he was, ready and willing to talk to us about the imminent release of his documentary about a stage production of Oscar Wilde's *Salome*.

Jessie and I always play fair: if someone is there for a specific reason like that, we don't want to shortchange them and make sure to discuss the actor or director's current project. I never would have dreamt of asking Pacino about *The Godfather*, *Serpico*, or *Dog*

Day Afternoon. He was the one who was relaxed enough to reminisce about some of those unforgettable movies. The scheduled hour wound up being an hour and a half. We walked away on Cloud Nine.

We never know what to expect. Amy Adams is one of the best actresses working today, with six Oscar nominations (so far) to prove it. Yet when Jessie went into fangirl mode talking about such early films as *Drop Dead Gorgeous* and *Psycho Beach Party*, she was all for it, happily sharing memories of making those pictures.

That's what makes each episode an adventure for us. When Richard Donner came to our recording booth at Meltdown, I'm sure he expected us to ask about *The Goonies*, *Superman*, and the other popular movies he's made. We did, but I was more interested in picking his brain about all the TV shows he directed like *Wanted: Dead or Alive*, *Perry Mason*, and *The Twilight Zone*, to name just a few. And you know what? He had a great time reminiscing about that period in his career. (Like many a guest, he apologized for the length of some of his anecdotes. We responded as we always do, explaining that unlike TV talk shows, we have plenty of time and we want to hear those stories.) One distinction Mr. Donner holds among our 200+ guests: he's the only one who admits to having been high while making some of his films and TV shows.

Jessie and I love character actors, who constitute the bedrock of Hollywood. Without them the stars wouldn't shine as brightly and the films we see wouldn't be nearly as entertaining. That's why we've sought out people like J.K. Simmons, Ed Begley, Jr., Dale Dickey, Alfred Molina, Stephen Tobolowsky, Bruce Davison, Robert Patrick, Giancarlo Esposito, Clifton Collins, Jr., Shea Whigham, Paul Dooley, Jacki Weaver, Lesley Manville, Simon Callow, William Fichtner, Beth Grant, Clancy Brown, and Tzi Ma. If any of those names are unfamiliar, just look them up online and I guarantee you'll recognize their faces.

One of our favorites was also a friend: Robert Forster, a remarkable guy whose career stagnated after a promising start. He spent many years unemployed, giving speeches free of charge on the power of positive thinking, and never became embittered. Quentin Tarantino gave him a great role in *Jackie Brown* that earned him an Oscar nomination and he never stopped working from that day forward.

His outlook on life was impressive, as was his work ethic. He learned this on his first day making a movie for director John Huston; the title was *Reflections in a Golden Eye* and Bob had been begging Huston to tell him what he wanted from the actor. Huston kept putting him off until the very last minute before they shot his first scene. Forster recounted this story in a perfect impression of Huston's voice: "Go take a look through the lennns."

"I walk over to the camera, the cameraman steps aside, I look through the lens. I turn back to Huston, he's got his hands fixed the way they show you the frame. He said (as Huston), 'Those are the frame lines.' And I looked again. I said, 'You mean that line that shows the cameraman what the audience sees?' He says (as Huston), 'Yes, those are the frame lines. Now, ask yourself this: what needs to be there?' That was it. In a little tiny Zen piece of information, he made me responsible and gave me the authority to deliver what was necessary inside the frame. He didn't tell me that I was going to have to do the detective work that you do when you realize that some guy wrote this and wants you to understand it."

He continued, "You've got to understand why you're in the scene and why that scene is in the movie, so when you hear 'action,' you can go for that little fraction of whatever it is we're shooting of this movie and know what is supposed to be there so that you can satisfy the needs of the writer. That isn't the end of it; the director may have a route for you, maybe you've got to make an entrance or an exit or move some props around or say some dialogue. You've got to figure out what the director needs of you so that you can do that for the director when you hear 'action.' And that isn't the end of it. The one listening for the words has got to hear them correctly; otherwise at the end of the shot somebody says, 'No good for sound.' And if you do something too big for the shot you're in, somebody behind the camera says, 'No good for composition.' And if you put the cup in the wrong spot, somebody says, 'No good for continuity.'

"You owe something to everybody on that set; everybody is your boss. The guy who set the lights wants you to be in 'em. And the one who is cutting this picture together wants you to deliver material that will contribute to the ups and the downs of the roller coaster car we're trying to put our audience into. And if I'm not believable going around the curves, the audience won't be there at the end of the ride. So, we owe the audience something, and for the other actor who may have to go up emotionally in a scene, you've got to build him a little ramp so that the other actor can do the scene, and for the one who hired me, I am supposed to help bring this picture in on time. I've got to be ready on my second, third, first take just so that we can help these guys make their schedule every single day.

"You owe something to everybody on that set. It sounds like a really hard thing to do, I realize that, but I know actors who I would not trust with a grocery list who can do that eight days a week. It is not so hard to create an action which advantages more than just yourself. I remind people and my children and myself that every action of every type can be, on a daily basis, made better by knowing that you have other people's interests and keep them in mind. See if you can't just deliver better strokes for the rest of your life."

Jessie and I were tempted to end the episode right then and there. Talk about life lessons! That humility—coupled with integrity—tells you why Bob was so special. We were devastated when we heard that he had died toward the end of 2019. We'd seen him just a few months earlier when he came to one of our screenings at

MaltinFest. Typically, he insisted on paying for his ticket. We refused him and his lovely partner, Denise, but he pressed a hundred dollar bill into Jessie's hand and wouldn't take it back.

We are luckier than most daily or nightly TV shows who are obliged to book guests for the sake of relationships with studios, networks, or publicists. We have just one criterion for a prospective guest: we have to be fans of their work. At least, one of us does: Jessie, being in a different demographic than I, is particularly excited when an actor she's grown up with like Josh Hartnett or Justin Long is available. She knows their credits by heart, but I may have to do some homework, checking YouTube interviews to get a sense of the person. Yet every time we book someone like that, the response is tremendous—and I almost always come away impressed.

We're both fans of Danny Huston's work on camera, and of course we greatly respect his heritage as the grandson of Walter and the son of John Huston—not to mention his half-sister Anjelica and his nephew Jack. But we couldn't have anticipated how much he loves talking about his family. He already sounds a lot like his famous father but he can also imitate him, which is mind-blowing. What's more, he carries himself like someone who just walked out of Old Hollywood: he is elegance personified.

Our engineer is a lovely guy named Aristotle Acevedo. He's more than a technician; he really cares about pop culture and is invested in the interviews he records, which makes it all the more enjoyable for us. We've shared some memorable adventures together. When we visited Carl Reiner at his home in Beverly Hills, Carl invited him to set up his equipment on a sofa nearby. When he added that Aristotle was in the exact spot where Mel Brooks sat almost every night to watch movies with Carl, Aristotle had to shake his head to take in that reality. It was much the same when we sat in Quincy Jones' living room, surrounded by memorabilia from his long career, listening to the coolest cat on earth spin his stories—and in no hurry to end our conversation.

We're never bored, and often the hour flies by without our realizing it. (The other advantage of podcasting is that there is no fixed running time for an episode.)

We've recorded "on the road" at film festivals in Savannah, Georgia; Champaign, Illinois; Traverse City, Michigan; and several times at Fantastic Fest and South by Southwest in Austin, Texas. That's where we've had fun talking to Tim Burton, Bill Hader, Chloe Grace Moretz, Dee Rees, Elijah Wood, Vince Vaughn, Jim Gaffigan, Bruce Campbell, the late Lynn Shelton and her significant other, Marc Maron, to name a few. There is a completely different energy when we work in front of a live audience. It's stimulating and it definitely keeps me on my toes. If Jessie was on autopilot—which she never is—she got a wake-up call when Bruce Campbell used her as a prop for a story he was telling, made a sweeping gesture with his arm, and smashed the microphone she was holding into her face. She has a lip ring and her mouth filled with blood, which Jessie tried to hide in the best show-must-go-on tradition. Bruce was working the crowd and didn't even realize what he'd done.

I've never considered myself to be in show business, but after bantering with so many comedians on Doug Benson's show, I've become comfortable being onstage with professional performers. When we're in front of an audience almost anything can happen, and I try to go with the flow. While interviewing Gilbert Gottfried in front of a crowd in Austin, Texas, I found myself joining in as Gilbert belted out the theme song from *Car 54, Where Are You?* I don't think I've ever sung in public before; it just seemed like the right thing to do at that moment.

From decades of attending the Telluride Film Festival, we've established relationships with people we see only once a year. They're almost like family. When I asked Ken Burns if he could possibly talk to us in 2019, he already knew he would be coming to Los Angeles to promote his seven-part PBS series *Country Music* and told his publicist to find an hour for us. He had just come from the airport and had a full agenda ahead of him, but he gave us his complete attention and was thrillingly eloquent—as he always is. Jessie realized that in all the time she's known Ken, this was the first time she'd ever discussed his work; their conversations are almost always about how his kids and grandkids are doing.

Our other Telluride-related coup was getting Werner Herzog to say yes. I first met him in the early 1980s in the Rocky Mountains, and while he has passed the *enfant terrible* stage, he remains a provocative and unpredictable presence on the filmmaking scene. We felt privileged to sit in his living room and listen to him expound on his ideas in that unmistakable voice. My favorite bon mot: he described directing as being "a lion tamer of the unexpected."

At the other end of the spectrum, we were lucky enough to land Jordan Peele when he was riding high on the success of his dazzling sleeper *Get Out* during Awards season. He told me, "One of the biggest regrets in my career is that I did not have someone in the Gremlins 2 sketch [on Key and Peele] pitch Leonard Maltin doing a review of the first *Gremlins* in the movie *Gremlins 2* and that Star Magic didn't green-light that in the room." Putting that statement into context, he explained, "*Gremlins 2* was like *Ben-Hur* for me. Like, let's be real. And *Gremlins 1*, I still will go to the mat on *Gremlins 1*."

One time we flew ourselves to Santa Fe, New Mexico, for the privilege of interviewing George R.R. Martin, who welcomed us to his combination art-house movie theatre, café, and bookstore. It turned out that the *Game of Thrones* author started out just the way I did, publishing his own fanzine.

Often, it's timing that plays a role in nabbing a guest—or losing one. A miscommunication had animation wizard Brad Bird arriving with barely 40 minutes before he had to dash off to the airport—with a promise to return that we're still counting on. A talkative guest and endless traffic delays made us late for our appointment with one of the busiest women in town, Ava DuVernay, the producer, entrepreneur, and director of *Selma* and *When They See Us*. We've known her since her days as a film publicist and were hyper-aware of the clock ticking as we approached the ARRAY campus she has built in L.A.'s historic Filipinotown. She so enjoyed talking about subjects she isn't usually asked about—like the aunt who inspired her love of movies—that she lingered past our exit time. We spoke in the newly opened screening room named for her Aunt Denise, lined with beautifully upholstered movie seats. "God bless her," said Ava, "she would love this, sitting with Leonard Maltin... in a theater that I own? Named after her? I could cry if I let myself, but I'm gonna smile instead." We smiled, too, happy to be in her company.

But for pure charm and graciousness there is none to compare to Angela Lansbury. She welcomed us into her home on the West Side of Los Angeles and we sat at her kitchen table to talk. She was 93 at the time but no one would ever know it; she moved easily and gracefully and her mind was sharp as a tack. In fact, she later sent an e-mail to Jessie saying that she'd listened to our episode and decided it was the best oral history she'd ever done! We can dine out on that compliment for years to come.

The Blessing Known as TCM

I don't know what I would do without Turner Classic Movies—and I know many people who feel the same way. For Alice and me it's our go-to channel, an oasis of comfort and civilization in an all too often crass, commercialized, user-unfriendly world.

There was no shortage of old movies on television when I was growing up; it's where I got much of my basic training as a film buff. But the films were not presented with any care: they were cut (sometimes slashed), interrupted, given no context, and often shown in inferior prints. Contrast that to TCM, where movies are revered and played uncut 24 hours a day. Wow.

Even better, I've gotten to work on a wide variety of projects for TCM, on the air and off, in Hollywood and on the road, and even on the high seas. I'm happy to have been in on their TCM Classic Film Festival from the very start in 2010.

Longtime show-business columnist, reporter, and historian Robert Osborne got the gig of a lifetime when TCM chose him as their on-air host and goodwill ambassador in 1994. He set a classy tone that helped put TCM on the map. Modest about his on-camera delivery, he told me, "You know, I never had any training for this." But his enthusiasm for the Golden Age of Hollywood was palpable, as were his many friendships with its leading lights. Stars felt comfortable talking to him because they knew how much he loved their work.

Viewers came to feel as if they knew the man. At the first TCM Classic Film Festival he was mobbed at every appearance, the silver-haired equivalent of a rock star.

The only problem for the people running the jam-packed, four-day festival was that Robert couldn't be in two places at once. I was more than happy to fill some gaps in that schedule. That's how I found myself chatting with Tony Curtis inside Club TCM—located in the site of the first Academy Awards ceremony, the Blossom Room of the Hollywood Roosevelt Hotel—at the first festival in 2010. Age hadn't dimmed his bravado or charisma, and after our conversation, fans clamored to get his signature in his latest book.

TCM shrewdly flew most of the staff from their home base in Atlanta to Los Angeles for the duration of the festival to serve as hosts, escorts, and such. They did their jobs with an extra level of care and provided a human connection to the institution known as Turner Classic Movies. There has never been a television network that created such a personal bond with its viewers. (Whenever I host or program a night on the channel, I know I'm reaching the right audience—and the response I get is heartening.)

Having shown that I could sustain an hour of conversation nonstop, I was handed a new headliner every year: Max von Sydow, Quincy Jones, Gina Lollobrigida, Shirley MacLaine, Lee Grant, Richard Sherman, Peter Bogdanovich. Each one was fascinating in his or her own way. In the green room I watched super-cool, confident Quincy Jones charm everyone he encountered. Onstage I held my tongue as Shirley MacLaine repeatedly teased the crowd with dishy stories of her private life and loves.

I soon learned the best places to hang out were the green rooms and makeup alcoves at the various screening locations. Alice, Jessie, and I could walk right in and spend time schmoozing with stars who were just about to introduce a movie or had just come from a screening. We never knew whom we might run into, from Keith Carradine to Anjelica Huston. I popped into the lobby of the Chinese Theater just before showtime and peered into the makeshift makeup room they'd created just so I could say hello to Kirk Douglas. It always blew my mind that he remembered me, and we had a lovely chat just before he introduced a screening of *20,000 Leagues Under The Sea.*

One afternoon I walked into the green room at the Chinese Theater multiplex and found Robert Osborne chatting with his old friend Robert Wagner. What an elegant pair they made, happy to be in each other's company. Wagner introduced himself to my daughter, saying "Hi, I'm R.J." I then did the kind of thing that children wish their parents wouldn't, reminding him that he met Jessie when she was still in Alice's tummy several decades earlier.

It was also fun to compare notes with other film experts who were participating. Many of them are friends, like Donald Bogle, the erudite chronicler of black performers and filmmakers; film scholar and biographer Cari Beauchamp; Bruce Goldstein, who programs Film Forum in New York City; and Randy Haberkamp, resident historian at the Academy of Motion Picture Arts and Sciences. Given the pace of the weekend, it was reassuring to run into TCM host Ben Mankiewicz and exchange a look that said, "Yes, I'm tired, but isn't this great?" Ditto, in recent years, for Alicia Malone, Dave Karger, and my old friend Eddie Muller, "the Czar of Noir."

Friends of mine here in L.A. were skeptical about the festival at first. Who would care about seeing *Casablanca* at ten in the morning? And why would they pay a premium price for a ticket?

It was my pal Cari who figured it out the second year: for the hundreds of people who flew in from all 50 states and beyond, this was Movie Buff Fantasy Camp. You could tell how they felt from the broad smiles on their faces and the look of excitement in their eyes as they walked from Club TCM headquarters in the Hollywood Roosevelt Hotel across the street to Grauman's Chinese

Theater, then down Hollywood Boulevard to the equally historic Egyptian Theater and back. They were in hog heaven.

Sure, they could see these films at home in Joplin, Missouri, or Miami, Florida, but they couldn't see them in historic movie palaces on a giant screen, introduced by one of their stars or a knowledgeable film historian, surrounded by an audience of like-minded movie lovers.

Every year I was asked to walk the red carpet on Hollywood Boulevard and work the press line on opening night, which I couldn't have managed without Jessie's help. We had to complete our task quickly as I'd have to leave by 6:00 to ride downtown and teach the last class of my spring semester at USC. It was challenging but adrenaline always helped.

My head spun for that dizzying hour because so many Hollywood veterans turned out for opening night, and I couldn't linger to chat with them. Wait—there's Herb Jeffries duded up, as befits the first black singing cowboy. And is that really Liza Minnelli I see out of the corner of my eye?

The last time Mickey Rooney attended, in 2013, he bounded onto the carpet and paid no attention to the cries of photographers eager to snap a picture. He only came to a stop when he ran into me and gave me a big hello. At that moment several professional fotogs took their shots, with my blue-haired daughter in the background. When he died the following spring, Jessie started hearing from friends far and wide that they had spotted her over Mickey's shoulder in photos of his last public appearance. (A few years later Jessie would not let me rest until I got her photograph with Julie Andrews on the red carpet. It was no easy task, given the crush of people who wanted a moment with the radiant star, but we succeeded. It helped that Julie is such a gracious person.)

Looking back over a decade, I have so many memories. I worked with the lovely Jane Powell at two events "on the road" leading up to the Hollywood festival—in Cambridge, Massachusetts, and Denver, Colorado. Then I had the pleasure of speaking with her onstage at the Chinese Theater auxiliary (which we call the Chinette) and introducing *Seven Brides for Seven Brothers*, which happens to be the favorite movie of both my wife and my daughter. Jane posed with my girls for a picture backstage that I cherish, after which we sat down in the theater and enjoyed the movie all over again for the umpteenth time. It took great restraint not to sing out loud.

I first met Mitzi Gaynor when I worked with her in Chicago, another "on the road" event where we spoke at the Music Box Theater before a showing of *South Pacific*. We actually met that morning while conducting press interviews to promote the TCM Festival and immediately hit it off. She has a wicked sense of humor and we delighted in needling each other. After a long, rambling but funny story that night, she turned to me and said, "Did I ever answer your question?" and I said, deadpan, "No." The audience howled; they loved it and so did she. We reunited on the TCM Cruise in 2019 and had fun all over again. The cruise took place during Halloween, and Mitzi scored a hit wearing her sailor's uniform from *South Pacific*.

Debbie Reynolds was also a cut-up and teased me about my long-term marriage as opposed to hers, to the delight of the people who came to see her in *The Unsinkable Molly Brown*. There is no direct way off the stage of the Egyptian, so TCM had provided a group of burly security people to escort her safely through the audience to an exit—but Debbie was in no hurry. In fact, she slowed the procession so she could make eye contact with as many fans as possible before taking her leave.

It was exciting to meet Hayley Mills and conduct back-to-back interviews—after a showing of *Summer Magic* at the Chinese, then into a golf cart that whisked us over to the Egyptian farther down Hollywood Boulevard to a packed house eager to see her in person and enjoy *The Parent Trap*. She couldn't have been more engaging, and the crowd was thrilled to have her there. TCM produced a lovely three-minute tribute that moved her to tears—in part, I suspect, because it also included her father, John Mills. She said it was watching how he dealt with fame and his fans that taught her lifelong lessons, while it was her mother, writer Mary Hayley Bell, who made sure she answered her fan mail. Incidentally, my best friend, Pete Hammond, who's interviewed everybody in Hollywood, could barely contain himself when he got to pose for a picture with Hayley Mills.

One year, TCM's talent wranglers scored a coup by getting Peggy Cummins (still beautiful at 87) to fly in from England. Eddie Muller naturally was the one to interview her before a screening of the film noir classic *Gun Crazy*. Afterwards, I found myself crossing Hollywood Boulevard to meet friends for dinner in step with Miss Cummins. She asked if I knew the actor who had just spoken to her and I said, "Yes, he's my friend Jimmy Karen. His uncle was the great actor Morris Carnovsky." She replied, "Oh yes, he played the judge in *Gun Crazy*." That coincidence had eluded me completely.

Show business keeps some people forever young. One afternoon I went from a chat with nonagenarian Eva Marie Saint, who was in a feisty, frisky mood following a screening of *Grand Prix*, to an equally lively conversation with the ageless Rita Moreno just before *The King and I*. These women are remarkable. Part of the secret is staying active. Director Norman Jewison doesn't consider himself old—and doesn't act that way, either. It was genuinely exciting to talk to him, veteran casting director Lynn Stalmaster, and composer John Williams after *Fiddler on the Roof* unspooled on the enormous Chinese Theater screen.

I've had the privilege, and thrill, of introducing a number of orchestras and conductors as they prepared to play scores for silent classics at the Egyptian Theater. There is nothing quite like watching a silent film that way. It's a participatory experience in which the audience plays a major part. Sitting in that palatial theater watching a Harold Lloyd comedy like *Speedy*, having just chatted with Harold's granddaughter Suzanne—the keeper of his flame—is a joy that's hard to express in mere words. Harold and his wife raised Sue, so she has a special connection to him both personally and professionally. She is the reason his great silent comedies remain in circulation today.

I am also the designated host of Sunday morning programs at the Cinerama Dome on Sunset Boulevard, where we've screened *This is Cinerama*, *Cinerama Holiday*, and even *Scent of Mystery* in Smell-o-Vision.

It's both poignant and sobering to realize how many people I've seen, or greeted, or interviewed at the TCM Classic Film Festival who are no longer with us: Tony Curtis, Debbie Reynolds, Ernest Borgnine, Diana Serra Cary aka Baby Peggy, and Carla Laemmle, who was 100 years old when she charmed a sold-out crowd who came to see *Dracula*—in which she appears in the very first scene. What a blessing to have been part of evenings like that, and how rewarding it is to know that moviemakers and stars of years past had a chance to meet their most ardent admirers.

I don't know what might have happened to film history had TCM not come along when it did. Collectors, archivists, and authors would have still followed their paths, but this channel has kept classic Hollywood vitally alive and brought it into our homes. It has provided a vehicle for us to make discoveries and pass our love of movies on to the next generation. And it has been a godsend during the Covid-19 pandemic.

Every morning I ride an exercise bike in my bedroom. As I do, I turn on TCM to see what's on. If it's a movie I've seen before (and like) it's just the diversion I need, the inspiration to keep on pedaling. If it's a film I don't know, I'll press record and catch the rest of it later. Either way I'm grateful that Turner Classic Movies exists—and even more grateful that I am a part of it.

Healthy Thoughts

For most of my life I took my health for granted. Like my parents, I was never seriously ill; the only time I spent in a hospital was when I had my tonsils removed at age 12.

My perspective changed when I married Alice, who had a partial thyroidectomy at the age of 19. It disrupted her life, to put it mildly, and incredibly, she required a second surgical procedure within a year of our moving to Los Angeles. Six months into our marriage, her father suffered a heart attack; he died three years later from a rare form of cancer. Dealing with doctors and hospitals, let alone mortality, was all new to me.

When we decided to have a baby, we couldn't have foreseen the problems that we would face. Alice had three miscarriages, the worst of which came after more than four months of bed rest. She had been carrying twins, and at that stage of pregnancy it was necessary for her to go into labor and deliver the fetuses. It was the lowest point of our lives—both hers and mine.

That's why we referred to Jessie as our Miracle Baby. Although it was treated as a high-risk pregnancy, Alice's experience was happily uneventful. Jessie was a joy from the moment she arrived, but in her teens she started developing problems that weren't easy to identify. She has lived with a variety of debilitating auto-immune diseases since that time. She refuses to surrender to them or to depression. In fact, she takes pride in talking about her problems on social media as a means of encouraging others like her with "invisible illnesses" and letting them know they are not alone. I am a private person, but I admire what she does for other people through her postings and videos.

As for me, I didn't know how to respond when my left hand started to shake, unpredictably and uncontrollably. A neurologist told me it was a "benign tremor," but I worried about how it looked on camera or in front of an audience. I decided to tell people about it before conducting onstage interviews, to disarm them and let them know I wasn't suffering.

Then, during an annual checkup my internist asked me if I was having trouble moving around in bed. I said yes, and he intuited that I had Parkinson's disease. My neurologist confirmed it.

This is not news anyone wants to hear, but I am fortunate. Medication helps a lot and, most important, I have a great support system with Alice, Jessie, and Scott all under the same roof. There is no denying that I am slower and clumsier than I used to be. I also have to articulate my words more carefully. Sometimes I grow impatient with myself, but overall I am functioning pretty well.

I never spoke about it because I was worried that it might cost me work, especially on television. Then one morning a reporter for the AARP website called to get my reaction to Alan Alda's admitting that he had Parkinson's. I looked at Alice and Jessie (who happened to be in the room) and decided that I would follow Alda's lead. To deny it or try to hide it would serve no purpose. Besides, I had confidence because I was facing this with my family's support.

I know how debilitating this disease can be, but I count myself lucky. I've accomplished a lot in the seven years since my diagnosis—including writing (and typing) this book. Parkinson's is not a death sentence if identified in its early stages. I am grateful that I can continue to do the work I love and hope to continue doing so for many years to come.

...and in Conclusion...

I know how lucky I am, getting to do something I love for a living. It's a good thing because I never had a backup plan. Chance and circumstance put me on television, then cable TV, then the Internet.

But I will take credit for making good choices. After all, I asked Alice to be my wife. I chose a life partner who shares my interests, not to mention my sense of humor and points of reference. (We joke that we can never split up. Who else would get half the jokes we make?) I surround myself with good people; my friends are journalists, authors, entrepreneurs, and archivists who are passionate about what they do, like me. I don't ever want to be the most interesting person at a dinner party.

Alice and I raised our daughter to be the same way. As an adult, Jessie appreciates that she got to participate in everything we did. That's why it seemed natural for her to join what has become our family business.

Every one of us faces a series of choices in life. I choose to be positive. I'm not blind to bad behavior or poor moviemaking. When someone asks me what's the worst interview I ever conducted, I tell the truth: I've encountered very few rotten apples over the years. And when I slog through a terrible movie, I console myself with the knowledge that at least I never have to see it again.

That's the closest I come to having a philosophy. I take life as it comes, one day at a time, and await the next phone call or e-mail that will set me off on a new venture. In November of 2020 I hosted a panel with Francis Ford Coppola, Al Pacino, and Andy Garcia to discuss the reconstructed *The Godfather Part III*. (This was executed via Zoom, of course; I never left my living room.) A friend in Paris just engaged me to narrate my first full-length documentary film about movie pioneer Georges Méliès. Most recently, I interviewed a popular Indonesian director of horror films named Jocko Anwar whom I met at the Sundance Film Festival last year. He says I'm his hero because he grew up reading my annual *Movie Guide*. And I've just finished my twenty-third year at USC, teaching my class via computer.

What other projects or assignments lie just around the corner? I can't wait to find out.

Index